History of the
AMERICAN PIANOFORTE

Da Capo Press Music Reprint Series

GENERAL EDITOR: FREDERICK FREEDMAN

Vassar College

History of the

AMERICAN PIANOFORTE

Its Technical Development, and the Trade

By

DANIEL SPILLANE

New Introduction by RITA BENTON

The University of Iowa

$ DA CAPO PRESS • NEW YORK • 1969

A Da Capo Press Reprint Edition

This Da Capo Press edition of Daniel Spillane's
History of the American Pianoforte
is an unabridged republication of the first edition
published in New York in 1890 by the author.
It includes an Index especially prepared
for this edition.

Library of Congress Catalog Card Number 68-16246

INTRODUCTION

Instrument making is a legitimate and important aspect of music history, but one that musicologists sometimes overlook or underestimate. Because it relates to the practical rather than the theoretical, and to the crassly commercial rather than the "purely" idealistic, professional historians may find it less than appealing as a subject for research. Yet the history of instrument making provides many insights into the nature of music written for instruments; and since it often involves musicians better-known for their composing or performing skills, as well as talented amateurs whose efforts support music, it is inter-woven throughout musical history with the fabric of the art itself. This remains true whether one believes that new designs in instruments inspire composers to feats of originality, or whether one believes, as many do, that it is more often the com-poser who makes demands on the ingenuity of the instrument maker, who must then find a way to satisfy those demands.

The meager literature on the history of instrument making in the United States is but one aspect of the general paucity of publications concerning the country's music. Oscar Sonneck's lament that "the literature on music in America is woefully in-adequate both in quantity and quality" is only slightly less true today than it was in 1913.[1] Sonneck's own achievement in filling some of the gaps is widely known; it established a standard of excellence that was rare for its time and place. But Sonneck had had the benefit of rigorous and systematic European academic training which indicated the necessity and the methodology for a program of research based on original source material. Fifteen years before the appearance of Sonneck's first book on American music, Daniel Spillane published his *History of the American Pianoforte,* in which he followed the same principle of reliance on documentary evidence. Spillane's lack of any systematic academic or historical schooling makes his achievement even more remarkable, and suggests a rather unusual personality. His life story confirms the impression, although it follows in the American tradition of "poor immigrant boy makes good."

Daniel Spillane was born in Cork, Ireland, in 1860, the son of a bandmaster. He was already playing several instruments at the age of ten, and by the time he was fifteen, he had composed several pieces, one of which was bought by a publisher. In 1880, he went to London to study composition and harmony, while also learning about piano construction. When he arrived in New York in 1883, his knowledge of piano regulating and tuning secured his livelihood. At the same time he wrote articles on piano literature and history for American and British music journals.

After the appearance, in 1890, of his *History of the American Pianoforte,* he devoted himself entirely to writing. *The Piano: Scientific, Technical, and Practical Instructions Relating to Tuning, Regulating, and Toning* was published in 1893, and reprinted in 1912. Meanwhile, Spillane was writing a succession of articles on pianos, organs, band and orchestral instruments for the magazine *Popular Science Monthly,* as part of a series on "The Development of American Industries since Columbus."

He also contributed nonmusical articles, poems, and short stories to various periodicals, and continued composing. During the summers of 1891 and 1892, he spent some months abroad fulfilling literary commissions from the *American Art Journal* and *The Music Trade Review*. Early in 1893 he became the associate editor of *The Music Trade Review,* and in June of the same year, editor of *The Keynote.* On October 21, 1893, at the early age of 33, he died in New York of complications following surgery. The several obituaries published during the ensuing days emphasize his sympathetic nature, generous impulses, aesthetic temperament, and strong character.

In preparing his *History of the American Pianoforte,* Spillane sought data in a wide variety of places: city directories, patent offices, contemporary newspapers, journals, and diaries, proceedings of early scholarly societies (*e.g.,* The Franklin Institute, to which he dedicated the work, and the American Philosophical Society), and in miscellaneous documents stored in historical societies dating from the colonial and early Federal periods. For supplementary information he consulted such familiar (though not aways correct) musical authorities as Rimbault, Brinsmead, Hipkins (in the *Encyclopaedia Britannica*), Fétis, and Oscar Paul, as well as such varied but basic compilations as Bishop's two-volume *A History of American Manufactures from 1608 to 1860* (1861–64), Ireland's *Fifty Years of a Play-Goer's Journal; or Annals of the New York Stage* ... (1860), and Felt's *The Annals of Salem* (1827).

Spillane's practical working knowledge of piano construction gave him exceptional equipment for understanding and explaining the intricacies of mechanical features and, wherever possible, he examined models before describing them. The earlier sections of his book, however, particularly those that review European developments in piano making, suffer from the conjectures and generalizations taken over from earlier writers who, in turn, had received them from their equally uncritical predecessors.

Spillane's decision to omit "a list of authorities and sources from which information has been derived," and instead to carry them "into the body of the work informally," was, of course, an unfortunate error by today's standards of scholarship, and sometimes leads to frustration. Is the "Dr. Hopkinson, of Philadelphia, a Scotchman," who prior to 1799 "exhibited a harpsichord with an iron frame," the Francis Hopkinson (lawyer and statesman rather than doctor) of Philadelphia who devised a new method of quilling harpsichords? Spillane claims that Dr. Hopkinson's improvement may actually have been for a piano, and is mentioned "remotely in a volume of 'American Philosophical Transactions.'" Perusal of the relevant volumes of *Transactions of the American Philosophical Society* fails to disclose any remarks concerning iron frames, although Francis Hopkinson's harpsichord quills, as well as several of his extra-musical interests, are documented there. More recent literature on Francis Hopkinson includes no mention of iron frames; nor does it seem likely that there is any confusion with the English piano maker named Hopkinson who was active in the latter half of the nineteenth century.

Some of Spillane's casual comments lead to interesting by-paths. He reports that in 1834 an industry-wide strike of New York piano workers was ignited by the ill treatment accorded the more recently arrived German workers by their colleagues of English descent. He implies that a differential wage scale existed between the two national groups, but explains that "matters were speedily readjusted on a new wage basis," and the strike ultimately resulted in the constitution of the first

piano-makers' trade society formed in this country. If the details
and exact motivation of the New York strike and union formation reported by Spillane remain elusive, there is evidence that
at least one American city already had a piano-workers' union
by 1834. James Sharp, of the Boston Cabinet and Piano-Forte
Workers, issued a call for a general convention of mechanics
belonging to various Boston trade unions in February 1834,
and at the convention held the following month was elected
first president of the newly formed Boston Central Labor Union.[2]

Concerning the labor situation in New York, two articles in
the weekly newspaper *The National Trades Union* of November 21 and 28, 1834, show that on those dates a union of piano
workers did not yet exist in New York. But by April of the
next year, a group was evidently organized, since on May 2,
1835, the same paper reports a meeting of the New York Trades'
Union, at which the striking Journeymen Cabinet-Makers expressed their thanks to the Piano-Forte Makers, "who assisted
them to procure employment at their respective branches, and
otherwise encouraged them in their strike."[3]

In view of his County Cork origins, some anti-English prejudice on Spillane's part would be understandable; the possibility
that he was less than objective in this respect should be considered in judging the accuracy of his frequent references to the
prejudice encountered by immigrant German workers, making
it difficult for them to gain a foothold in an industry which had
been dominated by artisans of English origin (see, for example,
pages 152, 186, 188, and 201). In any case, Spillane is unquestionably correct in attributing the subsequent tremendous advances in the design of American pianos to makers of German
origin, the most notable being William Steinway. The eventual
numerical strength of this ethnic group is indicated by the fact

that in 1868 the separately constituted "German Piano Makers' Association of New York" sent its own delegate to a congress of the National Labor Union.[4]

*   *   *

The early history of musical instruments in the United States, like most other features of its musical life, may be broadly characterized as an imitation of its counterpart in England. This was especially true of the larger cities; the more sparsely settled rural and frontier areas naturally suffered some cultural deprivation, although the surprising mobility of musicians in those days of primitive transportation strongly favored standardization. But even before 1720, during the period that Sonneck concedes might be called "the primitive period in our musical history, without fear of being convicted of hasty conclusions,"[5] musical instruments had already made their appearance. As early as 1633, inventories of two properties in New Hampshire, which had been settled only ten years earlier, listed fifteen recorders and oboes for one estate, and twenty-six oboes and recorders, as well as a drum, for the other.[6]

After 1720, the various indications of a flourishing musical culture increased, and references to organs, flutes, guitars, violins, harpsichords, and other instruments multiplied. These were imported along with other necessities and luxuries by general merchants. Some of the more affluent music lovers in Northern cities and among the plantation aristocracy of the South sent special orders to England for their instruments, as they did for music, books, furniture, and other symbols of the gracious living to which they aspired. Thus, in a letter written on June 1, 1771, to his friend Thomas Adams, then in Europe, Thomas Jefferson requested him to substitute a piano, which had captivated him at a recent hearing, for the clavichord which he had previously ordered.[7]

A few months earlier, the first public reference to a piano appeared in the *Massachusetts Gazette,* in a notice announcing a violin recital on March 21, 1771, in Boston's Concert Hall, between the acts of which "some select pieces on the forte piano and guitar" were to be performed by David Propert.[8] In 1774, piano lessons were first offered in newspaper advertisements in two cities. George James d'Argeau of Baltimore and H. B. Victor of Philadelphia both displayed the versatility typical of early American music masters in that they taught a wide variety of instruments.[9]

Among the earliest domestically manufactured instruments were the organ built in Philadelphia by Matthias Zimmerman before 1737, and the harpsichord constructed by Gustavus Hesselius (*not* Hesselins) in 1742 or 1743. Finally, in early 1775 John Behrent (sometimes called Brent or Belmont) of Philadelphia advertised his completion of "an extraordinary instrument by the name of pianoforte" and thus became the founder of an industry that, after a disruptive halt of about ten years caused by the Revolutionary War, was to grow by prodigious leaps.

Spillane's account of piano playing and making in the cities of Charleston (South Carolina), Fredericksburg (Virginia), Baltimore, New York, and especially Philadelphia, foreshadows Sonneck's later impression that "New England's share in the development of our early musical life has been unfairly and unduly overestimated to the disadvantage of the Middle Colonies and the South."[10]

A particular problem concerning pianos in the United States arises in connection with their capacity to withstand the abuse of extremes of weather: hot and cold, damp and dry. That these conditions impose severe demands on instruments was recognized as early as 1792, when Dodds & Claus of New York advertised improvements which rendered their pianos "much more acceptable than those imported. The introduction of their newly invented hammers and dampers is acknowledged to be a great improvement, as also the means they have taken to prepare their wood to stand the effect of our climate, which imported instruments never do." This and later claims to the superior ability of American pianos to withstand the rigors of the prevailing "continental climate" (as well as of overheated homes) cannot be dismissed as chauvinistic exaggeration. The importance of the meteorological factor was observed by the Belgian, Ernest Closson, who considered it to have exerted a beneficial influence:

> Although it was founded largely by foreigners, American piano manufacture nevertheless assumed its own special characteristics, aided by the fact that imported instruments stood up to the climate badly. In conformity with the national genius, the ingenuity of the national builders concentrated especially on the reinforcement of the various parts of the instrument, and the extension of the metallic parts, a development favoured by the excellent quality of American iron and the advanced state of the local metallurgical industry.[11]

As the native industry grew, the importation of pianos decreased correspondingly. After 1830, imports from England ceased almost entirely, while a few of the prestigious Erard and Pleyel pianos continued to arrive from France. In 1852 the Commissioner of Patents estimated that 9000 pianos had been manufactured the previous year, and in 1860 a total of 22,000 were made, more than half of them in New York state.

With respect to the Philadelphia Centennial Exhibition of 1876, Spillane, a not entirely unbiased commentator, reports that "there was no use trying to conceal the fact that the first-class American pianos exhibited excelled the best instruments of European makers in every respect." It may be noted, however, that Spillane's nationalistic enthusiasm was not at all unique. In 1879, Edgar Brinsmead wrote just as unequivocally that "the superiority of the English pianofortes over all rivals is due partly to the solidarity of their construction, which produces the lasting qualities for which they are so celebrated, and partly to the simplicity and excellence of the mechanism, the importance of which cannot be over-estimated."[12] And with a confidence which equals that of both statements, Oscar Comettant had written in 1869: "Even aside from the three large firms, Erard, Pleyel, and Henri Herz, France is still surely the country among all that produces the largest number of pianos that are beautiful in appearance, carefully made, and possess a good sound."[13]

Spillane would have been pleased at the subsequent growth of the American piano industry. In 1910, no fewer than 360,000 pianos were manufactured in the United States.[14] The advent of the radio undoubtedly acted to diminish the piano's role as a focus of home entertainment, and the depression of the early 1930's stimulated the downward trend, so that in 1937 the number of pianos manufactured was down to 137,000. By 1950 this had grown to 150,000; by 1958 to 158,919; and by 1963 to 214,195, according to the U.S. Census of Manufactures.

Musicologists will surely find much of interest in Spillane's work and may be surprised to discover its relevance to many aspects of American music.

Rita Benton

December 1968
The University of Iowa
Iowa City, Iowa

NOTES

1. Oscar G. T. Sonneck, "A Survey of Music in America," in his *Suum cuique, Essays in Music* (New York: G. Schirmer, 1916), 129. This essay was read before the Schola Cantorum, at New York, April 11, 1913.

2. Quoted from *The Man* (February 20 and March 6, 1834) by *A Documentary History of American Industrial Society,* ed. J. R. Commons *et al.* (Cleveland: Arthur H. Clark, 1910), VI, 87 and 90–1.

3. *Ibid.,* V, 237. In a list showing the "First Dates on which Trade Societies Appeared in New York, Baltimore, Philadelphia, and Boston, 1833–1837," the earliest dates cited are only slightly different from those given above. Boston: Cabinet and Pianoforte Makers, *The Man* (March 12, 1834); New York: Pianoforte Makers, *National Trades' Union* (November 28, 1835). No entries for piano makers appear under Baltimore or Philadelphia (*cf.* J. R. Commons *et al., History of Labour in the United States* [New York: The Macmillan Co., 1918], I, 474–5).

4. *A Documentary History . . .,* IX, 196.

5. Oscar G. T. Sonneck, *Early Concert Life in America (1731–1800)* (Leipzig: Breitkopf & Härtel, 1907), 8.

6. Irving Lowens, "Music in the American Wilderness," in his *Music and Musicians in Early America* (New York: W. W. Norton, 1964), 21–2.

7. Thomas Jefferson, *Papers,* ed. Julian Boyd (Princeton: Princeton University Press, 1950), 71.

8. Sonneck, *Early Concert Life,* 265.

9. Sonneck's article, "Benjamin Franklin's Musical Side," in his *Suum cuique,* 68; also his *Early Concert Life,* 76–7.

10. Sonneck, *Early Concert Life,* 10.

11. Ernest Closson, *History of the Pianoforte,* trans. Delano Ames (London: Paul Elek, 1947), 109.

12. Edgar Brinsmead, *The History of the Pianoforte* (London: Novello, Ewer, 1879), 142.

13. Oscar Comettant, *La musique, les musiciens, et les instruments de musique,* 2nd ed. (Paris: Michel Lévy, 1877), 691. The 1st edition was published in 1869.
14. Arthur Loesser, *Men, Women, and Pianos; a Social History* (New York: Simon and Schuster, 1954), 590.

TO THE PIANOFORTE.

—◆—

OH friend, whom glad or grave we seek,
    Heaven-holding shrine !
I ope thee, touch thee, hear thee speak,
    And peace is mine.
No fairy casket, full of bliss,
    Out-values thee ;
Love only, wakened with a kiss,
    More sweet may be.

To thee, when our full hearts o'erflow
    In griefs or joys,
Unspeakable emotions owe
    A fitting voice :
Mirth flies to thee, and love's unrest,
    And memory dear,
And sorrow, with his tightened breast,
    Comes for a tear.

Oh, since few joys of human mould
    Thus wait us still
Thrice bless'd be thine, thou gentle fold
    Of peace at will ;
No change, no sullenness, no cheat,
    In thee we find ;
Thy saddest voice is ever sweet,—
    Thine answer, kind.

—Leigh Hunt.

HISTORY

OF THE

AMERICAN PIANOFORTE;

ITS TECHNICAL DEVELOPMENT,

AND THE TRADE.

BY

DANIEL SPILLANE.

ILLUSTRATED.

NEW YORK:
D. SPILLANE, PUBLISHER,
23 EAST 14TH STREET.
1890.

BURR PRINTING HOUSE, FRANKFORT AND JACOB STS., N. Y.

CONTENTS.

CHAPTER XXII.
NEW YORK.

CHAPTER XXIII.
MISCELLANEOUS FIRMS.

CHAPTER XXIV.
KINDRED BRANCHES.

CHAPTER XXV.
KINDRED BRANCHES.

CHAPTER XXVI.
MUSICAL AND TRADE JOURNALISM.

APPENDICES.

PORTRAITS.

John Broadwood
Jonas Chickering.
William Knabe.
William B. Bradbury.
Isaac Woodward.
John B. Dunham.
Henry C. Watson.
Henry F. Miller.
William M. Thoms.

Sebastian Erard.
John Jacob Astor.
Henry E. Steinway.
John Firth.
George Jardine.
James A. Gray.
Albert Weber, Sr.
John C. Freund.
Napoleon J. Haines.

Henry Hazelton.

INTRODUCTORY.

In launching forth this, the first history of the American pianoforte, I cannot help pointing out the fact that it is the first work of the kind published in any country that treats on the instrument from the technical, historical, industrial, national, and personal standpoints concretely, while it attempts to create a broad and living interest in the pianoforte business by bringing it down to the present time as a development. The great technical minds that have been especially identified with the instrument in this country, however, stand forth in their proper sphere. In shaping the policy of the work, I have been actuated by a desire to elevate the character of the pianoforte business, as a whole, above mere commonplace commercialism, having in mind the large place the piano has filled for the past century, and in particular during the past twenty-five years, as a factor in our civilization ; as a source of household joy, a silent symbol in every home of the mysterious and humanizing influence of music. Believing the piano, as we know it, to be a development to which hundreds of minds, greater and lesser, have contributed, I have attempted to engraft that belief into the practical sphere of this history. If

the modern aspect of the work is not as complete in every
respect as it probably might be, it has resulted from the
apathy and distrust of members of the pianoforte firms to
whom I have applied for information as to their personal
and technical history. In many cases much discour-
tesy was experienced from persons whose sole interest in
the art business they follow is that of mere speculators.
If, however, impartial mention of them in these pages
in relation to American pianoforte history, past and
present, makes them prouder of and more interested in
the business they are associated with, the writer shall
have accomplished much indeed. In this connection I
acknowledge my indebtedness to the musical and trade
press, which has assisted my researches on modern history.

In relation to the earlier chapters, only people who
have essayed the task or gone over the field mentally
can estimate the vast amount of work and research en-
tailed in the compilation and writing of a volume of this
peculiar character, particularly in the present instance,
as no previous investigations of this nature have been
published beyond a few insignificant fragmentary articles.
Be this as it may, I wish merely to point out that I have
tried to rescue the remote history of the American pianoforte business, its antecedents and its people, from oblivion, and in my procedure have brought to light many
novel facts as well, all of interest to the historian of
American musical art.

For personal assistance in procuring early facts of in-
terest for these chapters I am indebted to Mr. Mendes
Cohen, Secretary Maryland Historical Society, and
Mr. W. Whitelock, of Baltimore ; Mr. J. W. Jor-

dan, Assistant-Librarian Pennsylvania Historical Society ; Mr. William H. Wahl, Secretary Franklin Institute, Philadelphia ; Mr. George H. Chickering, Boston ; Mr. Henry Kleber, Pittsburg ; Mr. William Steinway, Mr. W. M. Thoms, Mr. Henry Hazelton, Mr. Edward Jardine, of New York, Mr. Thaddeus Firth, of Maspeth, L. I., General Di Cesnola, Metropolitan Museum of Art, New York, and Mrs. Albert Weber, Sr., Port Chester, N. Y. To all these I tender my sincere thanks. The late Mr. James A. Gray, of Albany, also rendered me some services which I can only acknowledge here, owing to the recent death of that much-esteemed member of the trade. In compiling the chapters relating to Europe, I have been assisted by the writings of Mr. A. J. Hipkins, Mr. Edgar Brinsmead, Dr. Oscar Paul, Fetis, and Rimbault, while I have made personal researches in the British Patent Office records, as indicated. Several original facts in relation to William Southwell, of Dublin, were procured through the kindness of Mr. Augustine Southwell, of Philadelphia, his grandson. Unlike most standard European works by the authors named, no section has been devoted to a treatise on the acoustic or physical basis of the pianoforte. This is already elaborately and ably exemplified in most of the European writings indicated, all derived ostensibly, with modifications, from the works of Helmholtz, Tyndal, and through other familiar channels. I have made no attempt to illustrate the early actions of Cristofori, Broadwood, or any other early European developments of that nature, recognizing the fact that the works of those authors named stand as authorities for the European history of the pianoforte, past and present, in a detailed sense ; neither have I attempted to give practical chapters devoted to tuning, toning, and familiar branches of the business of interest to practical tuners, dealers, and others from the American standpoint.   All this has no rightful place in a work of this character. The field, moreover, is already covered by Mr. E. Quincy Norton, of Mobile, Ala., whose little book, "Construction and Care of the Pianoforte" (Ditson & Company, Boston), is the cleverest and most concise work of this technical nature ever published in any country, and is admirably explanatory, while the author is eminently qualified by experience for the task.   I have also secured several facts of interest from "Musical Instruments and Their Homes," by William A. and Mary E. Brown (Dodd, Mead & Co., New York).

I am aware that it is customary in historical works to give a list of authorities and sources from which information has been derived.   These are, however, in the present instance carried into the body of the work informally, while the vast numbers of old newspapers, magazines, annals, and historical works consulted for the purpose of procuring information cannot be given specifically owing to space, and would serve no end in reality, because properly the formality belongs to a class of literature that involves issues and disputes of consequence.   I have, however, taken pains in my chapters to bring forward proofs in support of technical points or facts of significance.   How I have fulfilled the task throughout and satisfied the musical public and the members of the pianoforte business remains to be seen.

February 17th, 1890.

HISTORY OF THE AMERICAN PIANOFORTE.

CHAPTER I.

THE ORIGIN OF THE PIANOFORTE.

THE CLAVICHORD—SPINET—VIRGINAL—HARPSICHORD—THE
FIRST PIANOFORTE—CRISTOFORI—MARIUS—SCHRÖETER—
EARLY LONDON PIANOFORTE-MAKERS—BROADWOOD'S IM-
PROVEMENTS.

FROM the first stages of civilization in which music
appears, the invention and development of musical instruments have always been governed by the progress of
the art itself, as well as by the growth of the mechanical
arts ; while music, in turn, grew in a distinct line with
the evolution of the human mind toward a higher plane
of intellectual and spiritual attainment. These three
conditions cannot be disassociated.

From the rude lyre of the ancients, which is the remote
precursor of the initial pianoforte of Cristofori, up to
the piano of the present day, is a huge step in human
achievement, yet the growth of musical art in all its

phases, has a manifest bearing upon the aggregate result meanwhile.

Looking backward, the most distinct technical revolutions in instrument development noticeable are Guido's
improvements in the organ keyboard and musical scale ;
the introduction of the clavichord and other variations
of that instrument ; the appearance of the virginal and
spinet, followed by the harpsichord, which became the
connecting link between the pianoforte, with its peculiar
sound-producing mechanism, and the race of relative
keyboard instruments briefly indicated in the foregoing.

The origin of the clavichord is involved in a haze of
doubt and supposition. From general appearances it is
probable that the Italians invented this instrument in
the fourteenth century, Italy being at that period, and
for several centuries following, the seat of European art
activity. It was subsequently copied by the Belgians
and Germans with special modifications. It continued
to be used in Germany for many centuries on account
of its extreme structural simplicity and low price.

Writers say that in his first musical journeys Mozart
played upon the clavichord, which formed part of his
baggage. In England the virginal superseded the clavichord toward the fifteenth century. This instrument
was an emphatic step toward the piano. In it wire was
substituted for gut, and a *jack* was introduced for the
first time so as to facilitate a rude form of escapement.
The spinet, which was similar in most respects with the
virginal, made its appearance about the same period. In
the latter the same action mechanism was used, the only
difference being that the spinet was built like a harp and
set down horizontally upon a frame-work, as exemplified

in the Rossi instrument illustrated elsewhere, at present in the possession of the South Kensington Museum, London. The virginal and spinet had but one string to each note, and the specimens now in existence have a keyboard range not exceeding four octaves. The New York Museum of Art possesses valuable examples of these instruments, purchased by the late Mr. Drexel, of Philadelphia, in his European travels, and presented to the city archives.

Toward the end of the sixteenth century the spinet and virginal were superseded by the harpsichord, which originated in Italy as early as the end of the fifteenth century. One example is illustrated here from the London South Kensington collection dated 1521. The harpsichord anticipated our pianoforte grands in shape, as shown in the illustrations presented. In this instrument the *jack* of the spinet and virginal was adopted, with a little modification. Two strings of wire to each note here appeared, which was another step upward toward Cristofori's pianoforte. The most notable harpsichord-maker and inventor known was Hans Ruckers, of Antwerp, one of whose instruments is among the Drexel collection in the Museum of Art. Handel always played upon Ruckers' instruments in preference to all others of his time, which is a sufficient guarantee of Ruckers' ability as a harpsichord-maker. Ruckers made many significant improvements in the instrument, assisted by his sons, John and Andrew, toward the seventeenth century, when he was famous throughout France and Germany.

The Italians, although the initiators, only adopted the harpsichord about 1702, when Father Zanetti, a Venetian priest, became noted for some innovations in the instrument, which gave it popularity. Crotone and Farini, two other celebrated Italian makers, later appeared. The latter substituted catgut for wire in the harpsichord, and gave the instrument the name of *clavictherium.* One Rigoli, of Florence, made vertical harpsichords, meanwhile, as early as 1621, but met with little notice. A noted French maker turned up toward the end of the seventeenth century named Richard whose fame lives.

Coming down more toward the invention of the piano, the names of Silbermann, Stein, Peronnard, Marius, Schobert, and Cristofori must be introduced. These were all famous harpsichord-makers, representing Germany, France, and Italy, variously. Many of these became identified later on with the promotion of the pianoforte.

A. J. Hipkins, at present of the celebrated firm of Broadwood & Company, London, one of our most eminent writers on piano history, supports the claim which gives Cristofori credit as the inventor of the piano, and places the date—after Rimbault—in 1709.

Bartolommeo Cristofori, of Padua, the originator of the instrument, was eminently known as a harpsichord-maker and is included in the above group. That he accomplished this significant achievement is shown.

Rival claims have been set up from a remote period. Fétis puts forth Marius as the first to exhibit a pianoforte, but beyond proving that the latter admittedly clever French harpsichord-maker submitted several hammer-harpsichords to the Academy in Paris in 1716, nothing is advanced to disprove the claim that Cristofori preceded the former in the production of the first instrument of this kind.

THE GREEN CLAVICHORD. EIGHTEENTH CENTURY.

SPINET BY PLAYER.

South Kensington Museum London.

PIANO BY CRISTOFORI.   A.D. 1726.

Kraus Museum, Florence.

Moreover, Germany—placing the year at 1717—claims the credit of the initial pianoforte for Schröeter, a child of the " Fatherland." It has been decisively proved, however—taking these dates advanced in relation to Marius's and Schröeter's instruments as a basis for a computative estimate—that Cristofori produced his first instrument in 1709, the date assigned. In " The Pianoforte," by Rimbault, an historical work published by Cocks & Company, London, in 1860, a translation of an Italian document, written by the Marchese Scipione Maffei, a Florentian scholar, in 1711, is given in support of the fact that Bartolommeo Cristofori, of that city, exhibited four pianofortes in 1709, which statement was originally published in the *Giornale* in the year indicated, accompanied with a diagram of Cristofori's action principle. This leaves no doubt as to the latter's position in pianoforte history.

Bartolommeo Cristofori was appointed custodian of the musical instruments of the Prince Ferdinand dei Medici, a Florentian noble, in 1708, and it was in the following year he exhibited his first instruments as designated. In Maffei's writings Cristofori's name is given as *Cristofali*, but this is proved to have been an error, as Mr. Hipkins points out in his history, because inscriptions upon existing pianofortes of the former's make give the name of this clever man as Cristofori, which fact should forever end any discussion on the matter. Notwithstanding this, most writers still insist upon using the name *Cristofali* in this connection.

The origin of the word pianoforte in musical instrument nomenclature is traced back to 1598, and is said to have originated with an Italian musical instrument-

maker named Paliarino. In some correspondence of
the latter, still preserved, dated in the above year, he
speaks frequently of a musical instrument called *piano e
forte.* Nothing is known, however, of the instrument
referred to. Cristofori is the originator of the title by
which the present "household orchestra," as some people style the piano, became known all over Europe.
The title alone ought to be sufficient evidence as to the
Italian extraction of the piano, notwithstanding that
these terms given are everywhere recognized by musicians.

It is said that Father Wood, an English monk, living
at Rome, made a pianoforte similar to Cristofori's instrument in 1711. He brought it to England later, where it
created a great sensation.

Schröeter, mentioned as a claimant herein, made many
improvements in the pianoforte in his time, and achieved
a high place in later years in his business. He claimed
to have made a pianoforte in 1717, in Dresden, without
having heard anything of Cristofori's instrument, which,
however, does not entitle him to priority even if his
statements were proved substantially. Christoph Gott-
lieb Schröeter was the son of an organist of some note.
He was born on the borders of Bohemia. Schröeter was
engaged throughout his life in conflicts with other rival
makers of pianos and harpsichords, which fact gives rise
to the impression that his original claim in connection
with the first pianoforte grew from pure imagination.
Schröeter's first pianoforte, exhibited in Dresden, caught
the popular fancy and its fame spread. In a little time
a host of imitators sprang up, among them being the
celebrated Geoffrey Silbermann, of Strasburg, who

made Bach's favorite instrument ; Spaett, of Dresden, and Stein, of Augsburg, all of whom reached a high plane of eminence in the pianoforte manufacturing business in after years.   Marius, the French maker, meanwhile made some improvements in his first pianofortes, which led to a French school of imitators, some of whom eclipsed their master in the production of these instruments.

England through all these years contributed nothing of consequence to the development of the harpischord up to about the middle of the last century, when the Tschudis settled in London.

Cristofori in the mean time had remedied many defects in his original action principle with valuable results.   In the first instrument he exhibited, the idea of " escapement" had been skilfully worked out, but no means had been provided to check the escape of the hammer after it had struck the strings, which led to a rebound of the hammer.   This was a serious difficulty in itself, but he finally overcame it.   Thus it is demonstrated that he substantially anticipated the bottom principles of an improved action.   There are several instruments of Cristofori's make in existence.   Two in Florence, dated 1720 and 1726, show a perfect anticipation of "escapement" and hammer "checking."   This great figure in pianoforte history died comparatively poor in 1731.   Before he passed away he had accomplished many other valuable improvements, such as strengthening and enlarging the case, and to a degree revolutionized the principles of construction throughout.

Up to 1760 all instruments were made in the form of grands, until Zumpe, a German workman, originated

the familiar "square" in London in that year.   Fétis,
who seemed to have had a particular love for disputing
dates, claimed that one Frederici made "squares" several
years earlier.   This is of little consequence, however.
Zumpe was a workman employed in the shop of Tschudi,
the famous London harpsichord-maker, and afterward
throughout his career exhibited great creative and inventive talent.   Zumpe started in business in London on
his own account, when he became famous throughout
England and the Continent.   His "damper" and action
improvements led up to many valuable results in time.
He amassed a large fortune during his life and died
rich and famous.

Previous to Zumpe's first achievement, pianoforte-
making had been comparatively a failure in England.
About 1760 a number of workmen settled in London,
whose arrival has since come to be set down as an epoch
of no small consequence in the manufacture of English
pianofortes.   These workmen were Germans and numbered twelve, whereupon they became known as the
"twelve apostles," which evangelistic title they earned
in some years to come.   Many of the descendants of
these men have been identified with the early development of the American pianoforte since that period, as
shown in future chapters.   Geib, Backers (Becker), and
Landreth were among this group of men.   Backers, who
was properly a Dutchman, became associated in a marked
degree with the English grand piano.   He was the inventor of what was known as the English grand action,
which has been handed down, with certain alterations,
even to this time.   The Broadwoods, of London, yet use
it—in an improved form, however.   Robert Stodart and

John Broadwood, two Scotch workmen, assisted Backers
very materially in his technical schemes. John Broadwood was the founder of the present London house.
These two workmen were in the employ of Tschudi and
were highly esteemed. Broadwood advanced so far in
the estimation of Tschudi that he married the latter's
daughter, becoming his partner and successor in the
great business he had built up in the course of events.

Toward 1790 Stodart, who had succeeded Backers,
made significant improvements in the character of the
English grand, which form of pianoforte the Stodart
firm in subsequent years became noted for throughout
England and the United States. Meanwhile John Broadwood set to work in 1780 and made some revolutionary
changes in the square by removing the pin-block or
wrest-plank from the front to the back of the case, further
making a perfectly unique adjustment of the scaling and
stringing conditions, so as to meet the new order of construction. His success was so significant that he turned
his attention toward promoting other radical changes,
one of which was the extension of pianoforte compass
in the keyboard. He now followed by introducing the
damper and soft pedals.

From these instances of ability given it can be seen
that "Broadwood the First" was a worthy initiator of
a famous name in connection with technical and acoustic
progress in the British pianoforte. His breadth of mind
in scientific directions is exemplified by the fact that he
recognized, upon deliberation, that science had necessarily something to do with acoustic principles, and
could be used toward the better development of the
piano. Acting upon these convictions, he called in the

assistance of Cavallo and Dr. Grey, of the British Museum, and with the counsel and assistance of these eminent scientists the laws of " striking distance" in relation to hammer adjustment were laid down. These principles spread through the different London shops in a short time, and from thence the Continental piano-makers got an inkling of the mystery. Upon the force of Cavallo's and Dr. Grey's counsel Broadwood experimented, and in some time adopted his method of building the upper bridge so as to give the hammers the necessary scope to hit the strings at the most favorable point consistent with the best quality of tone. Broadwood's shop was regarded during these early years as a " house of mystery," and every new idea propagated technically was eagerly sought for and copied everywhere.

Science, then, has played no small part in establishing the primary laws of pianoforte construction, not only in the acoustic department, but in the construction and bracing of the case, so as to make it capable of resisting extreme conditions of tension.

About the beginning of this century the most noted makers of pianos in Europe were Stein, Stodart, Broadwood, Pleyel, and Erard.

Ignace Pleyel was born in Austria, in 1757. His entrance upon this planet was eminently signalized by the circumstance that he was the twenty-fourth child born to his mother since her marriage to Martin Pleyel. But the good lady died soon after the birth of Ignace, whereupon the father of the celebrated piano-maker under notice married again and added fourteen children more to his previous record, thirty-eight in all, about thirty-five of whom lived and prospered. Pleyel became a clever composer in after years, and rose to be chapel-master of Strasburg Cathedral. He settled in Paris about 1804, and drifted into the business of manufacturing pianos in a short time, where he turned his celebrity as a musician and composer to account. He rapidly became owner of one of the largest establishments in Europe. About 1835 his son Camile and his partner Kalkbrenner—well known as a musician—were controlling the largest pianoforte trade, wholesale and retail, then in Europe.

CHAPTER II.

The Origin of the Pianoforte.

THE HOUSE OF ERARD—PLEYEL—PAPE—MORE ABOUT ENG-
LISH PIANOFORTE-MAKING—THE FIRST INTRODUCTION OF
IRON—HAWKINS—COLLARDS—THE UPRIGHT PIANOFORTE
—MARIUS—SOUTHWELL.

THE name of Erard is more historic than that of Pleyel.
The founder of this celebrated house was Sebastian
Erhardt, born in Strasburg in 1752, of German parents.
At sixteen he settled in Paris, where he learned harpsichord-making. He dropped incidentally into the pianoforte business, and in collaboration with his brother Jean
Batiste founded the house of Erard. Meanwhile young
Erhardt had changed the exterior expression of his name
to Erard, owing to the hostility felt during those years
toward the Germans by the French. The French Revolution drove the Erards to London, where they carried
on business for some time, but later returned to Paris.
Sebastian Erard patented some harp improvements in
1794, which gave him some note. His well-known double
action for the harp, which gave him special notoriety,
was *mock patented* in 1808. This was really the invention
of William Southwell, formerly of Dublin, who took out

SEBASTIAN ERARD.

JOHN BROADWOOD.

a patent for it in 1798 after moving to London.   He sold
the invention to Erard in 1808 among other matters.
Erard, acting under a private understanding with the
former, made a show of registering the invention, with
certain modifications, as his own, and thus achieved all
the credit and profit of the patent.

Sebastian Erard died in Paris in 1831 generally regretted.   The Erards adopted Backers's English grand
action for some time, until his famous Erard double escapement grand action was brought out.   This valuable
innovation made the Erard grands famous throughout
the musical world.   This was patented by Pierre Erard,
son of Sebastian, in 1821, at that time a partner of his
father.

A. J. Hipkins, in his article " Pianoforte," in the *En-
cyclopædia Britannica*, recalls an interesting circumstance regarding this action, related as follows : When
the British patent rights expired in 1835, the action had
meantime created so much notice that Pierre Erard was
anxious to have it protected for a new lease of time.   In
trying to effect this he carried the matter into the English superior courts at enormous expense, and finally
appealed to the House of Lords, which was considered
a most extraordinary course under the circumstances.
Having many influential friends among the British aristocracy and nobility, he was able to bring these factors
to bear for personal purposes, for noble and " superior"
people like to exercise their power just to assist a friend
at any moral expense.   In the Erard case, however,
Pierre Erard was striving to attain an honest right.
With the assistance of his noble friends he was able to
obtain an extension of his patent.   The Erards initiated

many improvements from 1800 up to 1840, apart from their improved grand action. One was their method of " bearing" for the strings. Their case-building schemes were also very significant factors in the improvement of the Erard pianoforte. The Erards claim—among many other important innovations—to have first introduced the shifting transposition action in the grand. From one of Foucaud's works published in Paris, in 1840, I learn that this invention was first tried upon a piano made for Marie Antoinette. Foucaud, however, only repeated what he learned directly from that firm. One Edward Riley patented the idea in London, in 1801, and this record is supposed to be the earliest publication of the transposition action principle in England. It has been recently reintroduced in London by several houses with much success.

The Erards are credited with having first designed and applied the string " agraffe," but this—in its modern shape—Foucaud attributes to Pape. Pape comes to our notice at this juncture.

It is a curious fact that the greatest French piano firms known were founded by natives of other European countries, not by Frenchmen. For instance, Pleyel was an Austrian, Erard a native of Strasburg, and properly a German, while Pape was born in Hanover. Jean Henri Pape saw the light in 1789. In 1809, when he was twenty years of age, he arrived in Paris, and in the following year entered Pleyel's establishment as a workman. Foucaud writes as follows in reference to Pape : " When he had become a skilful workman, not yet satisfied, he determined to travel outside of France and learn more. He turned toward England, for at that time—

1817—our English neighbors enjoyed a marked superiority in their pianos," which is complimentary to England.

On Pape's return to France from England he founded his own business house. M. Andes, writing of pianos and improvements in the Paris *Musical Gazette* for 1836, speaks at length of Pape's contributions to the development of the instrument, particularly of Pape's down-striking-action invention. Pape, it seems, exhibited his first piano built on this plan, with the action position above the strings, in 1827. This instrument was, it is scarcely necessary to remark, a horizontal piano. It was shown publicly in October of that year in Paris. Meanwhile the inventor claimed to have worked upon the idea since the previous year. Thomas Loud, Jr., of Philadelphia, however, took out a patent in Washington for a similar invention on May 15th, 1827, and clearly anticipated the celebrated French maker under discussion in this direction, while evidence, moreover, is in existence which proves that Loud took the editor of the *Franklin Institute Journal* to his shop in Philadelphia in April, 1826, and there showed him the basis of his technical schemes in advance of the patent, which was only applied for after Loud had worked out his experiments to a satisfactory issue. Pape was the first to introduce felt in Europe, according to M. Andes, but Alpheus Babcock, of Boston, unquestionably preceded him in this "new departure," for the latter was granted a United States patent in 1833 for the introduction of this hammer-covering material in pianos, which was, however, not availed of for many years after. Pape's first pianos, with felt, came out in 1839 ; but he previously advocated its use in 1835.

Pape invented a tuning-fork piano among his numerous experimental effects, which came to little. About 1838 he made some striking departures in the exterior structural plans of his instruments, which won him extensive notice. In this connection he exhibited a hexagonal and a cycloid piano. These improvements led up to no permanent reform, I may add. Pape was the first to introduce overstringing and iron bracing in French pianos unquestionably, and was altogether, taking him by the actual, aside from the experimental results, one of the greatest figures ever identified with the piano business in France. From the wording of a British patent granted to Pierre Frederick Fischer, merchant of Marlborough Street, London, in 1835, in which "overstringing" and the use and manufacture of woollen felt in relation to the piano are dealt with at considerable length in the specification, it becomes clear that Pape was the inventor in the background hereabouts. Fischer claimed to have had these improvements " communicated to him from abroad," and was not personally concerned outside of a legal point. Now Pape issued a pamphlet, I find, about this period in which he mentions felt, and makes a hidden allusion to a new method of stringing. On taking the wording and substance of both Pape's writings and Fischer's specification, side by side, it is almost apparent that Pape was Fischer's friend and the real person interested in the patent referred to. Meantime Hipkins and all other authorities on the piano in England have overlooked Fischer in relation to " overstringing "

Meanwhile I shall give a sketch of the first attempts to introduce metal into pianos as a case-strengthening and bracing agent and the authors.

This has an all-important bearing on the history of modern piano development, but more particularly on the American instrument as an individualized species.

The first noteworthy application of iron to the piano was made by Joseph Smith, of London, in 1799, not for compensation or resistance purposes designedly, but merely to promote a scheme that the inventor had patented in that year—October 3d—for introducing a tambourine, triangle, and other similar features into the instrument. It was in relation to this curious *pot-pourri* of acoustic effects—not by any means musical—that Smith happened to apply iron to the piano. Nothing came of Smith's scheme, need it be added. Prior to this, one Dr. Hopkinson, of Philadelphia, a Scotchman, exhibited a harpsichord made with an iron frame. Mention of it is made remotely in a volume of " American Philosophical Transactions." Hopkinson was a medical doctor by profession, and from what I can learn an Edinburgh graduate. The instrument Hopkinson introduced the improvement referred to may have been a piano, as the description published is very misleading, and the writer evidently did not know the difference between a piano and a harpsichord, so as to distinguish either individually.

Philadelphia was destined to be again more definitely and unmistakably identified with the permanent introduction of metal in the piano, as well as with the production of the *first* upright approximating to the present instrument in shape. The author of these improvements was an Englishman, John Isaac Hawkins, a civil engineer by profession, and necessarily a student of the nature and composition of metals, who had lived in Philadelphia for many years prior to the events herewith outlined. Hawkins took out a United States patent dated February 12th, 1800, for an upright piano, entitled a "portable grand pianoforte," a drawing of which is given in these pages, in which metal was extensively used. The general features of this remarkable instrument are discussed in another chapter. Hawkins took out another distinct patent in Washington on October 10th of the same year, for "improvements in the nature and construction of musical instruments." Isaac Hawkins, his father, also secured the "rights and privileges" of a British patent in the same year. Hawkins's pianos had little value musically. The inventor displayed special ability mainly in the ingenuity of his action, general novelty of the case, and his method of slinging the belly within an independent iron frame, as reviewed later. In these results sketched in the foregoing, Hawkins's peculiar relation to piano improvement is exemplified. However, not being formally a piano-maker, he failed from the practical standpoint to produce a permanent and positive improvement there and then. The examples he furnished his successors as to the use of iron, and economizing of space in piano construction have nevertheless been invaluable. The next striking introduction of iron in piano structure occurs in 1820.

To turn to the origin of the firm of Collard & Collard, an eminent house still in existence, I may point out that, owing to its connection from 1827 upward with James Stewart, originally a partner of Jonas Chickering in Boston, Collard & Collard's piano history has been somewhat moulded by American influences—that is, to the extent that Stewart, who was for upward of thirty-five

years foreman in that eminent shop, all along tried to
copy American ideas, as they evolved, into these instruments and occasionally in details successfully managed
to overcome the natural conservatism of his employers
in this respect, with effective results always, as could be
exemplified. Take in this connection the Collard & Collard improved square after the American lines, which up
to a recent date was exceedingly popular in England.
This was a specialty particularly known as " Collardian,"
so to speak, among musical people. Stewart's hand can
be traced in these improvements.

The house of Collard was founded originally in 1800 by
Clementi, the celebrated pianist and composer, in collaboration with Frederick W. Collard, a practical student
of pianoforte building. Clementi had previously been
connected with the firm of Longman & Lakey, but trans-
ferred his name and influence over to Collard in the year
given. This new establishment soon sprang into prominence owing to Clementi's great drawing influence as a
friend of the leading people of the period. In some time
Clementi dropped out, the house subsequently passing
through some titular changes. The present combination
name of Collard & Collard appeared in due time and
became a household word in Great Britain and Ireland.
F. W. Collard made many notable progressions in his
methods of construction after starting in business, which
helped to build up the reputation of the instrument. In
1826 James Stewart arrived from Boston, Mass. He carried two pianofortes across, such as those bearing the
inscription of Stewart & Chickering, and their general
excellence, taken in relation to Stewart as a part maker,
was such a manifest proof of Stewart's ability, that he

was thereupon engaged by the Collard firm to become foreman of their eminent shop.

Apart from names of firms given, many small places came into existence from 1780 upward in London, Paris, Dublin, Vienna, Florence, Berlin, and a multiplicity of small German, Austrian, and Italian cities too numerous to particularize. Among the London names were Geib, Loud, Davis, and many others familiar in early New York and Philadelphia records of piano-making. Thus a distinct relationship exists between these phases of English and early American history.

The upright, owing to its neat appearance and portable character, as well as its tone possibilities, is the favorite instrument with the masses at present in all countries where the piano is used. Therefore it deserves special notice here.

The abstract exterior form of the upright piano, as distinguished from horizontal instruments, is not by any means the materialization of a modern idea, for harpsichords were made upon this plan two centuries ago. Even Marius, the French rival of Cristofori, submitted a crude upright piano among the three instruments examined by the Paris *Académie des Sciences* in February, 1716. In the " Recueil des Instruments Approuvés par l'Académie des Sciences," published in that year, engraved plans of Marius's three *clavecins à maillets* are given, with explanations. Two of these instruments were horizontal in position, while the third harpsichord *à maillet*—which was the name Marius gave his invention— was a *vertical* one, in which the key impelled a rod furnished with the hammer directly upon the string. Nothing came from this example, however. I may add

ROSSI SPINET. SIXTEENTH CENTURY.

South Kensington Museum, London.

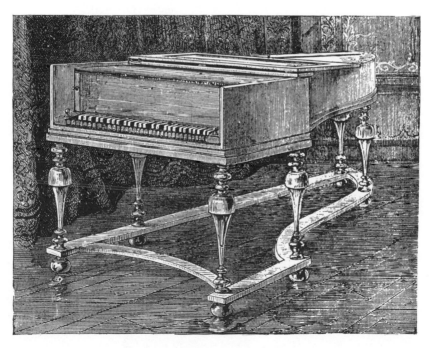

SILBERMANN GRAND PIANO. A.D. 1746.

From the original used by J. S. Bach in the Town Palace, Potsdam.

that this fact has been little commented upon in other histories.

Many attempts were made subsequently in Germany, Italy, France, and England to produce an upright piano by placing a square or grand on end or otherwise, so as to attain the results indicated. John Landreth performed the feat in 1787 by altering the position of a grand, and fitting it out with a special action, but his scheme proved a failure in the aggregate. Pardio, of Venice, about this year tried a similar idea, with the same results.

Stodart, of London, in 1795 invented an upright in the form of a bookcase, which came still closer to our present style of instrument in design, but it ended where it began.

Hawkins' instrument in 1800 was the first meritorious anticipation of our present upright, but it was proved in a short time to be of little account from the standpoint of utility.

CHAPTER III.

THE ORIGIN OF THE PIANOFORTE.

SOUTHWELL'S UPRIGHTS—HIS ACTION—SOUTHWELL'S " CABI-
NET "—WORNUM'S IMPORTANT DEVELOPMENTS IN ACTION
MECHANISM—TIMOTHY GILBERT, OF BOSTON—CHICKERING
—ALLEN & THOM'S METAL FRAMES—STEWART'S PATENT
— BROADWOOD'S HITCH-PIN PLATE -- MISCELLANEOUS
ITEMS.

PREVIOUS to Stodart and Hawkins's attempts William
Southwell, of Dublin, the subsequent inventor of the
popular " cabinet," placed a grand on end in 1794, and
to this experimental instrument he applied a special
upright action principle which, although imperfect just
then, ended in the production of his cabinet in 1807.
Southwell moved from Great Marlborough Street, Dublin, in that year, to London, where he lived for many
years.

Southwell's upright grand was exhibited in London
in the year signified, and attracted so much attention
that the great composer Haydn, then visiting the English metropolis, called at Southwell's shop in Lad Lane
and expressed himself delighted with the new field this

instrument outlined in piano-case structure, besides praising the musical results attained.

In this instrument Southwell exhibited for a positive certainty a compass of six octaves. In his patent, taken out on October 18th of that year—1794, the words " addition of treble keys," which occur in the opening of the specification, refer to this innovation   Southwell's new range exemplified in this piano ran from F to F. The instrument was found incapable of standing the enforced tension resulting from this extension of compass, and, therefore, was practically of little account.

Broadwood, meanwhile, learning of Haydn's distinguished interest in Southwell's schemes—a part of which was the latter's extension of compass in the keyboard—launched forth an instrument with six octaves, C to C, having a more decided value from a musical standpoint. This " scale," therefore, became generally copied all over the Continent.

Southwell's upright grand having been discarded for many reasons, this very clever man kept steadily at his ultimate purpose, and in 1798 produced a more convenient form of upright by placing a square on the side. To this he also applied a more perfected model of the action applied in his grand. This piano is illustrated in these pages from an instrument in the possession of W. Simpson, Esq., of Dundee, Scotland, thanks to Mr. A. J. Hipkins' historical work, in which it originally appeared. This piano was patented on November 8th of the year indicated.

In 1802 Thomas Loud, of London, produced an upright that, according to the specification of his patent on this instrument, was the real precursor in build and general characteristics of the perfected instrument of our time, but it is not known if Loud ever carried out his plans to a logical issue in London. Southwell now came out in 1807 with his "cabinet," which he patented on April 8th. This was a *bona fide* musical instrument, not a mere experiment in upright-case structure, and aside from its many obvious faults won praise from all sides. I have no hesitation in claiming Southwell to have been the real inventor of the upright pianoforte at this juncture. It is shown that he persistently followed out the idea of an upright for fourteen or more years, and ended by producing the *first* instrument of that character, out of which all subsequent uprights sprang. In this initial cabinet he succeeded in producing the first comparatively successful "scale" ever applied to the upright. Hawkins and his other rivals failed here. Moreover, Southwell introduced the first workable form of upright action ever seen up to that date, and passed all competitors in this respect. His method of case-building and the general characteristics of his instrument, in short, externally as well as internally, furnished the parent model upright out of which all other more improved instruments of that family have descended. Southwell's cabinet pianoforte was unquestionably—with all its admitted imperfections—the most significant innovation produced in connection with the development of the instrument for over forty years, and was the outcome—as I have tried to show—of many years of earnest effort and experiment. Southwell took out another patent in 1811 for improvements in this instrument of a many-sided kind, in which the action and other component features of the instrument are included.

Robert Wornum, a great figure in subsequent years, was granted his first patent in March, 1811, for an "improved upright with diagonal strings." This was a radical departure from, and an improvement on Southwell's piano. Wornum hereabouts becomes the connecting link. This instrument was known as Wornum's harmonic pianoforte. In this model the extreme height of the cabinet was reduced to about four feet six inches. This became the English cottage piano in after years. In 1826 Wornum produced his "piccolo" upright, being a reduced model of his first piano, thereby bringing the height down to three feet six inches. In this year he also patented a pezzicato pedal, also one "hopper" and two check actions. In the two models of uprights alluded to—produced in 1811 and 1826, respectively—Wornum exhibited a special action principle of much value, which attracted little attention in England. Pleyel, of Paris, however, took up one of these action schemes, slightly altered and fathered it, whereupon it became known as the French action.

About this period of the present century the United States had grown past childhood and was beginning to crawl along at a lively pace. Before 1826 I find that Wornum had been anticipated in his "piccolo" upright in this country by Loud & Brothers, of Philadelphia, and more than that, his last action was already almost developed and in use here. Uprights, however, never grew into popular favor in this country at that remote period. Wornum produced his celebrated "tape-check" action in 1843, which was a surpassingly important contribution to the piano.

This action, with some improvements added in this

country, has for years been used universally. Timothy Gilbert, of Boston, in 1841 brought out an upright action somewhat similar to Wornum's, minus the " tape check,'' which contained many ingenious features in anticipation of the former. This action of Gilbert's was furnished with a patent contrivance of value for assisting the quick return of the hammer, as well as with a novel " check'' screwed into the " jack rocker'' in the present way ; and, taken altogether, Gilbert's action deserves special notice. What became of it, however, may be surmised. Jonas Chickering adopted the " tape-check'' action in his up-rights after its publication in England for some time, with certain modifications, but public interest in the upright soon died out about this period, owing to the rapid improvement taking place in squares, hence it was found a waste of time to pay much attention to uprights.

Wornum's " tape-check'' action has become the reign-ing favorite in several European countries, but Great Britain has never taken kindly to it.

Past 1811 Southwell took out several other patents for details in pianoforte improvement, but never became identified with any of these innovations to a notable degree. His fame rested solely, meanwhile, upon the " cabinet.'' Southwell died in the " forties'' at an ad-vanced age at Rathmines, a suburb of Dublin, in which city he was born, and is buried in Glasnevin Cemetery. In devoting so much serious effort to the work of this eminent man in this chapter, the task is inspired by a conviction that his real place in English piano history has never been properly estimated or yet examined for obvious reasons. In helping to call attention to South-

well's real connection with the upright, the writer believes he is performing a duty due to Southwell's genius
and life-work, and thereby hopes to perpetuate his name
to some extent.

Southwell's family have given many eminent people
to the early American stage, let me add, among them
being Henry and Maria Southwell, both of Dublin,
familiar names years ago.

In relation to Thomas Loud's upright piano, patented
in 1802, I wish to point to the fact that Loud's specification contains in text a distinct anticipation of " overstringing." It is exemplified in these words: " Upright
pianos rendered portable by placing the strings in an
oblique direction, fixing the first bass strings from the
left-hand upper corner to the right-hand lower corner
behind the sounding-board, and the rest of the strings
in a parallel direction. By this means an instrument
standing five feet high and four feet wide will admit of
the bass strings being their full length, which is five
feet two inches."

Mr. Hipkins alludes to this patent of Loud's in these
words, in his history : " Thomas Loud patented a diagonal upright pianoforte in 1802." Here he dismisses the
subject. There is nothing in Loud's specification when
read correctly to convey any such impression. At the
same time a " diagonal pianoforte" is in every sense an
unknown quantity.

Loud, moreover, inserts the subjoined words in reference to his new pianoforte model : " The body of the
case does not as usual stand on a frame, but goes down
to the floor and stands on its own base, which affords
the opportunity *that is embraced* to carry or put the sound-

ing-board and strings thus low.'' The specification, if reproduced in full, would furnish unmistakable evidence
sufficient to satisfy any reader who is acquainted with
the outside details of piano construction, that Loud
meant '' overstringing'' in this patent in connection with
his portable upright.

Thomas Loud becomes of much significance personally
to American readers, because he emigrated to New York
in after years, where he died in 1834.   He built '' piccolo''
uprights, with bass overstringing, in this city, meanwhile,
as early as 1830, at least, or even earlier.   Loud's application of the innovation was very crude, and probably
only tested upon a few instruments, but they alone place
him in a very conspicuous position in British-American
piano history.   The British patent, taken out by Loud
in 1802, therefore, had clear reference to this important
method of stringing under notice.   The celebrated
Louds, of Philadelphia, spoken of in that chapter, were
either nephews or children of this clever piano-maker.
The patent here quoted was unfortunately entered in the
British Patent Office without drawings, otherwise there
would have been no room left for doubts or disputes.

Following out this method of stringing somewhat further, it was generally accepted for many years by all
authorities in England that the first person to introduce
'' overstringing'' there was J. Goodwin, of London.   He
took out a patent for this stringing system on March 8th,
1836, and for many years practised it.   On March 2d, of
the same year, Isaac Clark, of Cincinnati, O , was granted
a United States piano patent of a general nature, in
which overstringing is included, which precedes Goodwin by about six days.   If the latter happened to be the

English initiator of the aforesaid reform really—apart
from Loud—Clark's patent would discount him very
materially ; but it has recently been asserted that Geroek,
of Cornhill, London, made an overstrung cottage and a
similar square, in 1835, for Theobald Boehm, the celebrated maker of flutes, after the latter's designs.   A. J.
Hipkins brought this discovery forward a few years ago
as something singularly important, backed up by a fair
show of proof, yet for years Fischer's plan of an overstrung upright, almost identical with the present style,
could have been found on "sheet 2" of the official drawings accompanying this patent in the British Patent
Office, dated May 13th, 1835.

Meanwhile Loud made overstrung "piccolo" uprights
in New York long before this year—whether experi-
mentally or for regular sale cannot be learned—while John
Jardine, of the celebrated family of that name, exhibited
squares, which gives the United States priority in this
respect, even though the two makers named were originally Britons, one English the other evidently Scotch.
Notwithstanding this circumstance America is entitled
to the honor of the achievement pointed out, because it
is a well demonstrated fact, although, perhaps, a subtlety,
that the social and governmental institutions of this
country, in so far as they promote mental freedom, have
a stimulating and immediate influence upon the inventive faculties of persons brought up in Europe and settling here.

Continuing the subject of metal in piano development
from a previous chapter, the first notable European patent or invention produced, after Hawkins' "portable
upright iron frame grands," was Allen & Thom's system

of metal tube and plate bracing patented in 1820.   William Allen was the theoretical inventor of the idea, but James Thom, or Thoms, the foreman at Stodart's, put the invention into practical shape.   Allen was a tuner engaged in this concern meanwhile.   Like Thom he, too, was a Scotchman.

Allen & Thom's invention consisted of a number of metal tubes resting in metal sockets cast in plates, which were attached to the wrest-plank and to the block on which the strings were hitched.   The results which accompanied the introduction of the patent were so significant that the Stodarts secured it.   Broadwood and Erard now followed out this principle somewhat in some small improvements introduced between 1820 and 1823, which gave a further impetus to the use of metal in the pianoforte.   Pleyel, of Paris, in 1826, carried the idea further still, and exhibited in that year a grand having a regular network of small iron bars, crossing and recrossing, which were braced against the side of the instrument. This was no doubt suggested by Allen & Thom's invention, then in general adoption in Stodart's instruments. Pleyel's method did not survive, however, and little can be learned of it at present.

Samuel Herve is credited with having invented the fixed string pin-plate in 1821.   Hipkins states that the Broadwoods applied it to squares in 1822 with effective results.   Francis Melville, of Glasgow, Scotland, was granted a patent for metallic tubular bracing in 1825, which was designed evidently to be an improvement on Allen & Thom's invention, but nothing is known as to its outcome.

In 1827 James Stewart was granted a patent for his

method of stringing " without having loops or eyes in
single strings, by making one continuous string pass
round a single hitch-pin." This principle became copied
almost universally in a few years after this date all
through Europe. Stewart had previously arrived in
London from this country, where he was well known
as the first partner of Jonas Chickering. The idea of
stringing, formulated in this patent by Stewart, was carried over from Boston, where it was commonly known
as early as 1820.

James Shudi Broadwood took out another patent in
this year for a metal string plate for grands, which
became a permanent feature of the Broadwood instruments for several years, until such time as a better form
of plate took its place.

William Allen was granted another patent in 1832 for
a plate with tension-resistance and " compensating" improvements cast in one piece, the first of the kind ever
introduced in Europe. This was palpably a copy of
Alpheus Babcock's metal plate patented December 17th,
1825, in the United States Patent Office, which Hipkins
has very impartially always alluded to in connection
with the introduction of the metal plate in one casting.
The latter authority, however, is in error as to the real
nature and extent of Babcock's patent, as shown in another section. Allen could have learned in London
through Stewart, directly or indirectly, of Babcock's invention, for Stewart, no doubt, saw or learned of Babcock's iron frame pianos before he left Boston for England. At the same time Allen may have conceived the
basis of this invention without any exterior suggestions,
as he did in his former patent. Babcock, of Boston,

however, preceded him in this very important development.

Miscellaneous European pianoforte improvements were patented in the interregnum between the last date—1832—and the beginning of the century, of a nature too general and detailed to be included in these chapters. They do not always concern American pianoforte history directly, and are, therefore, in the abstract superfluous. The development of the pianoforte in Europe from this period upward becomes a matter of special history, and is entirely outside the scope of this work, unless in exceptional cases where points of comparison are made between special American and European improvements. The technical and musical relationship of European and American instruments is, meantime, perfectly apparent.

CHAPTER IV.

Boston.

A SPINET IN 1770 — REVOLUTIONARY PIANOFORTES — VON HAGEN — FIRST PIANOFORTES — CREHORE -— APPLETON-— OSBORN—STEWART.

THE historic city of Boston has for many years been credited with being the first place in which pianofortes were made on this continent. Although this is proved in a later chapter to be a fallacy, Boston still deserves precedence in this work, because it has in the past stood forth in the relation of a national school to the piano art business in this country. The *American* pianoforte deserves that distinctive title just as legitimately as the reed organ or harmonium, which in the abstract, like the piano, derived from Europe, is entitled to be known as the *American* organ, because in both cases these instruments are constructed in many particulars somewhat different to French, German, or English organs and pianos. Boston has been a national school, as I have observed, because some of the most distinctive features in the American piano, as it is to-day, originated there in part. Readers must take this in the broad sense.

First, there is the application of metal to the pianoforte, without which the modern methods of overstringing and enlarged resonating possibilities of the sounding-board, which result to some extent from the larger capacity of the case, would be impossible.   To Boston, coupled with the names of Alpheus Babcock and Jonas Chickering, we owe the first successful and permanent introduction of metal plates into squares and grands.   Timothy Gilbert, another Bostonian, also anticipated the present upright action in use throughout this country, and bequeathed to the trade many very potent technical ideas in connection with the improvement and development of the upright piano.   Jonas Chickering was incontrovertibly the first to strike out from the traditional methods which piano-makers at first trod in relation to the building of cases, for having of necessity studied the question of resistance *plus* tension, while developing his square and grand metal plates, he saw that the American pianoforte of the future would be large in body, therefore endowed with greater resonating facilities and tone-producing power.   The whole cast metal plate was the key to these conditions, and no unprejudiced person, standing on the ground of the technical historian, while gazing over the whole field of pianoforte development in this country, can take away from Jonas Chickering the credit of being the initiator practically of the significant innovations which are here coupled with his name, and these are linked unquestionably with the *nationalization* of the American pianoforte.

The United States Patent Office offers sufficient testimony on this point, as witness the official plates given. Opening with this plea for Boston, as the school from

which the most significant technical and acoustic traits
of our instruments have been derived primarily, let me
now proceed to sketch its history in connection with
the subject of this work.

The first mention I find of anything approaching the
making of pianos in Boston during the end of the last
century, is a notice published in the Boston *Gazette*, February, 1770, which speaks of an " excellent spinet," that
had just been finished by a resident of the city, " which,
for goodness of workmanship and harmony of sound, is
esteemed by the best judges to be superior to any that
has been imported from Europe." The State of Massachusetts, however, apart from the " Hub," may be credited with having produced the first violins made in this
country—assuming that an allusion to other musical instruments in this remote historical connection is permis-
sible—and Salem has long been spoken of as the place
in which the earliest organ known in this country was
set up. John Clark built the organ alluded to in 1743
for the Episcopal church of that town. This fact is
gleaned from " Felt's Annals of Salem." The Pennsylvania Historical Society, however, has furnished me with
authentic information regarding early organ-building in
that State, which advances a strong claim that one Matthias Zimmerman built an organ in Philadelphia before
1737, for his will was probated in that year, and in it he
bequeaths his organ to his nephew, hoping that he
would learn to play on it, further adding, " If not, it
can be sold, owing to its being so much of a curiosity."
Philadelphia also anticipated Boston in the matter of
producing spinets, for a Swedish organ-builder named
Gustavus Hesselins, made these instruments there as

early as 1742, as a matter of absolute fact.   Hesselins furthermore preceded Broomfield and others in the building of organs, as I have indicated, aside from Zimmerman altogether.

Ed. Broomfield, Jr., erected a large organ in Boston in 1745, and later on essayed to make harpsichords, of which no particulars can be ascertained.

Of pianofortes, the first reference that comes to hand is curiously enough truly historic, for I learn that the famous continental privateering frigate " Boston," sailed by the intrepid Captain Tucker, brought a British merchant ship as a prize into port in 1779, whereupon the cargo was sold for the benefit of the National Treasury, and among the general booty put up for sale " a London-made pianoforte" was included, also flutes, harpsichord wire and tools.   The ship was bound for New York, then occupied by the British, and carrying a general cargo of necessaries intended for the continental market ; for British merchants naturally put personal gains above mere party feeling of the time, and continued to ship goods to every port available.

After the battle of Lexington had been fought, meanwhile, frequent advertisements appeared in the patriot press of Boston and the State regarding flutes and drums for martial purposes.   This allusion, while it diverges from the subject of pianofortes, will no doubt be admissible at this point, because it throws light upon a picturesque phase of American musical history.   And let me here say, that " the musical" market at this period in Boston was made up mostly of consignments of these common-place musical instruments.   To our nineteenth-century mental palates the idea of rudely-uniformed soldiers

PIANOFORTE BY HAWKINS. A.D. 1800.

In the Possession of Messrs. Broadwood, London.

SOUTHWELL'S PIANO. A.D. 1798.

In the Possession of A. Simpson, Esq., Dundee, Scotland.

marching to battle without the accompaniment of a modern military band, and in its stead a few shrill fifes and noisy drums, may provoke a certain amount of ridicule; but let us not forget that the men of the Revolution did "passing well" under the circumstances. Without them and their rude musical, as well as dynamic accoutrements of warfare, the words American pianoforte, American musical art, or similar phrases, applied in the nationalist, though not necessarily insular sense, would scarcely be known to-day, for nationalism in art or life cannot exist without freedom, and this boon the patriot soldiers of the Revolution bequeathed to the race.

Passing over the Revolutionary epoch, I find that the pianoforte, toward 1790, superseded the harpsichord in the drawing-rooms of those rich Boston families that aimed at personally simulating, if not at really promoting an appreciation of musical art. According to a newspaper extract of 1791 there were upward of twenty-seven pianofortes to be found in the houses of rich Boston merchants and "esquires" throughout the whole city. These instruments were all London-made instruments, and were imported by general merchants along with other goods of a miscellaneous character from time to time since 1786, as explained incidentally in relation to early pianoforte importations in the New York chapters. Marquis de Chastellux, referred to elsewhere, saw pianofortes in Boston drawing-rooms as early as 1780, which fact he noted with astonishment.

Boston had two harpsichord and piano teachers in 1789, one of whom officiated as tuner and general repairer. About 1795 Peter A. von Hagen came to Boston from New York, and located there permanently, having been appointed in a short time musical conductor in the Federal Street Theatre. On his arrival in Boston his card announced that he was prepared to teach the piano forte or harpsichord according to the best London methods, adding the words, " Repairing and tuning of these instruments attended to with skill." Von Hagen becomes a significant figure presently.

The first mention I discover of the latter is in Ireland's *Annals of the New York Stage.* Here it is mentioned that in October, 1792, Mrs. Mechler (formerly Miss Storer, a very popular English singer and actress in New York prior to the war), who had long been absent from the local stage, appeared at a concert in Corré's Hotel in conjunction with Mr. and Mrs. von Hagen, recently from London. Von Hagen published the first copy of his *Musical Magazine* in December, 1797, from his address, 3 Cornhill, Boston, where he sold music imported from London, and in 1800 the Boston city directory gave his name in connection with the same house number and street.

Regarding the initial manufacture of pianos in Boston, it has long been generally accepted that the first instruments made there, were made by Benjamin Crehore, of Milton, a suburb of that city, some time around 1798–1800. These dates have hitherto been published and circulated as the probable period in which the first piano was made, not only in Boston but in this country. This latter feature of discussion shall be reserved. No specific or authoritative dates have ever been advanced in connection with Crehore's first instrument, or no proof can be traced in the directory or through such a source. Thomas Appleton, the organ-builder, who knew Crehore

and all the circumstances of his history, wrote a sketch
before he died, so as to throw light upon this phase
of musical instrument development here, which appeared
in conjunction with several others concerning pianoforte
history in the *American Musician* in 1887, but gave nothing of importance regarding Crehore in this connection.
Appleton wrote the statement referred to in 1871.

Many absurd and glamorous accounts have been published, from time to time, by way of illustrating how
Crehore became connected with pianoforte-making. One
foolish story tells us how he first repaired a violin for
Von Hagen, when the idea of making pianos suggested
itself to him. Another tale has it that he put glue in the
crack of a harpsichord sounding-board in 1797, whereupon he became so inflated with the awful success of his
attempt as a harpsichord repairer that he began to make
pianos. All these stories are unjust to Benjamin Crehore.
The facts are these, that Crehore was, as far back as 1791
well known in Boston, New York, and Philadelphia as a
maker of violins, 'cellos, and other instruments of that
family, besides guitars, drums, and flutes. In 1792 he
exhibited a harpsichord, with improvements suggested
by the pianoforte, and from this date forward became
known as a repairer of these instruments from the mechanical standpoint. His name also occurs in Annals of
the Boston Stage, for he became well known as a stage
carpenter and general expert around the Federal Street
Theatre in 1797. He evidently became acquainted with
Von Hagen about this time, and shortly afterward began
his initial attempt at piano-making proper ; or, he may
have made his first pianoforte still earlier. From Von
Hagen's subsequent relations with him, however, it is

probable that Von Hagen was connected with the production of Crehore's initial instrument.   Von Hagen was an excellent musician and posed as a tuner in his time. Crehore, being in no sense capable of reproducing the acoustic features of a pianoforte *solus*, he had some assistant clearly to attend to this department as well as the tuning, and Von Hagen was the man.

Von Hagen, in 1801, sold Crehore's pianofortes in his store on Common Street in conjunction with imported instruments, and continued in actual partnership with him up to 1807.

In the interregnum Von Hagen had his pianoforte warerooms also on Essex Street after 1805.   Crehore through all this time still assisted, on and off, at stage-carpenter work in the Federal Street Theatre.

Crehore was not the only person in the mean time that made pianos in Boston.

I find in the city directory for 1798 the names of "Bent & Green, musical instrument makers, 90 Newbury Street."   In 1800 the name of Green disappears and "William & Adam Bent, musical instrument makers, 26 Orange Street," appears in the directory, and continues at this address up to 1807, when "William Bent, pianoforte-maker, 24 Orange Street," comes to light. In 1809 he appears for the last time at 49 Newbury Street. Appleton stated that he visited the shop of the Bents as early as 1803, when they were then making pianos. "Their place," he says, "was on Winter Street, near Washington, when I became acquainted with them." They never appear on this street in the city directory, but it is possible that the Bents made a stray pianoforte as early as 1800, or, indeed, it is probable, and almost certain, judging from the wording of a vague press notice of that year, that William Bent was the "expert mechanic" whose "new grand pianoforte" created so much attention in 1799 in Boston. This could not refer to Crehore, for it spoke of the workshop of this expert as being situated in the rear of Newbury Street. Crehore, meanwhile, had his shop in Milton, as far as can be ascertained. If this theory is incorrect, then Crehore must have been the maker of this pianoforte referred to. The Bents went out of business in 1809. In Appleton's words : "William Bent invented the first leather-splitting machine, got a patent on it, and went to Philadelphia, where he carried on a leather business. Adam also retired from business and became a land speculator in South Boston."

In the Columbia *Sentinel*, from which many incidental items have been gleaned for these pages, I find the following notice in 1805 : "Mr. Mallet keeps constantly on hand and for sale at his musical repository, Devonshire Street, a handsome assortment of pianofortes, English and American." This was a newcomer in the field. The matter-of-fact way in which the word American is used here seems to indicate that there were many makers of these instruments in Boston at the period. Although frequent notices of this nature appear still earlier, there was always a sort of atmosphere surrounding these announcements, which indicated that those who could afford to purchase pianos had doubts as to the reliableness of American-made instruments, and this circumstance influenced the policy of Von Hagen and other advertisers. Mallet's card, however, has a ring of independence about it, as shown. Mallet sold Shaw's pianos about the year named. Francis Shaw was another maker, who came to Boston about 1804 from New York. He began in this year to make pianos on Chambers Street. A *Gazette* announcement speaks, in 1804, of the arrival in Boston of an expert pianoforte and musical instrument maker from London. Shaw, however, seems to have lived for a few years in New York before turning up in the "Hub." Shaw holds a significant place in early Boston records, for he took out the first patent relating to improvements in pianofortes, or to musical instruments of any kind, ever granted by the National Government to a resident of Massachusetts. This patent was issued on July 2d, 1806. Beyond the fact that several of Shaw's pianos are said to be in existence, little is known of his subsequent career.

Professor von Hagen had pianoforte warerooms on Essex Street up to 1808, when he retired from business and devoted himself exclusively to his professional duties. Benjamin Crehore, who undoubtedly is entitled to the honor of being considered the first maker of pianofortes in Massachusetts, survived the Bents. His workshop in Milton was the training school for such bright lights in our history as John Osborn and the two Babcock brothers, Lewis and Alpheus. The latter was taught tuning by Von Hagen, and after 1805 made this a specialty. Crehore made, probably, not more than ten or twelve pianos every year, and these he could dispose of—owing to native prejudice against this class of home-made luxuries among the exclusive people who alone possessed pianos in those days—only through Von Hagen's influence as a teacher of music. It is said that Crehore put the imprint of London and Paris on his instruments so as to sell them. This is entirely probable and natural. One thing must not be forgotten at this juncture, and it is that without a tariff on pianos at that time Crehore or any other native workman could not compete with the London and Paris workmen for obvious reasons.

In 1810 the Babcocks began making pianofortes in a small workshop at 44½ Newbury Street, Boston. In 1813 Thomas Appleton, already quoted, was taken into partnership by the Babcock Brothers for the purpose of combining pipe-organ manufacturing with pianos, Appleton being the organ specialist of the trio. Crehore at this time turns up as a journeyman piano-maker in the shop of Appleton & Babcock Brothers, having entirely failed on his own responsibility some time previously. Mallet and Shaw were accidentally responsible for this circumstance, owing to their successful competition. Crehore, no doubt, after leaving Von Hagen, weighted down by the disadvantage of living in a suburban village and having little facilities, financially or otherwise, for promoting success, got crowded out in the race, not a dishonorable *finale* by any means, for many clever men in all pursuits have come to this end. Hence, it is, why we find him working in the shop of Appleton & Babcock Brothers in his old age.

Crehore did not live in vain by any means. His name deserves an emphatic place in this history, because his shop, humble though it was, and entirely bare of technical examples of any value, brought forth Osborn and Alpheus Babcock. I have elsewhere issued eulogies in this connection. Crehore was born in Milton, of Gaelic stock, evidently Scotch-Irish, as his name denotes, and

died in his native village in 1819, after a useful life, poor
and forgotten.

In 1815 the Babcocks and Appleton, then at 18 Winter
Street, were joined by the Hoyts Brothers, who for many
years had been importers of small musical goods and
cheap pianos from Europe, when the firm of Hoyts, Babcock & Appleton was started.   Presently they moved to
a large building on Milk Street, said to be the site of
Franklin's birthplace, where they carried on business
until the great commercial panic and general business
depression of 1819, said to result from lowering the sea-
board tariff, visited the country, which affected them so
materially that they had to separate.   Lewis Babcock,
previous to this event, died in 1817, in Milton.   The
Hoyts dropped out of sight in 1819.   Thomas Appleton
returned to organ building on his own account, opening
his shop at the back of 19 Marlborough Street in that
year.   Many organs yet exist as examples of the latter's
professional skill.

Alpheus Babcock comes to light in the city directory
for 1821 at 11 Marlborough Street.   In 1822 he moved
to Parkanan's Market, Cambridge Street, where he carried on business with John Mackay, whose name occurs
further on in conjunction with that of Jonas Chickering.
It was about this period that Babcock originated his
famous metal plate for squares, which is illustrated in
these pages.   John Dwight, a pupil of John Osborn, yet
anticipated him somewhat in a " longitudinal metal bar,"
which, no doubt, furnished Babcock with the cue to his
plate scheme.

John Osborn—to return—one of Crehore's cleverest
apprentices, as his subsequent career proved, began busi-

J. Chickering

ness for himself in 1815 at " back of 3 Newbury Street." He became immediately noted for the superiority of his pianos, and in 1819 succeeded in introducing his instruments into general notice in New York and Philadelphia. Stray allusions to Osborn, about 1820–24, in occasional items in the Boston and New York papers, indicate that he was ranked as the very best piano-maker in the country.

In 1819 he moved to Orange Street, where he had in his shop as apprentices such subsequently eminent men as Jonas Chickering, Lemanuel and Timothy Gilbert, and less significant people, such—measured by results— as William Danforth, John Dwight, and Elijah Bullard.

James Stewart, a Scotchman, who emigrated to Baltimore in 1812 and learned piano-making of the Harpers in that city, where he carried on business until ruined by the industrial panic of 1819, came to Boston in 1820, where he became a partner of Osborn's. Stewart, according to Baltimore records, stood very high in the South as a maker, and has the honor of being very probably the first manufacturer to export pianofortes out of the United States, for he is shown to have shipped instruments frequently in 1817 from his shop, " 96 Hanover corner of Conway Street," in Baltimore to Havana, for the West Indian trade ; this being somewhat like sending " coals to Newcastle," for Havana at this time was a sort of wholesale depot for European goods intended for the United States market.

After a short stay with Osborn, Stewart and he quarrelled, whereupon they separated.

The intelligence and superior skill of Jonas Chickering, then in Osborn's shop, as a skilled piano-maker, had

ɒeen for a long time observed by the quick eye of Stewart, with the result that he induced Jonas Chickering to
become his partner in starting an independent business.

In 1823 Stewart started on Tremont Street, when
Stewart & Chickering first appears in the directory.
Next year they moved to 20 Common Street, where they
were located until 1826, when Stewart went to London,
where he afterward became noted in relation to the
Collard & Collard pianofortes, as shown in another
chapter.

CHAPTER V.

NEW YORK.

EARLY HARPSICHORD AND PIANOFORTE IMPORTERS—TRE-
MAINE—ZEDWITZ—PIERSON—PIANOFORTES—GILES—MAR-
QUIS DE CHASTELLUX — ASTOR — CAMPBELL — DODDS &
CLAUS.

SPINETS and virginals were known in New York as
early as the beginning of the last century, and toward
the Revolutionary period harpsichords became common
in every family having any claims to distinction—mone-
tary or otherwise. These were nearly all imported from
England, together with other articles of art and luxury
used in the households of the rich colonists. Learned
European travellers in this country before the Revolution
usually expressed their surprise at finding an unusual
degree of art taste and refinement among the educated
classes, even though Americans were in these colonial
days necessarily dependent upon Europe for intellectual
and artistic food in the shape of books, paintings,
music, musical instruments, and everything tending to
promote higher intellectual and artistic development.
In the face of this fact travellers from the old world were
naturally surprised to find colonial households, in many

cases, particularly in the cities, supplied with nearly all the luxuries known in London and Paris. That the people of the cities appreciated and understood things besides working, praying, and sleeping, is evidenced from the promotion of journalism and drama in these centres at a very remote period. Great orators and scholars like Henry, Carroll, Franklin, the Adamses, and such figures in pre-Revolutionary and subsequent history, were not fed intellectually upon a mere course of stereotyped school studies and rustic pastimes. Those men read deeply, knew what was going on in the old world—although seven and eight weeks after date —and were by no means so antiquated as some writers would have us believe. Their personal letters, speeches, and general utterances indicate that they were men of great culture and breadth of character, fully in touch with literary, art, as well as political progress. All of them, from Washington upward, knew indirectly something of music, and appreciated it thoroughly. In connection with the prominent people of that great epoch, which marks the impulse of this country toward national greatness, we read of spinets, harpsichords, and pianofortes. The Carroll harpsichord, the Washington pianoforte, and facts of this kind are mentioned in standard histories. Jefferson and his contemporary lights alluded to drama, music, and painting in their public utterances and private correspondence in most familiar and appreciative terms, and in the houses of all of these men were to be found harpsichords and pianofortes at a very early date.

Spinets, virginals, and harpsichords were brought over from London by general merchants in the same

manner as paintings, books, fine furniture, and other
luxuries and necessaries were imported. Usually ship
masters studied every want, and in some cases contracted
with colonists for the purchase of special articles in England. All the ships engaged in this trade before 1783
were mostly British, and for twenty or more years after,
they held the sway on the seas as international traders.
General merchants of New York, such as Hayman Levy,
Peter Goelet, Campbell, and Gault, John Arthur, Riving-
ton, and others, imported harpsichords—and occasionally
a pianoforte for a special customer before 1776—in an informal manner ; meanwhile they brought over furniture,
paintings, clothing, pots, kettles, ladies' hoops and fineries, books, and a thousand other articles in the same
ship. In those days of American life storekeepers did
not devote themselves to one or two specialties entirely,
which has since grown to be the order of things. In
many cases these rich merchants were owners or part
owners in trading ships.

As regards spinet or harpsichord-making in New York,
the earliest account of this nature on record is, as far as
can be learned, that one Tremaine, a skilful cabinet-
maker and musician, incidentally made a harpsichord of
" a most agreeable and melodious volume and tone character," which was used in the old John Street Theatre
in 1759 at a benefit performance arranged by a " company of London thespians just in town." Tremaine
was before this year, like Crehore, associated with the
stage of this old house occasionally as a stage carpenter
and general handyman. He subsequently became an
actor. Annals of the American stage say that he made
his *début* in 1759 at Williamsburg, Va., appearing after-

ward in New York. Tremaine was probably the first musical director in this country, for he essayed about this year to act in that capacity. He held a place on the New York stage until after the Revolution as an actor, and seems to have been generally respected in his profession.

Passing over 1759, the next circumstance in this line of research I discover, is an announcement in an issue of the New York *Journal* for 1773, stating that " David Walhaupter, at the upper end of Fair Street *makes* and repairs harpsichords, guitars, and all sorts of musical instruments." They had pianofortes in New York in this year also, for I find in another issue of this paper that " Herman Zedwitz, violin teacher just from Europe," advertises a concert at " Hull's Assembly Rooms at the sign of the Golden Spade," and on following out the subsequent numbers of the newspaper referred to for news of this concert, I find among other things that " the accompaniment of Mr. Hulett on the pianoforte was very chaste and always appropriate to the variations of Mr. Zedwitz's playing," as this precursor of our latter-day musical critics oddly expresses it. Thus we see that the residents of New York at that period were not so backward, in a musical sense, as they are generally supposed to have been.

In 1774 Herman Zedwitz established a sort of " trust " in the business of chimney cleaning, and offers through the *Journal* to take " contracts per year or quarter " for dusting out the sooty interiors of flues. " None but competent boys employed," he assures his patrons. Rather an incongruous association of professions, truly. New Yorkers scarcely appreciated the genius of Herr Zedwitz, very evidently, as a violin virtuoso, when he had to recruit his financial status, between professional *séances*, by sending small boys up chimneys.

In 1775 one William Pierson announces from his address " at the sign of the Dial, Hanover Square," that he teaches vocal music and the harpsichord, also tunes harpsichords and other musical instruments. This issue of the New York *Journal*, May 14th, 1775, published while yet the guns of Lexington echoed in the people's ears, contains quite a number of musical and dramatic items, all contrasting very incongruously when compared with the general columns of the paper, which is filled with patriotic letters, resolutions, and exhortations, all breathing the spirit of war. David Wolhaupter rises to the occasion, for he asserts typographically in that issue that his " military drums equal anything imported." John Holt, the patriotic editor of the *Journal*, prints another paragraph informing his readers that excellent drums could be purchased at his store.

In addition to the facts recited I find various concerts announced during 1773, 1774, and 1775, many new names appearing meanwhile, among them being that of William C. Hulett, mentioned previously, who became quite prominent afterward. Among announcements of goods received from England by city merchants, in these years, musical instruments appeared in quite a casual and ordinary manner. Peter Goelet, in his new supply of goods just imported in the " Earl of Dunmore," advertised April 29th, 1773, specifies over three hundred different articles, ranging from " masons' trowels up to oil paintings," through " skillets, spades, books, paint-pots, to guitars, fiddles, flutes, and other musical instruments.''

A " large box of harpsichord wire and hammers" is also
included in this particular list. What is meant by the
word " hammers" is rather vague, unless piano-hammers
were meant, harpsichords having no such action principle. More likely these were tuning hammers. This
list of goods published referred only to articles generally
displayed for sale. In special cases, when harpsichords
or pianofortes were brought over by these general importers, it was by a previous contract, therefore these
facts were never announced. In the different other lists
appearing, musical instruments, such as guitars and
violins, appear invariably. Peter Goelet, however, was
regarded, as far back as 1767, as an importer of musical
instruments and music in a special sense above all others.

A curious advertisement is printed in the New York
Packet for October 7th, 1773, signed Peter Paracelus
Puff, which reads " French fiddle-strings ; or, music without a master," in which the aforesaid Peter expresses
willingness to show off his invention to visitors at his
warerooms corner of Dupe Street, playing several airs in
the interim for any gentleman desiring the dose. There
is an atmosphere of mystery about this invention and
Peter Paracelus Puff, that I have failed to fathom anyhow.
I gather, however, that Mr. Puff was a wag.

A more definite reference to pianofortes appears in the
New York *Journal* during 1774. An auction of goods
saved from the wrecked ship " Pedro " is here announced
at P. McDavitt's auction store " near Coenties Slip," and
among other things mentioned three " hammer harpsichords slightly damaged" are included. These, no
doubt, were pianofortes specially ordered for some families in Baltimore, for which port the ship was destined.

The Revolutionary period interposes between the year 1775 and 1783, therefore nothing can be learned of direct relevance to this work about harpsichords, pianofortes, or musical instruments through the New York press of the time. People did not, however, during those years forget to take what pleasure they possibly could out of life, for work and commerce went on about as usual within New York, and, as a writer says : " Never before was there so much amusement and diversion in the Dutch town. The tavern roofs nightly rang with the loyal songs of the soldiers, and the streets and byways of the city were gay with life and military music." This continued during the occupation of New York by the British. Meanwhile, anticipating a permanent stay in the city, the officers of the regiments settled down to the regular routine of life, determining, soldier fashion, to extract as much pleasure as possible from the surroundings. Owing to the presence of such an unusual number of soldiers within its limits the city was turned into a constant scene of gayety. The John Street Theatre was taken possession of, rechristened the Royal Theatre, and performances were regularly given by the military officers throughout those years, records of which are partly given in Ireland's " Annals of the New York Stage."

In the " Travels and Adventures of Captain Giles," a Scotch military officer who was stationed in New York during a portion of this period, I find a very significant allusion to early pianofortes in New York. He also gives some interesting pictures of New York life during these years. From Captain Giles's work one learns that in the winter of 1778–79, while the soldiers of Washington, not three hundred miles away, were starving and perishing for want of shelter, the wives and daughters of the rich New York merchants gave themselves entirely up to the gayety and enjoyment of picturesque military surroundings, fairly revelling in the originality of the situation   The author of '' Knickerbocker Life in New York'' reiterates some of these anomalies.

Apropos of this period Giles writes : '' There was surely never before such a demand known in the stores of the merchants for rich silks, laces, and fineries The Bowling Green presented a rich spectacle in the summer afternoons.   The rich uniforms of our officers, their gay conversation and brilliant accomplishments won the hearts of the fair colonists.   If the York ladies were the only foes we had to fight,'' he very piquantly asserts, '' the king would still have possessed the colonies.'' Evidently the gallant captain was somewhat of a musician, for he speaks of going to one Campbell's, in Maiden Lane, for strings and music-books.   Elsewhere he says, in reference to a dramatic performance given at the Royal Theatre, '' We were at a loss to procure musicians for the play owing to trouble with Carew and Sanson. Stevens refused to ask the colonel, and we were much chagrined to think of the injury to the play, when a lucky accident came to our rescue.   This was Sunday morning, and Stevens, the witty fellow, travelled all the taverns. He came across a French harpsichord player, who was agreeable to our wishes and price, and next got a pianoforte at Campbell's store.   That night we had it taken on a sleigh to the theatre, when the driver, a burly Dutchman, Stevens, and myself unloaded it.   We kept it concealed until Monday afternoon, when we exhibited it to the astonishment of poor André and the other players, who were delighted beyond measure." The play Giles refers to was Kelly's " False Delicacy," in which Major André, afterward executed as a spy, acted as prompter. This gallant officer, it seems, acted as a scene-painter at the Royal Theatre, from time to time, during his life in New York.

The Campbell mentioned by Giles must have been the person of that name connected with Campbell and Gault.

Throughout those years when the British occupied New York, we learn that musical instruments were freely imported, and the ladies of the city vied with each other as never before to excel in personal accomplishments and graces.

Marquis de Chastellux, whose " Travels" created so much notice when first published sixty years ago, is quoted by the author of " The Republican Court" for the purpose of showing the condition of art in this country over a century ago. M. de Chastellux visited Boston and Philadelphia in 1780, and in his work expresses the surprise he felt at finding many pianofortes in the houses visited, and to note that the ladies had a keen appreciation of good music and art. This writer pays particular attention to the fact regarding pianofortes, because outside of a few centres in Europe they were yet little known. From his references elsewhere to harpsichords and other musical instruments he did not mistake the former for pianofortes by any means. In " The Republican Court" may be also seen citations from many other writers, tending to throw light upon this period of American life, from which further evidence may be deduced going to show that harpsichords and pianos were

better known in this country at that time than is generally supposed.

It has long been an established belief that John Jacob
Astor, the first member of that family—known through
their extraordinary wealth—was the first to import pianos
into this country. Astor only imported his first instruments in 1789, therefore it is a manifest absurdity in the
face of the evidence here given to accept this tradition
any longer. The first Astor was such a notable figure,
however, in the early days of the piano business, that he
deserves more than a cursory allusion. That magnificent
monument to his generosity and patriotism—viz., the
Astor Library, which is to every bibliographer a source
of wealth and inspiration, and to the public a priceless
treasure, alone entitles the founder, in his relationship
to pianos, to serious notice in these pages.

John Jacob Astor was born in Germany in 1763, and
on reaching the age of manhood gave his first evidence
of strong individuality by starting for London to seek
his fortune. After a short stay in that metropolis, where
he was employed for some time in a pianoforte house,
he determined to investigate his chances in the new
world. In 1783, accordingly, he sailed for Baltimore,
having a small collection of flutes as his sole stock in
trade, so writers give it. On the voyage hither he made
the acquaintance of a New York fur merchant, and became interested in this business as a possible field for
advancement. Meanwhile a lucky storm caused the ship
to head for New York, where young Astor determined to
land. He disembarked his very small cargo of personal
effects, and immediately entered into the field of strife
with characteristic promptness. He subsequently en-

gaged in the fur exporting business, which was for a
great many years his real specialty. He established
trading stations in remote sections of the North and
Northwest, and developed the resources of his business
with such infinite skill that he quickly laid the basis of
the immense fortune he was possessed of at his death.
His connection with pianos all along was momentary
and casual. When he began to export furs in 1789 he
imported occasionally a few pianos, so as to fill up time
and help to defray expenses, but this was never at any
time regarded by Astor as his staple business. When in
a few years his fur business assumed proportions, he
eschewed all relations with pianos, Michael and John
Paff succeeding him in this branch. What John Jacob
Astor did in the rôle of importer of pianofortes was done
by numerous other merchants years before his arrival in
the United States, as shown. He was not the first to
import pianofortes, and is not entitled to be known as
the "father of the music trade," as he is frequently
termed by speakers and writers. Moreover, he never,
as can be proved, took any particular pride in the part
he played in piano history, and had modest and sensible
pretensions in this connection. The first legitimate
pianoforte and music-store—apart from Campbell's, alluded to, whose history, however, is buried in doubt—
was Gilfert's, and this was in existence as early as 1786.
A regular line of pianos and musical instruments was here
kept on hand. For many years the name was known
in New York in relation to pianofortes and other features
of musical art, which shall be recounted in due place.
Additional evidence in reference to John Jacob Astor's
real position as a piano dealer is furnished elsewhere.

One Campbell turns up in the first New York directory published in 1786, which cannot have been the Campbell formerly spoken of. In this year, however, an announcement appears in one of the city papers that " Samuel Campbell, of 44 Hanover Street, has received new music for German flute, harpsichord, and pianoforte : Glee, ' The Hermit,' by Goldsmith; overture by Rossini; solos for guitar, with a number of modern songs," etc. This individual, some say, only came from Scotland in 1783, therefore it cannot be the Campbell whose name occurs in conjunction with pianos.

So much now upon the importation of harpsichords and pianofortes. Evidence is here adduced to show that unquestionably pianofortes were commonly made in New York as far back as 1785. The first point is that evidence is in existence going to show that one George Ulshoefer, a German musician, also a harpsichord and pianoforte-tuner, exhibited a pianoforte of his own make in the coffee-room of the City Tavern in 1785, where it was used at a concert given in aid of an old musician named Philip Harrison, formerly, back in 1762, connected with the New Theatre situated in Chapel Street. Ulshoefer claimed to have made every part of the instrument himself, which is hardly probable. George Ulshoefer's " patent high-strung pianoforte," the instrument was styled.

Here is more culminating evidence about the early production of pianos in New York taken from the first number of the *Diary* or *Louden's Register* issued on February 12th, 1792 :

" Messrs. Dodds & Claus, musical instrument manufactory, 66 Queen Street, announce that the forte piano is become so exceedingly fashionable in Europe that few

polite families are without it. This much-esteemed instrument forms an agreeable accompaniment to the
female voice, takes up but little room, may be moved
with ease, and consequently kept in tune with little attention, so it is on that account superior to the harpsichord. The *improvements* which Messrs. Dodds & Claus
have made in the forte piano have rendered it much more
acceptable than those imported. The introduction of
their newly-invented hammers and dampers is acknowledged to be a great improvement, as also the means they
have taken to prepare their wood to stand the effect of
our climate, which imported instruments never do, but
are sure to suffer from the saline quality of the seas.
One great advantage to the purchaser is that Messrs.
Dodds & Claus make it an invariable rule to repair every
instrument that may prove defective in the workmanship
if applied to within two years after delivery.''

Thomas Dodds, organ builder and musical instrument
maker in general, 66 Queen Street, appears in the first New
York directory issued in 1786. Clements Claus came from
London in 1788, where he took out a patent in relation
to a new stringed instrument in 1781. Claus was, however, a native of Stuttgart, Germany.

Thomas Dodds, apart from the citation given from
Louden's Diary, made harpsichords and pianofortes in
1786 at the address given.

In May, 1785, one Joseph Adam Fleming, harpsichord
and pianoforte-maker '' from Europe,'' advertised himself in the *Independent Journal* from 27 Crown Street, with
this significant postscript: '' Harpsichords and other
instruments made, sold, bought, and exchanged or *let
out at quarterly payments.*''

CHAPTER VI.

PHILADELPHIA.

THE FIRST PIANOFORTE MADE ON THIS CONTINENT—-JOHN
BEHRENT — JULIAN — ALBRECHT — TAWS — MORE ABOUT
HAWKINS—THOMAS JEFFERSON.

THE first pianoforte made on this continent, to all appearances, was that produced by John Behrent, in Philadelphia in 1775.

When we consider how much the instrument has contributed toward human happiness and the promotion of art and culture in Europe and America, the honor falling to Philadelphia through formal recognition of the fact, is by no means inconsiderable. Apart from this point the "Quaker City" was the principal seat of the trade up to about 1835. The Franklin Institute of Philadelphia, moreover, gave a most significant stimulus to the development of the piano art business in this country, when it established its system of annual exhibition fairs in 1824, devoted to progress and invention in the mechanic arts, which have been a permanent feature of this useful institution since that year. This was the parent of the New York Mechanics' Institute founded

THE CARROLL HARPSICHORD,

Made by Tschudi & Broadwood.

Now in possession of W. H. Rohlfing, Milwaukee, Wis.

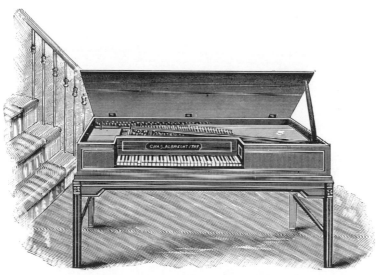

THE ALBRECHT PIANO, A.D. 1789.

Pennsylvania Historical Society.

several years later, and perpetuated on exactly the same lines. The usefulness of these societies is duly accredited incidentally throughout the course of the work at every available point. Institutions of this nature are necessarily built up in such a spirit of philanthropy, republicanism, and magnanimity, that they are always rare, therefore they should always command more emphatic recognition.

Philadelphia, from the earliest period in American civilization up to about 1840, when Boston usurped that place, was the centre of art and literary activity on this continent, and there music was fostered and encouraged above all other cities, in early years particularly. It is in relation to these facts curiously meet that the first pianoforte made in this country should have been produced in that city.

The honor of having brought out the first American pipe-organ is not less worthy of emphasis at the writer's hands, for evidences go to support this theory. The spinets and virginals made by Gustavus Hessilens in Philadelphia in 1742 were undoubtedly the first manufactured in America, but as these instruments have been absorbed in the pianoforte and have no longer any utilitarian value, mention of the matter is of moment only from the antiquarian standpoint.

If I may be permitted to put forward the fact in connection with a semi eulogy of the " Quaker City," I will add that the barrel-organ, " that curse and plague of the modern high-class musical individual," materialized in Philadelphia for the first time in American history under the hands of Charles Taws. Taws arrived in New York in 1785 from Scotland, and settled down in Philadelphia some years past that date, where he carried on musical instrument making, which will be exemplified in proper time.

In relation to violin-making in Massachusetts, where the first of these instruments made in this country originated, it may be interesting to know something of the maker and particulars as given.

Geoffrey Stafford, a "lute and fiddle-maker" by trade, who figures in the relationship indicated, was a Londoner of questionable reputation, who was landed in Massachusetts by order of His Majesty King William's government, as a transported convict, some time in 1691, along with a batch of two hundred other exiled Anglo-Saxons of the same social standing. Stafford was a notorious ruffian, although acting betimes as a sort of technical spirit medium to interpreters of the divine art, or, in other words, occasionally making lutes and " fiddles," and the Prince of Orange's party having used him for their ends determined to get rid of the gentleman for his country's good by shipping him to the American convict settlements. The eminent individuals composing the convict section of the early settlers at that date were sought to be utilized by the infamous Governor Fletcher as protection against the Indians and French. The " protection" these worthies did, however, was on their own account as freebooters when they found themselves armed. Some became pirates, but a gang in which Stafford was leader struck out across country and established themselves near Albany in this State, where they were a perpetual terror. Once Stafford sallied frontierward with his gang and cleaned out several settlements of the Mohawks, whereupon Governor Fletcher, in a

fit of drunken admiration, sent for Stafford to come
and consult with him about an Indian campaign and
other matters. Stafford, who had previously made violins in the " Bay State," came on to New York at
Fletcher's invitation, bringing with him a violin and lute
that he curiously managed in some way to make near
Albany.

Fletcher gave Stafford a regular military commission,
we read, and fell in love with the latter's violin playing.
Stafford made Fletcher a violin specially, and dallied in
" New Amsterdam" some time so as to sample and com-
mune with the governor's whiskey, until he threatened to
become a permanency in the executive household.

One evening, however, the genial Mr. Stafford, while
in his cups, ran Fletcher's favorite body-servant through
with the governor's sword, just for a lark, killing him on
the spot, Fletcher meanwhile looking on highly amused.
Presently Stafford, who, in spite of his artistic occupation proper, was a remote anarchist, prodded the governor's paunch with the tip of his sword in a playfully
significant manner, whereupon the fun terminated.
Stafford made violins and lutes between whiles, but
meantime got " strung up" to a tree by a Dutchman
upon whom he committed a robbery. He left a family,
some of whose descendants now claim to have originally
come over on the Mayflower.

It would be no compliment to Boston to print the foregoing sketch in that section. Although Stafford is probably of some consequence personally, as a picturesque
and romantic feature in a dry historical work, the natives
of Massachusetts will hardly care to perpetuate his memory in bronze, marble, or otherwise. Leaving facetious-

ness and striking out into the subject under treatment, the question of the first pianoforte presents itself.

According to testimony and facts gathered and generously placed at my disposal by Mr. John W. Jordan, of the Pennsylvania Historical Society, on its behalf, John Behrent made pianofortes in 1775 in Philadelphia, as an incontrovertible matter of fact. This date leaves no doubt as to the priority of this city in regard to the first American pianoforte.

In this year Behrent advertises that he had just finished " an extraordinary instrument, by the name of the pianoforte, in mahogany in the manner of the harpsichord." Behrent, who possibly was a German or Swede, as his name suggests, lived in that year on " Third Street below Brown, nearly opposite the army barracks " in the city named. Behrent is given as Belmont in Bishop's historical work on American arts and industries, where this fact was also published in 1864, but I am assured from the authoritative source named that *Behrent* is the name.

J. F. Watson, the historian, took particular pains years ago, among other matters, to trace up the condition of early art and music in Philadelphia, and his MSS., now in possession of the State Historical Society, furnish proofs of an incontrovertible nature regarding Behrent and the first pianoforte, put forth in an unpretentious manner, as the writer had evidently no idea of inviting a controversy or provoking a conflict of claims on this ground, because he could not have known of the statements launched in late years concerning Boston, or of any other specified claims regarding the location of the probable first piano, which the initation of the American musical press has called forth from time to time.

The War of the Revolution, which opened in this year, probably put a stop to Behrent's future progress as a pianoforte-maker, for he is heard of no more in connection with pianofortes as far as I can ascertain. In 1785, however, no sooner had the war terminated than James Julian, of Franklin and Arch streets, came forth and announced "the great *American pianoforte* of his own invention," which goes to indicate that Julian was a strong nationalist in art, as well as an early maker of pianos. Julian's name frequently appears in this connection in Philadelphia papers of the time. This is the second great link in the chain of proofs concerning the "Quaker City" and original American piano making.

The name of Charles Albrecht now comes up. Albrecht began making pianofortes in Philadelphia some time before 1789, and made excellent instruments for their time, many specimens of which are in existence to day. One stands in the art rooms of the Pennsylvania Historical Society dated 1789, and another was presented by the late Mr. Drexel to the New York Museum of Art, which was made about the same period. The latter has a beautifully finished and inlaid case, that is almost a composite work of art in itself, and speaks much for Albrecht's skill and æsthetic perceptions. It contains some distinctly original ideas in detail in the form of the case, which go to show that the person referred to was no mere plagiarist of mechanical principles, but an improver. Albrecht's instruments are copies, with some improvements, of pianos imported at that period from London. Albrecht's name appears in 1791 in the Philadelphia city directory as a joiner, and the following years as musical instrument maker. Between 1785 and 1791 no directory was issued, therefore he cannot be followed up, but his name, after 1791, occurs regularly up to 1824, as told later.   Albrecht was, it is safe to assume, a German.

Charles Taws arrived in New York, as shown in that chapter, in 1786, and remained for some time in the city, where he tuned harpsichords and pianos, besides earning his livelihood in other ways.   He was an excellent scholar, and we find him in 1787 teaching some branches of learning in a private school.   In 1788 he went to Philadelphia, and soon after began to manufacture pianofortes there in a modest way.   Watson, the historian, saw one of his pianos in 1795, but it is certain that he made some still earlier, and for that matter he may have made instruments while in New York.   Alexander Wilson, the Scottish poet, who came to Philadelphia in 1795 from his native country, speaks of a Scottish pianoforte-maker with whom he passed many pleasant hours in Philadelphia in 1797.   " This very ingenious and learned ' Scotty,' " Wilson says, in 1810. "invented a complete change afterward for the shape of the pianoforte, and had it sent to Paris and London."   It is hard to tell here what Wilson meant in this description, but Taws must have been the fellow-countryman to whom he refers. Wilson was the composer of the well-known Scottish ballad, " Connell and Flora," and was the author of the first American work on ornithology produced here. This book was the first to treat of the birds peculiar to this country in an intelligent manner.   Samuel Bradford, of Philadelphia, in the face of many risks, owing to the elaborate character of the work, produced it, when it made Wilson famous at a bound among scientific people.

The latter was also a musician, and this accounts somewhat for speaking of his casual acquaintance with the
pianoforte-maker referred to.   Taws became associated
in some manner with Reinagle, of the Philadelphia Theatre, mentioned in a New York chapter around 1800, and
was evidently somewhat of an authority on acoustics, for
the New York papers of the year 1801 tell us that Mr.
Taws, the eminent musical instrument expert of Philadelphia, was in town at that time in company with
Mr. Reinagle, " to inspect the architectural plans that
Joseph Corré, of the Mount Vernon Gardens, had prepared for rebuilding his present play-house, being an expert in acoustics.''   It is also mentioned in stage annals
that Reinagle, in addition to being a director and manager, was interested in musical instrument making,
having a share in some business in Philadelphia after
1800.

As I mentioned, Taws made pianos earlier than 1795,
the year in which Watson saw the instrument referred
to, because his name appears in the Philadelphia city
directory for 1793 as a musical instrument maker, and
this gives us the right to assume that he, at least, made
pianos in 1792, the previous year.   Up to 1796 he was
located at 60 Walnut Street.   Then I have traced him
through each successive issue of the directory record
up to 1833.   He did business at various times in the
interregnum at 61 South Third, 63 South Third, 115
Pine, 74 Union, and 73 Union streets, when his name
disappears in the year 1833, his place being then 73
Union Street, as given above.   His death, therefore,
must be placed as being somewhere around this year.
Meanwhile a James B. Taws appears in 1829 at 80 Gas-

kill Street, and in 1837 a Lewis Taws, 16 Howard Street, is given for the first time, the former as " musical instrument maker," the second as being an " organ-builder." These were sons of Charles Taws, and became well known later in the city under consideration. Apart from the foregoing, Mr. Jordan, of the Pennsylvania Historical Society, states that Taws was in business on Third and Union streets in 1789.

Charles Albrecht made pianofortes up to 1825 at 95 Vine Street, and finally at 3 South Third Street, where he was located during his last years. Christian F. L. Albrecht comes in business in 1825 at 98 Sassafras (now Race Street), and continues in the concurrent issues of the directory up to 1842, when the name of Albrecht disappears as far as I can discover, but reappears presently. This was a son of Charles Albrecht's very probably.

John I. Hawkins, who is mentioned in Chapter II., in relation to the introduction of the upright and iron plating in piano development, was not practically connected with the business even in the remotest manner, as far as can be ascertained, until he appeared as a manufacturer of his specialty instrument in Philadelphia toward the end of 1799. In February, 1800, his first United States patent was granted. He lived then at 15 South Second Street, where he made and sold his iron " portable grands." His card states that his instruments could be purchased " at little more than half the price of imported *grand* or *square* pianofortes." Hawkins must have been associated in an indirect way with some practical piano-maker, or he would scarcely have gone into the business at all. This assumption cannot be verified nevertheless. Hawkins' American patents are out of print, but luckily

his father's British patent explains all. It reads *ex parte :*
" Now know ye that the said Isaac Hawkins do hereby
declare that the said invention of improvements was
communicated to me in confidence by my son, John
Isaac Hawkins, residing in Philadelphia, North America,
and is described in the following." Here follows a detailed description of Hawkins' inventions, which relate
to the upright pianoforte and apply equally in a number
of directions. For instance, Hawkins includes metallic
elastic wire strings in his list. These strings were supposed to be made with links of heavy wire formed like a
chain for use in the bass section of pianos. This wire
chain was also intended to be applied to lathes and
machinery of all kinds, as stated in the patent. Curiously enough Hawkins' invention hereabouts has been
introduced practically during recent years in the way he
pointed out, and somebody else gets the credit of the
invention. But to return, Hawkins' American patents
related to upright pianofortes explained in the European
section. Hawkins was an Englishman, as seen, otherwise one would be likely to assume that Wilson, the
ornithologist and poet, spoken of, had reference to him,
when he writes of his temporary friend and acquaintance
the learned " Scotty," who had invented a complete
change for the shape of the pianoforte and had it sent
to London and Paris. Or would it not be possible that
Taws, the Scotchman, being a practical piano-maker and
expert, actually made the " uprights " attributed to Hawkins and allowed him to send the model to his father in
Manchester, England, for patenting purposes ? Wilson's
remarks may have some significance in this connection.
Hawkins was not a musical instrument maker at all, we

must remember, being by profession a civil engineer. The model piano made by him must have been put to-gether and suggested by some practical person of experience, being no mere copy of another instrument.

But, departing from all idle supposition of this nature, and giving Hawkins credit on the face of his results, Hipkins' description of one of Hawkins' pianos in the possession of the Broadwoods, of London, will be interesting : " The real inventor of the upright piano, in its modern and useful form, was that remarkable English-man John Isaac Hawkins, the inventor of ever-pointed pencils—a civil engineer, poet, preacher, and phrenolo-gist. While living at Philadelphia, U. S. A , Hawkins invented the cottage piano—portable grand, as he called it—and his father, Isaac Hawkins, took out in the year 1800 the English patent for it. One of these original pianinos belongs to Messrs. Broadwood. The strings descend nearly to the floor, while the keyboard, a folding one, is raised to a convenient height between the floor and the upper extremities of the strings. Hawkins had an iron frame and a bracing of iron rods, within which the belly was entirely suspended, a system of tuning by mechanical screws, an upper metal bridge, equal length of string throughout, and metal supports to the action, in which a later help to repetition was anticipated, the whole instrument being independent of the outer case. Hawkins tried also a lately revived notion of coiled strings in the bass to do away with tension. Lastly, he sought for a *sostenuto*, which has often been tried," etc.

This elaborate and very explicit diagnosis of Hawkins' original upright piano, from Mr. Hipkins' clever pen, indicates that the former was a most remarkable improver ; rather more like a revolutionist, indeed, for he aimed at almost a radical departure in piano construction. As I have elsewhere remarked, Hawkins' work came to naught, owing to the musical worthlessness of his instruments.

What became of this remarkable individual ultimately cannot be learned from any source. It is only known that he gave up making pianos in 1802 in Philadelphia and left the city. He may have afterward settled in some other place in the pursuit of his profession, but here the historian must draw a blank.

Thomas Jefferson, the father of democracy, happened to see one of Hawkins' " portable grands" in 1800, while visiting Philadelphia in that year, for the following letter exists among his correspondence. It accurately points out the peculiar structure of Hawkins' instrument and the other original features of stringing and wrest-pin arrangement alluded to. Jefferson writes to his daughter, in 1800, as follows : " A very ingenious, modest and poor young man, in Philadelphia, has invented one of the prettiest improvements in the pianoforte that I have ever seen, and it has tempted me to engage one for Monticello. His strings are perpendicular, and he contrives within that height to give his strings the same length as in a grand pianoforte, and fixes the three unisons to the same screw. It scarcely gets out of tune at all, and then, for the most part, the three unisons are tuned at once."

If this is not Hawkins' pianoforte mentioned, then there must have been some other inventor in Philadelphia in 1800 who either copied from the former or *vice versa*.

CHAPTER VII.

BOSTON.

SOME STATISTICS — MORE ABOUT STEWART — OSBORN —
DWIGHT—MACKAY—JONAS CHICKERING—HIS PATENTS—
GOODRICH—THE GILBERTS—CURRIER'S PATENT.

FROM statistics concerning piano-making in this country given by Bishop in his " History of the Arts and Industries of the United States," I am able to give some
accurate idea of the extent of the business in 1829. It
was officially shown that in this year 2500 pianos were
made, of the aggregate value of $750,000, of which 900
were made in Philadelphia, 800 in New York, 717 in Boston, and a considerable number in Baltimore and other
minor places. Boston was not far behind New York in
numbers, and taking the commercial possibilities of the
two cities into consideration, Boston made an excellent
showing. I have shown in the previous Boston chapter
the people who constituted the business there in 1820
and before, meantime giving further facts here.

James Stewart was granted a patent on November
14th, 1822, for an improvement in the arrangement of
sounding-boards, while in Boston, which was the second
issued to a resident of this city since the Patent Office

was established. Stewart's numerous inventions subsequently, while in connection with the Collards in London, from 1827 upward, amply show that he was by instinct a revolutionist and improver.

Alpheus Babcock and John Mackay carried on business at 7 Parkman's Market until about 1829, when the latter became a partner of Jonas Chickering. In December of this year Alpheus Babcock went to Philadelphia, where he joined J. G. Klem, a very clever German, and for years the agent in that city for the Babcock pianos, and began business soon after.

Babcock while in Boston made pianos for John Mackay and G. D. Mackay, a brother and business associate of the former, yet his instruments all bore the maker's seal of " A. Babcock, Boston." Messrs. Mason & Hamlin have in their possession one of these instruments used in early years by no less a person than Dr. Lowell Mason, the celebrated American composer. Babcock's iron plate is specially discussed in relation to Conrad Meyer in a Philadelphia chapter, therefore readers not previously acquainted with the nature and scope of this invention and its difference from other methods of plate bracing briefly described in our European section elsewhere, can learn the points of advantage and technical distinction involved. Babcock's pianos ranked very high as far back as 1822. In 1824 I find that he was a prize winner at the first Mechanic Arts Exhibition of the Franklin Institute, Philadelphia. The committee's report upon the disbursement of premiums contains the subjoined in reference to Babcock : " Premium No. 47 (to the maker of the best horizontal piano) is adjudged to A. Babcock, of Boston, for specimen No. 327, which is a horizontal piano made for J. Mackay, of Boston. It has received the high approbation of the judges. Every part of its interior mechanism has the highest finish, and its tone and touch are excellent. The strings of the lower octaves are covered with flattened wire. It entitles its maker to the *silver medal,* having been considered the best of the four square pianos exhibited.''

In 1825 Babcock also had an instrument at the second annual exhibition of the Institute with the same successful results. In the judges' report on this year's exhibits, we read as follows : ''Loud & Brothers' two square pianos shown exhibited evident proofs of their skill ; one of them is a particularly fine instrument, which was near getting the premium. This was, however, adjudged to Alpheus Babcock's piano, in which the highest finish is observable in every part of its interior mechanism. Its touch and tone are excellent. The maker received the *silver medal.''*

In this exhibition Babcock had to compete with Mickley and Loud & Brothers, of Philadelphia, and William Geib, of New York. The instances adduced here are given just to show what a high place this clever Boston maker occupied in the business in those years.

John Mackay, of whom I have spoken, although reputed to have no practical knowledge of piano construction or its details, took out a patent for a new method of covering (and boring the shank-holes of) hammer-heads on August 14th, 1828. This was while yet in connection with Babcock. Mackay's patent was reissued in 1839, being evidently regarded of value.

Mackay was originally a ship merchant and bore the title of captain. He acquired some knowledge of, and a taste for the piano business while trading between England and Boston in past years, carrying general merchandise after the manner of sea captains referred to in the New York chapters, and possessed considerable wealth, with which he backed up Babcock. His brothers, W. H. and G. D. Mackay, were to some degree also interested in his music trade ventures.

Jonas Chickering's name has been made the subject of many ridiculous stories as to his original *entrée* into the pianoforte business. Like the tales associated with Crehore's first attempts at making pianos, it has been circulated around for many years that Chickering the first got the idea of making these instruments from having been called to repair one at his home, which is a manifest absurdity. Jonas Chickering was born in Ipswich, N. H., and learned cabinet-making. Proving a very skilful pupil, and imbued with all the ambition that follows in the train of inherent ability, he soon turned toward the city of Boston. Here he became employed in Osborn's shop, and *formally* acquired a knowledge of pianoforte making Timothy Gilbert, who was a companion in Osborn's, was also a young cabinet maker.

Jonas Chickering became, therefore, regularly and truly a pianoforte-maker, apart from the incident that he was at first a cabinet maker, which in reality ought to be counted as an advantage. Jonas Chickering came of good stock—if allusion to this fact has any significance —and it was no disgrace in the early days of the Republic for the son of a respectable family to learn an artistic trade, but quite the contrary, it was looked upon as a most creditable thing in every way.

John Osborn, from 1815 up to 1835, when he died in

New York, was one of the leading makers in the United States, which will be shown as we proceed.

I find Osborn in 1820 and 1821 at 12 Orange Street. In 1822 and 1823 he carried on business at 1 Boyleson Square. Later on he appears at 471 Washington Street, where he had his business until the end of 1829, when he moved to Albany. His fate subsequently is shown in a New York chapter.

Reverting to Captain Mackay, it is certain that his connection with Jonas Chickering had a very marked influence upon the fortunes of the new concern after 1830.

The latter not only acquired in Mackay a rich partner, but a business man of considerable ability, who immediately upon the growth of superior travelling and other facilities for the transportation of goods around this year, sought to spread the Chickering piano everywhere throughout the United States.

It is said that as early as 1839 Chickering & Mackay had penetrated every commercial point available for the sale of their instruments, then ranking high in price and character, and succeeded in establishing the first agencies known all through the country, thus becoming the pioneers of the music trade. Mackay from the first had charge of the commercial side of the business, and was responsible to a great extent for its policy and success, while Mr. Chickering attended zealously to the technical department. Captain Mackay met with a sad fate in 1841.

In this year Mackay sailed from Boston bound for South America, for the purpose of obtaining some cargoes of wood for the business in Boston, and, strange to

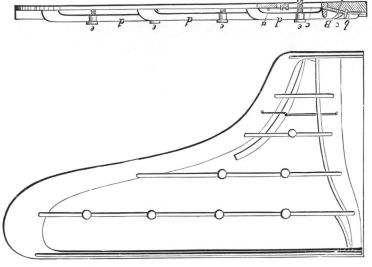

JONAS CHICKERING'S FULL SOLID-CAST GRAND METAL
PLATE.

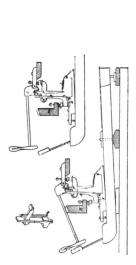

N. J. HAINES' SQUARE ACTION.

Patented May 24, 1859.

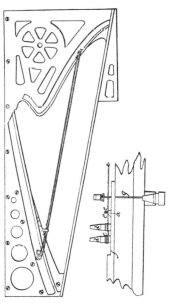

JONAS CHICKERING'S FULL SOLID-CAST PLATE FOR SQUARES,
AND DAMPER IMPROVEMENT

say, neither the ship nor Mackay was ever heard of afterward. This threw back the business on the hands of
Jonas Chickering, who retired somewhat from the shop
department and devoted himself more to the details of
the shipping and commercial duties involved, until his
sons were able to assume some of the responsibility,
when the firm became Chickering & Sons.

About 1822 another piano-maker appeared on Common
Street named John Dwight, previously alluded to. He
must have been of an inventive turn, for he took out a
patent for the application of a "longitudinal iron bar"
to the piano on July 29th, 1824, thus anticipating a
minor feature of Babcock's plate by about sixteen
months. Dwight subsequently became a partner of
Daniel B. Newhall. This firm exhibited some pianos in
1839 designed to meet a want then felt for low-priced
instruments, and as far as can be learned devoted themselves entirely to this class of trade. Dwight & Newhall
patented a very ingenious method of adjusting the keys,
I may add, in 1841, which was intended to supersede the
method then as now in use. It did not succeed, however.

In 1808 William M. Goodrich, an organ-builder, began
business in Chamber Street, and in 1822 was manufacturing pianos at 81 Market Street. Goodrich became known
toward 1827 in this connection. In 1828 he exhibited
one of his instruments in Philadelphia, at the Franklin
Institute, which created no especial notice.

Lemanuel and Timothy Gilbert, two of John Osborn's
apprentices, began business separately in 1829. Timothy
was in partnership with E. R. Currier and became quite
noted in after years, more for ingenuity and inventive-

ness, however, than anything else. T. Gilbert's instruments were always undergoing new changes, and he seems to have never settled down to any one method or principle for any length of time. Lemanuel Gilbert began originally on Washington Street. He was out of business for some time, but came back about 1839 to his old quarters. In 1841 he was granted a patent, which was a modification of the square English fly action. In this design no under hammers, or hoppers, however, are used, the jack setting in the hammer-heel after the style of the present square action. It is claimed that this was the action afterward used by Chickering & Sons, but this is not correct, for the square action used by the latter firm before 1860, or thereabouts, contained "hoppers," and was materially distinct from any of the Gilbert action patents, either those of Lemanuel or Timothy. The former became quite noted in his time among piano-makers as an expert, but seemingly did not meet with substantial business encouragement. Any of his old pianos seen by the writer bear no comparison with instruments by Nunns & Clark, New York, Chickering, or Loud Brothers, Philadelphia, made about the same period. Lemanuel Gilbert went out of business in 1863 and died in Boston some time afterward. He patented a variety of improvements during his time, an upright action, with a method of projecting the whole hammer line in close proximity to the strings—after the manner of our present upright action soft-pedal—being the most significant. In this patent a number of other very ingenious principles are also included. This was taken out as early as June 18th, 1850.

Timothy Gilbert & Company some time past 1840 became a very important house in the trade, and had many agencies scattered over the country. The pianos turned out by Timothy entirely surpassed those made by Lemanuel Gilbert all along. On February 10th, 1841, the former was granted a patent for a number of ideas and inventions relating to uprights and squares worked out in one paper. The specification and drawing illustrates an upright action, an entire metal back and plate for uprights designed to carry the sounding-board independent of wooden connections, and a number of lesser improvements which came to nothing. The action, however, is significant. This outlined many ideas afterward claimed by Wornum (" tape-check" action) in England. His square action, patented in 1847, resembles the old Chickering principle to a considerable degree, and was no doubt ingenious, but time has established the superiority of the ordinary French rocker action beyond dispute, at least over Gilbert's scheme. There were " hoppers" used in Gilbert's action, also the usual fly and jack, fastened permanently to the key, but with no method of regulating the position of the jack and hopper under the heel of the striking hammer, just as in the old English action.

Several other patents taken out at various dates between 1850 and 1860 relate to minor details. T. Gilbert & Company established a direct agency in New York in 1848 at 339 Broadway, Berry & Waters being agents, and seemed to have made it remunerative, for they continued to sell their instruments in this way for several years, until Horace Waters took up the agency, which he held for some time.

In 1847 T. Gilbert & Company created a great stir by

producing their organ-pianos, which were reviewed in
the Boston and New York press of the year as if they
were something marvellously new.   They were made
after the designs of Obed Coleman, who held a patent
for the invention dated April 17th, 1844.   There was
also a British patent taken out on October 10th of the
same year.   Coleman sold his patent to Gilbert & Company for a small figure in 1846, having made no practical
use of it in the mean time.   Little came of this, however,
it having been proved that the piano section, at least, required to be tuned every month to keep it in toler-
ably good condition.   T. Gilbert & Company went out
of business nominally in 1868, but the name has been
used since that time by several successors.

Going back to Jonas Chickering, the various inventions and improvements made by his firm since 1823
remain to be treated of briefly.

Jonas Chickering's square metal plate, of which a diagram is furnished, was patented October 8th, 1840, together with an improved damper arrangement.   An application had been made in relation to this patent in
1837, but upon a slight technical point it was put back.

In 1843 Chickering's plate for grands, made in one
solid casting, was produced and patented.   This was a
most significant improvement beyond question, and was
the great stepping-stone to the overstrung grands now in
use.   Here is a brief digest of Chickering's official specification and claims : " Patent No. 3238 having thus set
forth my improvements, I wish it understood that I am
aware that the strings of a pianoforte, in their passage
from the hitch-pins to the straining screws, have been
passed through holes made through a pin screwed in a

block, and from said pin bent or inclined upward to the straining screw, and therefore I do not claim such an arrangement as mine. *But*, what I do claim consists in this improvement—viz., that of supporting the strings by passing them through a solid ledge cast directly upon the lower part of the inclined front plate, through apertures of which ledge the strings are to be passed in the manner set forth ; the tone being, therefore, particularly in the treble, greatly augmented and improved. I also claim my particular method of constructing the metallic frame of the grand pianoforte,'' etc.

JONAS CHICKERING, Boston.

The patentee here had reference to what are now known as '' agraffes,'' and which were introduced by Erard of Paris in his instruments, about 1808 or earlier. Mr. Chickering improved upon the original principle by casting the agraffes in the plate as outlined. This is one of the ideas patented in the above. The grand solid cast plate was the principal object of the patent, but the drawing in this case explains itself, hence the absence of specified explanation.

About 1843 Jonas Chickering, with Nunns & Clark, New York, Boardman & Gray, Albany, and the Louds, of Philadelphia, held the leading place in the business in this country, but outranked all others in commercial enterprise. Jonas Chickering was deeply interested in the progress of musical art in Boston also, personally, all along, since his rise to distinction in his own profession, and was honored by being elected Vice-President of the old Handel and Haydn Society of the city in 1834, over which musical organization he afterward presided as

President.   This justly-celebrated musical society was
founded in 1815, and produced some of the standard
oratorios by Handel and Haydn in that year for the first
time in this country—that is, formally, with the assistance of an orchestra, organ, and trained chorus.   The
organization had $9000 in funds in 1834, also a Chicker-
ing & Mackay pianoforte, and an organ built by Thomas
Appleton at a cost of four thousand dollars.   An ancestor,
as I am informed, of the present Bourne family connected with piano-making in Boston, named Abner
Bourne, was associated with Jonas Chickering in pushing the affairs of the society, but the latter was particularly identified with its artistic successes.

Chickering & Mackay, in the order of events, made uprights as early as 1830, one of which stands at present in
the rooms of the New England Conservatory, Boston.
Some of these Chickering & Mackay pianos were exhibited in the Franklin Institute, Philadelphia, from time
to time, and won high encomiums.   Meanwhile as time
progressed and new ideas became established, the Chickering instruments were improved, and maintained from
the very beginning, as shown, a first place.   It would
be a tortuous task to follow up and elaborate in these
chapters all the little modifications in the direction of
progress, made from time to time in the cases, action,
stringing, and acoustic departments of these pianos—
beginning at Stewart & Chickering's time up to the present instruments—made under the personal supervision
of Mr. George H. Chickering at their factory in Boston.
However, the gross results are apparent in the present
high character of the Chickering & Sons pianos.

Jonas Chickering, after a useful and exemplary life,

died on December 8th, 1853, at the house of a friend, death resulting from the sudden rupture of a blood-vessel. On December 1st, 1852, the previous year, the entire stock in trade of Chickering & Sons, involving a loss of a quarter of a million dollars, was destroyed by fire, the disaster resulting in a dead financial loss to the extent indicated, which great calamity, however, seemed only to stimulate the firm to renewed efforts in trade. At present Mr. C. F. and Geo. H. Chickering uphold the genius of the name, and are thoroughly educated in the details of the manufacturing and commercial departments of the business, besides being in complete touch with art in the truest and fullest sense. The American art historian of the future must rightfully assign to Chickering & Sons a place of honor in his chapters, dealing with the progress and growth of domestic music, for they have well earned it in conjunction with a few other firms hereafter mentioned.

Let me add that they have maintained a New York branch house for over thirty-five years, and have been during that period as much a part of the metropolis as they were of Boston. Patents and improvements introduced by the firm since 1853 are given in casual form further on.

It has been accepted without contradiction for many years that seven-octave pianos were not known in this country until after 1845, at least so old manufacturers say, but the facts shown elsewhere as regards Jardine's and Loud & Brothers' grand, made in 1825, and said to have contained ninety keys, go to prove as one example that the prevailing idea is not at all correct. Although Loud & Brothers' instrument may have been made on experimental lines and never carried further, the incidental fact that they made such a piano is specially valuable to the historian.   Now for another peculiar incident :   In 1831 Ebenezer R. Currier, of Boston, took out a patent for a pianoforte " with a shifting action like the grand for horizontal instruments, also the placing of the keyboard midway so as to give a compass of *seven octaves*, according to the stringing diagram and other models." I cannot find out what became of the patent after that year, but it is sufficiently significant in itself to merit especial comment, for it proves to us that many people made seven-octave square pianos before 1840, at least, for experimental, if not for practical purposes.   Currier also patented a down-striking grand action, of which the diagram is given on account of its peculiarity and ingenious construction.   It is somewhat after the plan of Loud's square action of 1827.   Currier was also a pupil of that clever man Osborn, and in this year was a partner of Timothy Gilbert.   They carried on business at this time at 398 Washington Street, which Timothy Gilbert & Company occupied for upward of twenty-five years after that date.

CHAPTER VIII.

New York.

AFTER the evacuation of New York and the termination of the Revolutionary War, there was an earnest
prayer went out for new colonists ; immigrants skilled
in the arts, sciences, and mechanical pursuits, as well as
simple settlers to " hew down the forests and tickle the
rich soil into waving corn-fields." The soldiers had
sheathed their swords. The Franklins, Jeffersons, and
Adamses came into the breach with the principles of
our new government outlined and ready to put into practice. These scholarly men, without whose minds, as
well as the voices and pens of the many other eminent
patriots of the period, Washington's work would have
been in vain, saw the necessities of the hour. They knew
that the safety, status, and future strength of the new
Republic rested upon immigration, and they encouraged
it in every manner. There was consequently a strong
tide of emigration to these shores. Laborers and farmers,

artisans and skilled mechanicians, artists and musicians, came hither.   They helped to extend the frontiers of civilization westward ; they laid the foundations of cities, and some sowed the seeds of art culture.   In 1786, three years after the peace was concluded, as a look in the directory indicates, New York contained quite a number of musicians and musical instrument makers, nearly all new arrivals, some of whom—as previously indicated— became very eminent in after years.   We find in the New York *Independent Gazette* of that year—May 23d—that " Charles Taws, organ-builder, lately arrived in this city from Britain, builds and repairs finger and barrel-organs. He also repairs and tunes pianofortes, harpsichords, and guitars."   The address appended is " 26 Frankfort Street."   Taws already appears in a Philadelphia chapter, where he cuts a prominent figure.

Here, in particular, is an important item appended.   It is an announcement copied from the New York *Independent Journal* of 1785 :

" Mr. Reinagle, member of the Society of Musicians in London, gives lessons on the pianoforte, also harpsichord and violin.   He is preparing for a public concert.

N. B.—He is prepared to supply his friends and scholars with the best instruments and printed music on the same terms sold in the shops, only allowing for freight and package."

The postscript given is yet another proof of the correctness of my position as regards Astor, if any more proofs are needed.   I feel confident, however, that it has been clearly shown how musical instruments came to be imported into this country originally apart from Reinagle's advertisement.

Reinagle, like Taws, became very prominent afterward in Philadelphia as the musical director and subsequently manager of the Philadelphia Theatre. Meanwhile he was interested in the piano business established by Taws. His son Hugh became noted very early for his musical precocity, but died very suddenly of yellow fever in New Orleans some time during the year 1820.

Duplessix & Mechtler, French musicians, instructors of the pianoforte, turn up in 1786, as well as many other teachers, all of which goes to show that in the preceding interval between 1783 and this period pianofortes had become more general.

I find that when Joseph Corré, formerly host of the City Tavern, opened the Mount Vernon Gardens in 1791 as a musical *rendezvous*, after the Franco-German concert-garden plan, he had one of Dodds's pianofortes in use. In 1800 Corré began to give theatrical performances. His resort became famous subsequently in connection with the introduction of clever foreign artists, the first performance of what can be termed Italian opera given in this country taking place there. Corré was quite a character. He was formerly cook to Major Carew, an Irish officer in the British army. When the latter evacuated New York on the eventful morning of November 25th, 1783, Corré stayed behind very wisely and determined to make personal terms with his conquerors. We find him afterward presiding as host over the policy and destinies of the City Tavern in the early part of 1784.

Corré was a Frenchman by birth, but became assimilated with Germany somewhat, because he wedded a daughter of the Teutonic race in New York.

In May, 1786, the following announcement appeared

in the *Independent Journal :* " For sale, at the printing-office 251 Water Street, the first number of the *American Musical Magazine* containing an excellent piece of music entitled ' The Season Moralized,' price one shilling." This was the first musical journal or anything approaching thereto ever produced in this country, and was the forerunner of *Gilfert's Musical Magazine* known for several years past 1790 as a standard publication. In the diary of Dr. Alexander Anderson, known as the " father of American engraving," for 1792, frequent mention is made of Gilfert and other persons associated with musical instruments and music in that year in New York. Here are some very interesting examples : " March 23d. —Went to *Gilfert's Musical Magazine* and engaged to engrave letters for the title of a piece of music for his magazine for twelve shillings. 24th.—Scoured a copper plate. Began Gilfert's plate. Called at old Mr. Pierce's in Chatham Street to look at the old violin. No sooner had I struck a note than his wife denounced music as leading to the devil. I went again in the evening and brought it away, promising to return it in the morning or pay five dollars for it. Was so much pleased with the tone of it that I put it in *Mr. Claus's* hands to repair and varnish. 26th.—Called at Scoles's. He found much fault with my engraving for Gilfert." Anderson was a passionate lover of music, as we find by his diary, and extensively mixed up with dramatic, literary, and musical people of his time. Here are more of his jottings for the same year : " April 25th.—Furnished Freneau's engraving. Walked on the Battery. Called at *Gilfert's Musical Magazine* and got a tuning-fork for my father. Before dark I finished the border for Mr. Corré. He came and paid me ten shillings. After playing a tune on the violin I took a short walk with my brother. 28th.—I took my violin to Mr. Martin's to undergo a little attention. May 1st.—Got my violin from Martin's. May 4th.—Bought a violin bow at Gilfert's for twelve shillings. May 26th.—Began Gilfert's plate. 28th.— Finished Gilfert's plate, and having obtained a proof at Burgers's delivered it and received four dollars. June 8th.—Paid Claus two and one half dollars for repairing and varnishing my old violin.''

Numerous other allusions of this character appear in Anderson's diary, which throw an interesting light upon this phase of early New York life. In a number of Louden's paper, *The Diary*, Berry & Rogers, 35 Hanover Square, advertise among other goods '' Ass-skin books, flutes, guitars, and fiddles, with music for the same,'' and equally curious facts in the same issue.

Ulshoefer's name appears in the record of the Park Theatre in 1795 as a '' first violin'' under Hewitt, but presently disappears. This is all I can learn of him so far.

In this year—1795—frequent advertisements appear in the *Journal* from Gilfert & Aspinwall, 207 Pearl Street, announcing the arrival of pianofortes, invariably headed '' Consignment of patent pianofortes from London.'' J. J. Astor and many others were also bringing over instruments during this period, so it is safe to assume that there was a vast number consumed throughout the territory everywhere, and with this field open to conquer, it is not, therefore, surprising that numerous Englishmen and Germans came over about this time to set up business, having no doubt—particularly English

piano-makers—learned of the large consignments of instruments going to the United States from time to time
from London.

Thus it is that in 1799 the names of Morgan Davis and
Thomas Gibson appear as " musical instrument makers
in general." These two individuals were evidently
legitimate pianoforte-makers, for they turn up in partnership as Gibson & Davis, pianoforte-makers, in 1801,
at 63 Barclay Street, and were well known even thirty
years afterward. Davis must have been a Welshman
judging by his surname, and particularly by his Christian
name, which is as peculiar to Wales as Guido is to Italy,
or Ivan to Russia.

Some of Gibson's descendants are still in New York,
and inquiries made of them elicited the information that
their ancestor was a Scotchman, who had learned his
business legitimately in London. Mr. Henry Hazelton
remembers Gibson's shop in Barclay Street. I have
traced Gibson & Davis together through successive
directories up to 1820, when they separate.

From this date forward Davis makes pianos at 61 Barclay Street, while Gibson occupies the old number, 63.
They were in business up to 1836 in the same street and
location precisely. Next year Davis disappears and presently Gibson follows suit. Both died, apparently. The
names appear nowhere after 1839. If either of these
piano-makers left children they must have become
journeymen in the trade subsequently. The Davises
appearing afterward in Boston, I find had no relationship to the Morgan Davis treated of.

In 1791 Mr. Hammond, the first official representative
ever sent from Great Britain to the United States, ar-

rived. This was several years before the consummation of Jay's famous treaty, which was considered at the period a wise piece of diplomacy by those skilled in governmental and diplomatic philosophy, although the populace, in their ignorance of the necessities and requirements of government, were furious at what they considered a disgraceful compromise between the two countries, and accordingly denounced everybody having any connection with the treaty virulently. Hammond's appointment was the result of action taken by London tradespeople and merchants, evidently, for I find that a large body of merchants and representatives of London houses waited upon the Foreign Secretary, in 1790, and vehemently urged him to see that the American trade did not slip through their fingers through the prejudice of the king and others. In this year Spain commenced shipping goods of all kinds in large quantities to Havana, for the purpose of meeting the wants of American merchants, and other European countries on good terms with Spain were taking advantage of the fact by shipping goods to this port, which was fast becoming a supply centre for the Southern American States, through Baltimore, Charleston, and other convenient centres. This alarmed and stirred up the British Government, and the treaty with Jay was the culminating point.

In this deputation several of the prominent English pianoforte houses were represented, among them being Broadwood, Stodart, and Southwell. The appointment of a British representative, and later the consummation of a regular treaty between the two countries, had, however, an undesirable and unlooked-for effect in a few years for European makers, because men who were unsuccessful in England and Germany began to seek these shores. They founded a rival trade within the States subsequently, and assisted, partly by the operation of a tariff in later years, built up the basis of the American pianoforte art business of the future. London piano-makers, in particular, came over on the first appearance of peaceful relations between Great Britain and the United States, beginning with Hammond's appointment. Davis and Gibson were among these men. The Geibs and John Montgomery were also among the more recent arrivals after this event, including Shaw, spoken of in Boston records. These were not necessarily all English, however, although coming from London shops, because many of the best men connected with the early New York pianoforte history were Scotchmen by birth, although labelled Anglo-Saxon *pro forma*, a few were Welshmen, and an odd individual Irish.

The Germans began to come over as early as 1818. About 1840 they had secured a firm foothold in New York, while they predominated in Baltimore and were very strong in Philadelphia.

John Montgomery, a Dublin harpsichord and piano-maker, in 1800, was in business at 52 Barclay Street. His advertisement reads that he was making pianofortes " on the best London principles." He disappeared from sight in a few years. The Geibs, a most eminent family in relation to the business, come to the surface in the city directory for 1802 and 1803 conjunctively. In this issue John Geib & Son, organ-builders, 55 Warren Street, appears, also " Adam Geib, teacher." In 1805 and 1806 John Geib & Son were still in business at the above address, while " John & Adam Geib, pianoforte-

ISAAC WOODWARD.

JOHN JACOB ASTOR

makers, Mount Vernon,'' appear for the first time. This was a union of Adam Geib, the teacher, and John Geib, a practical pianoforte-maker, who arrived fresh from London. The name of Geib became very prominent later in New York.

John Geib, the inventor of the grasshopper action, also the '' buff stop'' for squares, which was patented November 9th, 1786, in London, was the father of the John and Adam Geib, piano-makers, referred to. The family was German originally, as the name indicates. John Geib, Sr., of '' grasshopper-action'' fame, was one of the '' twelve apostles,'' who came to England from Germany in 1760 and founded the piano business there. It was through these men Broadwood, Stodart, and other makers acquired a knowledge of piano making, which goes to illustrate the far-reaching influence of the Germans in music and art.

The Geibs—John and Adam—appear in the 1807 directory on '' Leonard near Broadway.'' Before 1809 John Geib evidently died, for his name disappears out of this record, while Adam remains at the same address for several years. John Geib, Jr., started in business in 1815. On October 3d, 1817, he took out the second patent ever granted to a resident of New York for improvements in the '' shape and structure of the upright pianoforte.'' In 1821 this inventor was in business on the '' Bowery near Bedford Street,'' while Adam Geib and William, another of the former's nephews, appear at 23 Maiden Lane, where Geib & Walker, and subsequently William Geib alone carried on the piano business up to a recent date. The Geibs are mentioned further on in relation to exhibitions of pianofortes and relative matters.

Among the piano-makers that came over from London about the beginning of the century were George Chartres and Joseph Waites. They were in business in New York in 1804. In 1815—July 8th—George Chartres was granted the *first* patent issued to a New Yorker for a pianoforte improvement. The patent—drawing and specification —has unfortunately been lost among the others mentioned. This may have been a valuable innovation also. Many of Chartres's old pianofortes are yet to be found throughout New York State, as I am informed, and future investigation may reveal something in this respect.

The Kearsings came over still earlier than Waites and Chartres. They arrived in New York in 1802 and began business at Bowery corner North, as the usual newspaper announcement states. For many years subsequently John Kearsing & Sons were in business. Up to 1830 this family led in New York, although their output of instruments per annum was perhaps insignificant in a modern sense. In 1831 a United States patent, dated June 13th, was granted to H. O., G. F., and W. F. Kearsing for an improvement in square actions, of little value, evidently, for it has not survived. T. Kearsing & Sons held a place in the trade up to 1840, when the name disappeared from the list of piano manufacturers in the business directory. In recent years the name of George Kearsing, one of the group mentioned in relation to their patent of 1831, appeared. This old maker was in business in 1868 and upward, but got crowded out by more modern methods and larger facilities. Members of the family are yet in the business as journeymen.

A clever German named James Alois Gutwaldt came to this country in 1811 and began making instruments in Brooklyn, some of which were sold by the Paffs on Broadway.

A good many of the music teachers and musicians in New York at that time were Germans, and they came to Gutwaldt's aid. He sprang into rapid esteem and his pianos created quite a furore. His grands were frequently mentioned with great commedation by the press in connection with concerts from time to time past 1813. Through some unknown cause his popularity died out finally, and we hear little of him after 1830. It is asserted, however, that he was employed past this period in Firth & Hall's piano shop as their foreman for several years, but this I find is erroneous. Gutwaldt took out a patent on August 27th, 1818, for "an improvement in the framework of grands."

In 1815 John Firth made musical instruments in a small way at 3 Warren Street, notwithstanding that it is asserted, and accepted generally, like many other fallacies, that he was not practical. Furthermore, it is said that he only appeared in New York in 1828. In 1820 William Hall came into the trade and began business on Wooster Street, near Prince Street. Firth was in this year on Hester Street, near Rynders Street. In 1824 the firm of Firth & Hall was founded. In this year they opened an extensive place at 358 Pearl Street and became immediately very successful. Mr. James A. Gray, of Boardman & Gray, Albany, learned tuning and practical piano-making in their shop between 1831 and 1835, when they were manufacturing pianos.

Meanwhile the informal business started by John Jacob Astor in 1789 fell into the hands of John and Michael Paff in 1802. These are the piano-dealers mentioned in connection with J. A. Gutwaldt.   After some little changes the business fell into the hands of William Dubois, who nominally became their successor.   Dubois, it is asserted, was born in the West Indies, but had handled pianos, as a ship merchant, between here and London. As he knew nothing practically about pianofortes and was not even a musician, this accounts somewhat for his initiation into the trade under the circumstances.

In 1819 Robert Stodart arrived in New York from England, and imported pianos made by his uncle, Robert Stodart, then in business in London.   The latter was in turn a son of the original Stodart mentioned in the English chapters.   Stodart Jr. evidently found that these high-priced instruments would not sell in the face of the very ordinary class of imported pianos brought over previously by Astor and others and then sold in the city, for he began manufacturing in 1820.   In 1821 he joined forces with William Dubois, and thereupon the firm of Dubois & Stodart began manufacturing, the former furnishing the capital.   This firm immediately became very prominent.   Mr. Henry Hazelton, of Hazelton Brothers, one of the oldest men in the trade, learned his business in this house, having been apprenticed in 1831.   Their business place in that year was on Broadway.   In a few years after this a Mr. Chambers became a partner, whereupon Stodart withdrew and began manufacturing in a new field.   In 1836 George Bacon, father of Mr. Francis Bacon, became a partner, the firm becoming Dubois, Bacon & Chambers.   In 1841, or thereabouts, Dubois withdrew.   Mr. Raven, who had served his apprenticeship with William Geib & Company, was taken in, whereupon the firm became Bacon & Raven subsequently. In 1856 the firm became Raven & Bacon, owing to the demise of the senior Mr. Bacon, Mr. Francis Bacon, one of his sons, taking his place in the firm. This house has all along, since 1836, been very prominent in the trade, and musical circles have regarded their pianos with much favor. Many of our most eminent piano men have at some period been employed in the workshop of this house, and the name of the firm will be known for many years to come, in consequence of its association with the early days of American pianoforte-making.

CHAPTER IX.

PHILADELPHIA.

FIRST IMPORTERS IN PHILADELPHIA—THE BLAKES—THE
FIRST UNITED STATES PATENT CONCERNING PIANOS—
McLEAN—MORE OF HAWKINS—THE LOUDS—THE FRANK-
LIN INSTITUTE—ALBRECHT—MEYER AND BABCOCK.

THE principal importer of pianofortes in Philadelphia
toward the end of the last century was Blake, whose
descendants have since that period been connected more
or less with the business in that city. George E. Blake,
one of this family, in recognition of his traditional and
direct connection with the piano business, was chosen to
act on the "Committee on Musical Instruments" connected with the first exhibition of the Philadelphia
Franklin Institute, and filled this honorary post during
several subsequent years.

There was a strong feeling existing about 1790 in favor
of encouraging local industries, and this was expressed
even in that remote year in relation to American-made
pianos. For instance, the *General Advertiser* of Philadelphia, in 1790, speaks of American musical instrument-
making as having arrived at great perfection in that city,
and says : "An ingenious artist has completed several

pianofortes in point of workmanship nothing inferior to
the imported. Their *superio ity* as it is, is, in fact, due
to the circumstance that wood seasoned in London does
not stand this dry climate, and further that Philadel-
phia-made pianofortes are braced with screws instead of
glue." This is really a most significant item of newspaper history in connection with the business, and serves
to show that the radical obstructions to the utility of
European instruments in this country were anticipated
and understood from the first.

The first patent issued at Washington in relation to
pianofortes after the department was founded, was
granted to J. Sylvanus McLean, of New Jersey, on May
27th, 1796. This was the sixth year after the establish
ment of the Patent Office.

It has long been known that pianos were made in Bordentown, N. J., during the latter part of the last century,
in a small way, and incidentally it has been asserted that
it was in this village that Hawkins made his experiments
in "uprights" in 1799, but this cannot be verified.

Hipkins also stated in his earlier writings in connection with Hawkins that the latter lived in Bordentown,
N. J., originally, when he produced his "portable upright
grand," but how the London historian discovered his
information cannot be learned. This is, however, not
true, to the extent that Hawkins lived in Philadelphia in
1799–1800, and several succeeding years. Moreover, he
took out his patents while in that city. He may yet
have lived in Bordentown before coming to Philadelphia.

McLean probably is the piano-maker that lived in the
former place, although his name cannot be traced in
local annals or records of any kind. There was an ex-

pert cabinet-maker, amateur painter, and musician, however, lived in Elizabethtown, N. J., in 1790, or thereabouts, whose name corresponds partially with the inventor under reference, who may have been the real person sought after in regard to the first pianoforte patent.

This is, meanwhile, all conjecture, only made interesting by reason of its historical suggestiveness.   McLean's
patent was for " alterations in the scope and make of the
pianoforte."   No further specification was ever issued,
and the original drawings in connection with the record
were destroyed in 1836 and have not been replaced.

McLean may have really anticipated Hawkins's upright
in this record ; or more, given the suggestion to the
latter ; but further light cannot, unfortunately, be thrown
upon the matter.

Resuming with Philadelphia, the name of Loud comes
uppermost at this point.

Thomas Loud, Jr., was in business in the " Quaker
City" as early as 1816.   In 1817 he was located at Prune
and Fifth streets.   In 1818 he took his brother into partnership and moved to 361 High Street, now Market,
where they carried on business as Thomas & John Loud.
In 1822 Philologus was taken into partnership, whereupon
the name of Loud Brothers appeared for the first time.

Loud Brothers, in 1824, were the most extensive
makers of pianos in this country.   In this single year
they claimed to have made six hundred and eighty instruments, which was a large output for such a comparatively remote period, particularly when the use of
pianos was limited almost to the very wealthy classes.

In 1825 Loud Brothers were well represented at the
second exhibition of the Franklin Institute.   They were

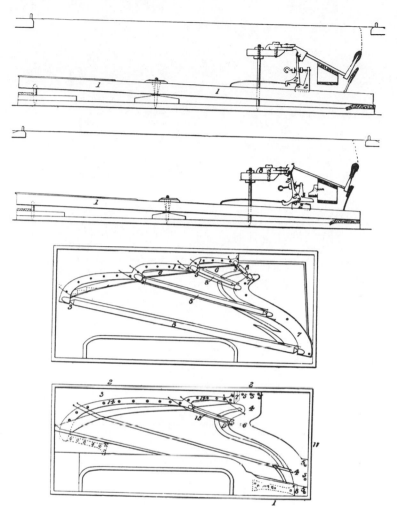

T. Loud's Actions and Separable Plates with Compensating Tubes.

Patented December 7, 1837.

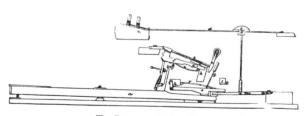

T. Gilbert's Action.

Patented August 7, 1847.

outclassed in one direction by Alpheus Babcock, of Boston, to whom the premium for the best square was awarded, but carried off the premium for the best upright piano.

The "Committee on Premiums" set forth a description of Loud Brothers' instrument in this manner : "Premium No. 46—to the manufacturer of the best upright or cabinet piano—is awarded to Loud Brothers for specimen No. 172, being an upright pianoforte of rosewood, which is considered a masterpiece of these excellent artists. It is finished in the best style, has a fine full tone and a very good touch ; it is, moreover, a beautiful piece of furniture and decidedly entitles the makers to the *silver medal*, being the best of the four upright pianos exhibited."

In the "Judges' Report" of this event, besides giving the same views in relation to the upright selected for the premium, they express the following opinion upon another upright exhibited by Loud Brothers, as subjoined : "The mahogany upright by the same makers is not of so high a class as the preceding, and is not exhibited with the same pretensions. Its tone is not so equal, although resembling the former in quality. Its touch is also inferior, yet it deserves the character of an excellent instrument."

The Louds were famous in their day and were very progressive and revolutionary in their methods. In 1826 they won particular notoriety owing to a grand they made for an eccentric Louisiana planter named Gordon. This individual was a driver of a Broadway stage in New York ten years before, who, owing to the death of a Southern relative, found himself suddenly lifted into the arms of "Queen Money." Upon coming into possession of several large Southern plantations, besides a solid bank residue, he became anxious to outdo all his Southern neighbors in the matter of display. This had some meaning, principally because he found these supporters of the American Constitution too proud to acknowledge him as an equal on account of his former occupation. Gordon thought of a commonplace manner of revenging himself, as he thought, upon these people. He accordingly erected a magnificent residence, furnished it in the most elaborate way imaginable, filled his stables with the best-blooded horses in the country, and carried his schemes to the most eccentric point. The most peculiar feature of Gordon's actions was that he engaged an excellent orchestra to play specially for the amusement of himself and his visitors, who were mostly persons from the North. He went to Loud Brothers in Philadelphia, and paid them an extraordinary price to make him the most elaborate and remarkable pianoforte ever made in the United States up to that year. The Louds in their effort to be extraordinary, therefore, in accordance with the price agreed upon, produced an instrument having a compass of seven and one-half octaves, the most extensive range ever reached before that period ; but it was absolutely worthless from a musical standpoint, so musicians said.

The case is described as being a marvel of cabinet art, the designing being done by the best artists of the period. It was adorned externally all over with paintings in the allegorical style, and created an absolute furor in New York and Philadelphia among musical and art people, aside from the fact that it excited the enmity and curiosity of the fashionable people to an extent entirely human and easily understood.

Inquiries recently made in New Orleans and elsewhere in Louisiana failed to elicit any information pertaining to the fate of this remarkable instrument. There are so many Gordons scattered throughout the State, however, that it would be a gigantic task in itself to trace the Loud Brothers' piano referred to by this means, assuming that it is still in preservation, and the " end" would hardly repay the labor expended. The only value the instrument possibly could have in the eyes of readers of a work of this character, is that it would serve as an interesting and serious example of early art in American piano-making if illustrated in these pages.

On May 15th, 1827, Thomas Loud, Jr., took out a patent for his down-striking action, illustrated elsewhere, which was a very ingenious piece of mechanism and a remarkable development in action evolution, for its time, but it came to nothing practically.

In 1835 the same inventor took out a patent for a cast metal plate, with compensating tubes, after the manner of Thoms & Allen's plate for grands, patented previously in London, with the difference that Loud's tubes were supposed to rest in sockets cast in the frame, which was produced in two entire castings, unlike Babcock's plate. This frame, however, was only a mere strip of cast-iron adjusted with small screws in the woodwork, outside the hitch-pin section, and this was a copy of Babcock's scheme.

On December 7th, 1837, Loud patented a further extension of this plate idea, illustrated in two figures given elsewhere. In the same patent he published two square actions, which were a compromise the-oretically between the common English and French actions, with special methods of adjusting the play of the *jack* underneath the hammer-heels in each design, as exemplified in the drawings given. The actions have neither hoppers nor "rockers," and the manner of regu-lating "escapement" in each is also original to an extent, as the plates indicate.

The actions never survived, but Loud's "compensat-ing tubes" were generally adopted in New York in 1838, applied by various makers in such a manner as to defeat the object of Loud's patent. Albany shortly followed suit.

Various arrangements of this idea may be met with in old instruments of the period, in which tubes are ap-plied in different ways, but invariably always so as to permit the strings to rest on a wooden back-bridge, because there was a general distrust of metal manifested. In Nunns & Clark's squares of 1838, for instance, one end of the large compensating tube rests in a socket cast in the hitch-pin plate, runs across from end to end, skirting the lowest bass strings, and rests in another socket, which is adjusted to the woodwork of the case. This became the accepted system of bracing after 1840 in most manufacturing centres, until the more general adoption of the whole metal plate in recent years.

The Loud brothers were in business at 306 Chestnut Street in 1837. In this year they met with a reverse in fortune and suspended manufacturing. Mr. W. White-lock, a very old member of the Maryland Historical Society, who knew the Loud brothers intimately, has kindly furnished me with a few important facts about this very significant family of early piano-makers. He writes : " When I first knew them, in 1831, the firm was ' Loud Brothers,' and was composed of the sons of the emigrant Loud referred to. They were Thomas, Philologus, John, and Joseph. They were induced to purchase a gold mine in North Carolina and failed in consequence. Thomas subsequently engaged in business with his son Thomas C. Philologus removed to Macon, Ga., and subsequently died in Albany in that State. John was the husband of Marguerite St. Leon Loud, an authoress of some repute fifty years ago. Joseph migrated to California, and returning died in Philadelphia last summer, leaving a son. A sister of Joseph married Dr. T. T. Smiley, of Philadelphia, and left a large family." The writer of the foregoing means that Loud Brothers failed through the cause intimated sometime past 1831.

After the break-up of the original firm of Loud Brothers referred to by Mr. Whitelock, Loud & Company appeared in business in Philadelphia at 170 Chestnut Street for a few years, when they disappeared. Thomas C. Loud, a son of Thomas the inventor, appeared in 305 South Tenth Street about 1838, and continues in the directory up to 1854. Thomas C. Loud, assisted by his father, during the intervening years retrieved the status of the name in connection with pianos, and up to about 1848 did a very large business. John Loud, another of the old firm, enjoyed some distinction as a maker up to 1842, when he went out of the trade as a manufacturer.

The last patent taken out by Thomas Loud was in 1847 and concerned an action, but it was of little consequence.

In seeking out information regarding this family, one

of the sons of Thomas C. Loud informed the writer that his father was born in Philadelphia on July 12th, 1812, which goes to show that the family arrived in the "Quaker City" several years before they started in business.

A very notable figure appeared in Philadelphia about 1828 in the person of Conrad Meyer, known up to a recent period, both in connection with a standing dispute concerning the introduction of the modern iron plate and as an old piano-maker of repute.

Meyer was born in Marburg, Hesse-Cassel, and emigrated to Baltimore in 1819, where he drifted into the workshop of Joseph Hiskey, a countryman of his own, and rapidly acquired a knowledge of the details of piano-making. He subsequently settled in Philadelphia. In the directory he appears for the first time in 1829 at 108 North Fourth Street. From 1830 to 1839 he manufactured at 50 South Fifth Street. In 1840 he moved to 152 South Fourth Street, where he had his business for a considerable period.

Meyer exhibited a square in 1832 at the Franklin Institute, but it won no distinctive notice. In 1833 I find he exhibited a square containing some application of iron in the shape of a plate. In this annual exhibition of the Institute Nunns & Company, of New York, A. Babcock, and C. F. L. Albrecht, of Philadelphia, won the honors. Of the first-named makers' piano the committee writes : " We consider Messrs. Nunns' upright piano of great merit. We consider it the best of the kind for purity and sweetness of tone that has ever come under our notice." Loud Brothers also had an upright made of American bird's-eye maple in this exhibition. A reference to Meyer occurs in the manner of an addendum, as follows : " We also think it worthy to notice a piano by Conrad Meyer having a shifting or transposing action, also a piano with *an iron frame,* which has some good qualities."

Meyer achieved great prominence in recent years in relation to the introduction of the full iron plate in the piano, which has some bearing on the latter instrument. He exhibited a square with one of these plates at the Philadelphia Centennial Exhibition in 1876, that he claimed to have been the one made in 1832 and exhibited in 1833 at the Franklin Institute. He asserted that this was the first plate on the modern lines ever attempted in this country, therefore he claimed to be the inventor and initiator of the system of solid iron plates now in general adoption in grands, squares, and uprights. Here Meyer's piano was formally examined, his record searched, and comparison with other systems instituted, which resulted in an abstract acceptation of the latter's general claim by the committee, no piano-makers or others, however, having in the mean time come forward to raise a point of dispute, based on any evidence to the contrary.

Discredit had been thrown previously on Babcock's iron plate, illustrated herein, by certain firms, which resulted in giving Meyer's statements a reliable color. Meyer's pianoforte was taken to Paris in 1878 and placed in the Universal Exposition during that year. It attracted considerable attention from piano manufacturers, experts, and people identified with musical trade journalism, particularly owing to the circumstance that Meyer had his claims previously accredited in 1876 in Philadelphia.

European writers on the piano, therefore, took all the facts stated in connection with Meyer's instrument, as trustworthy, and constant reiteration of the accepted statement that Meyer was the first to produce and patent a plate cast solid on the modern lines, from 1878 upward, by standard authorities, has resulted in placing the inventor named in a prominent place in pianoforte history in relation to this improvement.   Moreover, it was all along put forward in a matter-of-fact style that Conrad Meyer *patented* this innovation in 1832, and this has become an accepted phase of American pianoforte history throughout Europe.   At this point it will be necessary to give a brief history of Alpheus Babcock's plate, which is the precursor of all modern attempts at plate-casting on the lines intimated.   To recapitulate :

Babcock, while in Boston, in 1825, took out a patent for a metal frame complete, with hitch-pin section made in one casting.   This is shown elsewhere.   It is incontrovertibly the basis of every subsequent attempt in that direction.   This record is dated December 17th in the Patent Office.   Now, while it is known very generally that Babcock was granted this patent, a very general misconception prevails as to the absolute nature and scope of his iron frame, and many absurd statements have been perpetuated in reference to it.   The standard British authority, Mr. Hipkins, writing in 1880 on Allen's cast-iron frame patent of 1831, writes as follows, on Babcock's : " Allen's proposal of one casting had been anticipated in America by Alpheus Babcock, of Boston, U. S., who, in 1825, patented a cast-iron frame for square pianos.   The object of this frame, like that of Allen's first patent, *was compensation.*   It *failed*, but Babcock's

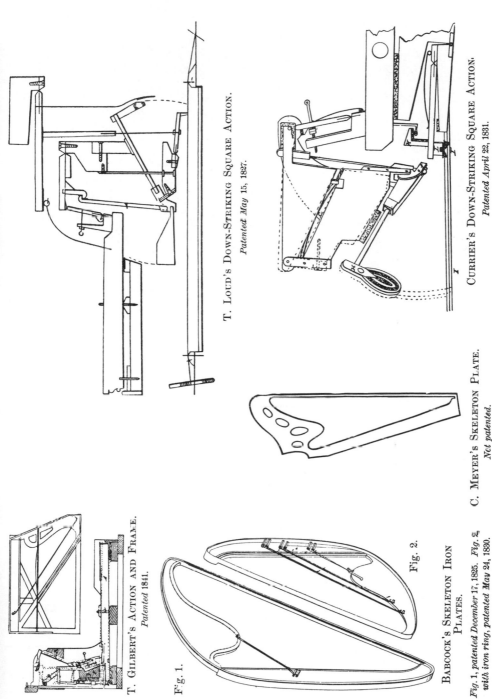

T. Loud's Down-Striking Square Action.
Patented May 15, 1827.

Currier's Down-Striking Square Action.
Patented April 22, 1831.

C. Meyer's Skeleton Plate.
Not patented.

T. Gilbert's Action and Frame.
Patented 1841.

Fig. 1.

Fig. 2.

Babcock's Skeleton Iron Plates.
Fig. 1, patented December 17, 1825. Fig. 2, with iron ring, patented May 24, 1830.

single casting laid the foundation of a system of construction which has been largely and successfully developed in America. . . . Conrad Meyer, of Philadelphia, claimed to have invented the metal plate in a single casting in 1832. Whether Meyer was aware of the previous efforts of Allen and Babcock or not, he has the merit of having made a good square on this plan of construction in 1833."

In a very valuable work issued by Steinway & Sons in relation to the historical growth of the American pianoforte, during the progress of the Centennial Exhibition in 1876, I further find this reference to Babcock: " In the year 1825 Alpheus Babcock, of Philadelphia, was granted a patent for the construction of a cast-iron ring somewhat resembling the shape of a harp in a square piano, for the purpose of increasing its power of resistance to the pull of the strings. By this invention the principle was first practically introduced of casting the iron hitch-pin plate, together with that portion which supported the wrest-plank *in one piece*. In 1833 Conrad Meyer, of Philadelphia, exhibited at the fair of the Franklin Institute a square which was constructed with a full cast-iron frame, substantially the same as used at present." Steinway & Sons' estimate of Babcock's innovation is nearer the correct standard than that of the British historian, but reflects the general opinion prevailing as to the utility and significance of the invention under consideration. Another firm states in a pamphlet, that " Babcock made a cast-iron ring in 1825 which was *never* put into practical use." There is a supplementary assertion put forth also, that " Conrad Meyer, of Philadelphia, took out a United States patent in 1832 for a full cast-iron frame."

Having procured an official drawing of Babcock's patent at the National Patent Office, after considerable difficulty, owing to the fact that the original record was destroyed in the fire of 1836, and knowing the nature of Meyer's plate, the writer assumes to be in a fair position to discuss facts, not conjectures, by comparison. The iron plate exhibited in the Meyer square claimed to have been made in 1832 is illustrated in these pages, and is practically similar with Babcock's in every way.

Reviewing the foregoing, I wish to show, in the first place, that Babcock's plate, shown in these pages, was not intended for compensation, as so many authorities assert. It contains no suggestion of compensating rods, tubes, or other contrivances, such as Thoms & Allen's and Loud's plates exemplify, arranged so as to "give and take," with the process of tuning and atmospheric changes. It is in every respect a frame identical with that exhibited in Meyer's square at the Centennial Exhibition and elsewhere, except in a few minor details.

Babcock's plate patent was not a failure when applied, as is believed. Moreover, it was applied practically, not merely recorded in Washington. Turning to the records of the Franklin Institute, Philadelphia, we find among the records relating to the pianos shown at the fourth annual exhibition in October, 1827, the following reference to a Babcock instrument : " Especially mention is made of a horizontal piano by A. Babcock, of Boston, of an *improved construction*, the frame which supports the strings being of *solid cast-iron* and strong enough to resist their enormous tension. This instrument was finished in the highest manner possible, not merely on the exterior but throughout, and the maker has maintained the high character which he had previously acquired.''

Not only is the above fact a significant proof upon one issue, but it can be shown that, for several subsequent years past 1830, the clever Boston maker continued to use his iron plates. Many of these instruments, I am informed, are still in existence, and in themselves furnish positive evidence that Babcock knew the absolute worth and practical value of his invention.

Another point I wish to show is that Meyer never applied for a patent in 1832, or at any time in connection with the plate exhibited in 1876, and therefore was never granted one. More than this, there is no proof whatever that the particular instrument exhibited by Meyer in 1833 at the Franklin Institute was similar with that shown in Philadelphia in 1876 and in Paris in 1878. If they were identical, then, Babcock, who lived in Philadelphia in 1833, must have assisted and allowed Meyer to use his invention. This is by no means improbable.

Babcock arrived in Philadelphia in December, 1829, from Boston, where he began manufacturing in conjunction with Klem, his former agent. In 1830 he took out a patent for '' cross-stringing pianofortes,'' together with an iron ring intended for string-hitching purposes, which no doubt gave rise to the expression, '' Babcock's iron ring.'' This patent is illustrated elsewhere in the plate.

While defending Babcock's position as an inventor, it is not claimed that his frame was entirely acceptable from a modern standpoint, or entitled to be regarded as an anticipation of the plate introduced by Chickering in 1837, for this was the complete link between the Steinway improved overstrung grand plate of 1859 and all prefatory attempts resorted to prior to 1825.

CHAPTER X.

CHARLESTON AND BALTIMORE.

EARLY PIANO-MAKING IN CHARLESTON—THE FIRST PARADE
OF MUSICAL INSTRUMENT-MAKERS—WATTS—BALTIMORE
—HARPER — STEWART — HISKEY — GAEHLE — KNABE AP-
PEARS—KNABE & GAEHLE—KNABE & COMPANY.

AFTER the close of the Revolutionary War Charleston
and Baltimore were naturally the two most important
ports south of Philadelphia. Looking over old journals
of these cities published during 1786, or earlier, we find
by the advertising pages that articles generally needed,
and not to be had through home production were imported from Europe in precisely the same manner as in
the Northern seaport cities. The Southern States, from
the earliest date of their settlement up to the recent Civil
War, maintained a very exclusive set of people, to whom
the patronage of music and the allied arts was a fashionable duty almost, therefore it is not surprising that the
largest share of early harpsichords and pianofortes
brought over from Europe before the commencement of
this century was absorbed in the South.

The first notice of harpsichord or pianoforte making
in Charleston or Baltimore that I find is an advertise-

ment from Charles Watts, pianoforte-maker, in the Charleston *City Gazette* of 1791, September 10th—found in the library of Mr. W. M. Thoms, editor of the *American Art Journal*—where he addresses his business constituents in the following manner : "Charles Watts, cabinet and pianoforte-maker, duly acknowledging past favors, most respectfully informs his friends and the public that he has moved to the corner of Broad Street and Market Square, opposite the State House. Those ladies and gentlemen who are pleased to patronize him in the above branches, may depend on having their orders completed with care and punctuality. N.B.—Harpsichords, pianofortes, and spinets completely repaired. July 19th, 1791."

In another issue of this journal the following advertisement appears . "For sale, remarkably cheap, an excellent harpsichord chosen in London by the late Mr. Yarnold. Inquire at the printing-office."

Watts arrived in New York from England in January, 1789. On June 8th I find that the *Daily Gazette* contained an announcement that "Charles Watts, musical instrument-maker, 29 Broad Street, corner Princess, is just arrived from London, and has brought over for sale two of his forte-pianos, one of a new construction with brass dampers. He likewise tunes, makes, and repairs all kinds of musical instruments."

Watts was in New York up to March in the following year, when he went to Charleston. He was a pianoforte-maker by trade and well known in London before his departure for this country, but evidently had to advertise himself partly as a cabinet-maker, through necessity, in New York and Charleston.

In the number of the Charleston *City Gazette* first quoted
from, I find among articles for sale at 16 Elliot Street,
the subjoined : " A few excellent violins and flutes, and
some music, canzonettes, duets, etc."

We are all prone naturally to look back with reverence
on the distant past.   Influenced by this wholesome spirit
the historian and the sympathetic reader delight in re-
suscitating what would be considered insignificant events
and facts from the standpoint of to-day, wrapping around
them an atmosphere of idealism that is entirely permissi-
ble.   As a sentimentalist of that stamp, the writer dwells
with peculiar emphasis upon facts, such as the subjoined,
given throughout these pages promiscuously.   What I
wish to dwell on here, is that, probably the first time
in the history of this country that the music trade
or profession was represented at a public celebration or
national event, was in Charleston, on May 25th, 1788.
On this day and date there was a State celebration held
in that city to commemorate the adoption of the Federal
Constitution, to which the Southern States then in being
gave enthusiastic support.   Curiously enough we read
of " musical instrument-makers," as marching in one
line of the parade, to the number of twenty-three.   It
turns out that these were composed of Baltimoreans and
visitors from Philadelphia, including those resident in
Charleston.   What they were, or how many of them
were harpsichord or piano-makers is not known.   From
my discoveries in connection with early history, I am of
opinion that Baltimore had one or two harpsichord-
makers about this year, besides several musical instrument-makers, devoted like Wolfhaupter, in New York, to
small musical instruments.   Charleston also had several

makers of musical instruments as far back as 1786. These, added to the visitors from the cities named, formed the body parading at this event.

These men may have made a miserable exhibition from a modern comparison, but one cannot help looking back through the dingy pages of history at this handful of mechanics with reverent eyes.

Coming to the "Monumental City," the earliest piano-maker that I find in Baltimore annals is John Harper. His name appears as early as 1802 in the directory, and I have learned that he made pianos for many years after that date. Stewart was a product of his shop. A resident of St. Louis has an old Harper, recently. spoken of in a newspaper of that city, that the present owner *claims* to have been made in 1792. It is an old family relic, and can be traced indirectly back to that date, when it was purchased in Baltimore.

James Stewart, who is more fully treated of elsewhere, began business in 1814 in the latter city. at 96 Hanover Street, corner of Conway. He moved to 175 Hanover Street in 1818, where he was located for a short period. Stewart was famous throughout the South from 1814 up to the beginning of 1820, when he failed and went to Boston.

Joseph Hiskey, whose name has been handed down to recent times, through his pupil, Conrad Meyer, and other old makers, became a leading manufacturer of pianos in the South as early as 1820. In that year he lived at 7 Water Street. He moved to "corner of Howard and Saratoga streets" in 1821, where he continued to make pianos for a great many years following. It is related that James Lick, the celebrated founder of the observatory bearing his name, and famous for his astronomical inquiries, worked as an apprentice in Hiskey's shop, and made pianos afterward as a journeyman in New York and Philadelphia.

Conrad Meyer, as stated, was another eminent pupil of Hiskey's shop, but owing to his subsequent connection with Philadelphia he is treated of in that section at more length.

Hiskey was a German and remarkable for his cheery, hearty manner. Many old men are alive in Baltimore who remember him perfectly well in his later days. His name went out of business in 1845.

Henry Hartye appeared in Baltimore in 1826, and began making pianos on Hanover Street in 1827. He became far more remarkable as a piano-maker than Hiskey. One of his instruments was considered so excellent, when exhibited at one of the fairs in Philadelphia, that the British Minister resident in Washington purchased it on sight, and ordered two others of the same kind for the purpose of shipping to English friends as presents.

Hartye was another remarkable member of the Teutonic race, a people that have been significantly identified with the progress of American art and music since the Revolution. Hartye took out a patent on May 12th, 1836, for an improvement in the English system of applying metal plates to the pianoforte. His claim, regarding novelty, rested upon the method formulated of carrying the tuning-pin through the metal plate into the wrest-plank underneath. This he claimed to be original. Hartye's application of iron to the wrest-plank was, no doubt, a rough anticipation of a system well known and in general use to-day.

The idea primarily can be traced as far back as 1800 in the United States, when Hawkins, of Philadelphia, carried his tuning-pins in the metal "wrest-plank" of his uprights ; but in either case it was not entirely new.

Thomas Loud, of Philadelphia, imitated Hartye in 1837 by introducing a metal strip, to be secured on the wrest plank of the piano, which he named a "metallic supporting brace," intending it to carry the tuning-pins. This was included in Loud's patent of 1837, which is partially illustrated in these pages.

Hartye became a very popular manufacturer of pianos in his time and effected a few reforms in structure, but his name has long ago been forgotten, unlike that of Babcock, Stewart, Osborn, or even Hiskey.

Louis Fissore, a French piano-maker, who had worked in Pleyel's shop in Paris, arrived in Baltimore in the early part of 1833. He landed in New York originally and evidently did not meet with any encouragement in the metropolis, hence his early appearance in the former place. He took out a patent on July 22d, 1833, for an improvement in metal plates. The index to the patent, however, reads simply, "Improvements in pianofortes." The announcement appears here that "Louis Fissore, an alien," was a resident of Baltimore, Md., only three months at the date when the patent was issued. This record is among those destroyed in 1836. Fissore's patent appears in a condensed form upon the *Journal of the Franklin Institute* for January, 1833. Of it the editor writes descriptively : " The improvements here patented depend principally upon the employment of cast-iron to constitute a part of the frame of the instrument, the novelty in this part *not consisting in the use of this material,* but in the particular manner of its construction and adaptation.   The tuning-pins are passed through a cast-iron plate and are fixed in such a way as not to depend for their tightness upon being driven in, but upon a washer passing over a square shank at the back of the plate, the pin being drawn up to a shoulder by means of a screw-nut.   A particular kind of tuning-hammer is also employed, the key part of which is operated upon by pinions, which give to it a slow, and, consequently, a powerful motion from that of the handle.   Fissore's claims are : His manner of constructing and connecting the iron frame, and his manner of fixing the tuning-pins and the instrument for tuning.''

The plate designed by Fissore was very evidently a variation of those used in Europe at the time, with compensating tubes and such appliances.

Little is known of this inventor beyond that his name turns up in New Orleans for a few years past 1840, when it disappears finally.   He probably became a journeyman and remained in that position throughout his life.

In 1833 the pianoforte art business in Baltimore received a most decisive contribution in the person of William Knabe, the subsequent founder of the great house of Knabe & Company, one of the most respected firms known in relation to art and commercial life throughout the South and North.

William Knabe, the elder, was a native of Kreutzburg, Germany, where he was born in 1803.   He acquired a knowledge of piano-making in all its branches in his native country before arriving in the United States, and immediately went to work in the shop of Henry Hartye upon his arrival in Baltimore in 1833.   Added to his acquirements as a practical piano-maker, Mr. Knabe was possessed of a superior education, his parents having intended him in youth for one of the learned professions which the Napoleonic wars made impossible.

As the portrait given in these pages represents, he was a man of decided mechanical genius and of no uncommon order, as the rapid growth of the Knabe pianoforte to artistic eminence in comparatively remote years exemplifies. His face indicates a keen faculty of perceptiveness in its shrewd lines around the eyes and mouth, tempered by kindliness of disposition, and this physiognomic estimate is fully borne out by facts as to his living character.

When Knabe had acquired a knowledge of American piano-making methods, and could use the language effectively, he bethought him of getting into business. He found a partner in Henry Gaehle, another practical piano-maker, and these two began business in 1839 as Knabe & Gaehle. This association continued up to 1854, when the partnership was dissolved.

The name of Gaehle continued in the trade and became well known subsequently in Baltimore in relation to piano-making. William Knabe succeeded to the privileges and rights of the former house, thus retaining the legal right to date the origin of his concern from 1839, the year in which the Knabe & Gaehle pianoforte first appeared. The house now became Knabe & Company.

The rise of the Knabe piano to artistic and commercial eminence, as early as 1860, when it was well known throughout the country, resulted from sterling merit in the instrument, as well as from the keen executive ability of William Knabe, who, in addition to being a clever piano-maker, was a shrewd business man. In 1860 Knabe & Company were located at 135 and 137 North Eutaw Street, where they had a splendidly appointed factory. They controlled the Southern trade, to a great extent, about this year, owing to the growing antipathy felt toward every article coming from the North, and were everywhere highly esteemed.

William Knabe was a very popular citizen of the " Monumental City," as can be gleaned from Scharf's " Annals of Baltimore," and took an active part in popular affairs. He died in 1864, generally regretted by all classes.

Mr. Knabe's sons, William, Jr., and Ernest, who had previously been very carefully trained in the details of practical piano-building, as well as fitted for the commercial management of the concern, together with Charles Keidel, a relative by marriage, became the heirs of the house, which continued to be William Knabe & Company up to the present time in nomenclature.

William Knabe, Jr., up to his recent death a member of this firm, was born in Baltimore in 1841, and received a collegiate training, besides a practical education in piano mechanics inside his father's shop.

The Knabe firm have introduced many new improvements in the Knabe piano within the last fifteen years, especially in the " scaling" and other acoustic departments, many of which it would be impossible to protect by patent. Apart from innovations of this nature, several important patents have been taken out incidentally by the firm for use in their instruments. William Knabe, Jr., died in January, 1889, at Aiken, S. C., at the age of forty-seven.

Reviewing the modern history of the concern briefly, I find that in 1864, while the Civil War was yet being fought, and the commercial relations of North and South necessarily in an involved condition, Knabe & Company established a direct agency in New York. *Watson's Art Journal*, the predecessor of the present *American Art Journal*, for that year, comments upon the circumstance in a eulogistic notice. From that source I learn that J. Bauer & Company, 544 Broadway, became Knabe & Company's representatives, and filled that position for several subsequent years, until, in 1873, the New York branch fell under the direct management of the firm.

Knabe & Company suffered considerably during the great Civil War, but the return of peace beheld them ready to loom up with the " New South." Their invasion of the North in 1864 opened up a wide field for the artistic future and popularity of the instrument, until the Knabe piano has grown to be as well known throughout the North as any of the celebrated instruments made in Boston or New York.

Gaehle seems to have been a permanent name in the Southern manufacturing trade, for Gaehle & Company appears in the Baltimore directory up to very recently, even all through the years of the Civil War, when the piano business was seriously depressed in that city. This concern was known only in connection with a popular price class of instrument all along.

John J. Wise, another Baltimore maker, began business in 1829, and became noted as a manufacturer, before 1852, particularly. Previous to 1840 Wise was next to Hartye the most important piano-maker south of Philadelphia. He was a frequent customer of the Patent

Office, and introduced a great many little improvements in actions and other mechanical directions during his career.   On November 19th, 1833, he was granted a patent for an ingenious method of tuning and stringing, that has since been frequently tried and found impracticable, which does not deserve exemplification here.

His square action, produced in 1839, however, was an excellent modification of the familiar French action, with a few special points of improvement that are very interesting and novel, though by no means so startling as to win emphatic notice, beyond that they have been reproduced since that year by inventors, as original.   Wise took out another patent in 1848 for sound-board improvements, and is found frequently after this date in patent reports.   The Wise pianos were exhibited in various institute annual exhibitions from time to time, and always with honor.   After 1850, with the uprising of the new order of piano firms having large shops fitted out with special plant and all facilities for doing things on a huge scale, including the principal factor of all—capital—the Wises sank into a third-rate place.   They did not leave the business, notwithstanding, for in 1860, John Wise & Brothers—evidently sons of J. J. Wise—carried on business in Baltimore at 31 Hanover Street.   The war did not annihilate them either, for they appear in 1876 and since then.

Many new piano-makers sprang up in Baltimore toward 1850, among whom was Joseph Newman, afterward a very well known inventor and manufacturer in that city, in connection, however, with several members of his family—the firm's formal title for some time being Newman & Brothers.   From 1850 to 1860 this concern,

Charles M. Stieff, and J. T. Stoddard, were three of the best-known makers in Baltimore outside of Gaehle & Company and Knabe & Company.

Newman took out a patent for an "improvement in sounding-boards," in 1857, that excited some attention, owing to a controversy which it gave rise to. He became associated some time past 1853 with W. R. Talbot, a piano-maker who settled in Baltimore from Albany, where he was well known, and out of this partnership Newman Brothers & Company grew and continued for some time.

Joseph Newman's patent, spoken of, was for a double sounding-board, with two sets of strings, which was copied from James Pirsson, of New York, who introduced and patented it in the United States in 1857. Pirsson's double grands made upon this plan were well-known instruments in their time, as our New York chapters show, from the standpoint of their eccentricity.

Newman made pianos on the lines indicated in his patent and exhibited some, but they never achieved permanency or popularity, therefore they were abandoned quickly. He, however, made the upright a study for some time, and brought out some notable improvements in case structure and action construction in connection with this popular form, that were really worthy of appreciation. Nothing could induce the public in the United States to adopt the upright as a popular instrument thirty or less years ago, therefore Newman wasted his time like many others on a profitless task. Talbot, who is mentioned here, died in 1884. Little is known of the Newmans in recent years, and they have dropped out of all records concerning piano-making.

C. M. Stieff survived the war, and grew into a very respectable position in the Southern States as a piano-maker, which has been maintained for many years.

J. T. Stoddard also deserves mention in relation to the piano art business as it was from 1860 up to 1876.

Returning to Charleston, a writer from that city in 1838, has a letter in the New York *American Musical Journal* for August, in which he advocates the production of a work on the art of piano-tuning. "Even in Baltimore," he goes on to say, "and other Southern cities, I find that outside of piano-making shops tuners of average ability are very scarce, and in most cases cannot be had at all. Cannot this be remedied?" Pianos were made before 1840 in Charleston. Cornelius Bogart, one maker, took a patent in 1851 from this city for an improvement in sounding-boards. This, to some extent, was an anticipation of Driggs' sounding-board arrangement spoken of elsewhere. The difference in the former is that Bogart made his sounding-board of several kinds of wood, which were glued and fitted closely after the manner of the mandolin, cut out so as to set in that formation naturally. Like a thousand other inventions of a like nature Bogart's "improvement" amounted practically to nothing.

CHAPTER XI.

ALBANY.

MEACHAM & COMPANY—BURY'S PATENT—CLEMENCE & BURNS
—OSBORN, MARSHALL, JAMES & TRAVER—HAZELTON—
BOARDMAN & GRAY—MYRON A. DECKER—BUFFALO—
ROCHESTER---UTICA AND TROY—MUSIC IN ALBANY.

ALBANY loomed up as a possible centre for a great city early in the century. It was confidently believed at one time that the simple fact that it was the capital city of New York State would of necessity bring it up to a point of development where it would rival the largest cities on this continent. This belief no doubt induced the early piano-makers recorded here to concentrate there before 1840, in preference to more important commercial centres, such as Buffalo and Rochester.

There is a very general impression abroad that the first maker of pianofortes in Albany did not appear before 1830.

On this subject the late Mr. James A. Gray, who at his death was the oldest and most representative piano-maker in that city, wrote shortly before his demise in reply to inquiries among other matters mentioned throughout these pages : " The first organized maker in

Albany was, I think, Meacham & Company, musical instrument-makers, the pianos being made for them by John Osborn, who, about 1835, was prominent as a manufacturer in New York. I have also heard of a Stewart as having made pianos in Albany previous to the above.''

In this connection I have discovered that J. & H. Meacham, musical instrument-makers, State Street, were in business as far back as 1813, when the first Albany directory was issued. In 1825 Sylvanus B. Pond was taken into partnership by the Meachams, when the firm of Meacham & Pond appeared. The latter subsequently came to New York and became a distinguished member of the music trade of the metropolis. Meacham & Pond, and later Meacham & Company were well known up to 1850, throughout the State, in connection with the pianoforte and music trade of the capital city, but have been almost forgotten in recent years.

" Harley Hosford, musical instrument-maker, 97 State Street," is given in the first Albany directory. Hosford made organs and pianofortes in a small way in this year, and as early as 1810 was known in relation to pianofortes in that city. He was, moreover, a teacher, and identified, probably, to some extent, with musical progress in Albany after the beginning of the century.

Hosford was, as far as can be ascertained, the first maker of pianos in Albany, although his relation to the business was of an insignificant character. Nothing can be learned of his subsequent fate.

A patent was granted to Richard Bury, of Albany, on August 21st, 1819, for a pianoforte with glass strings. In this instrument strips of glass were " adjusted, tuned, and placed in such a position as to be operated and played from a piano keyboard, the mechanism employed to strike the strings being on the cabinet-piano-action principle, having hammers covered with a woollen felting substance so as to conduce toward the production of the best quality of tone.''

Bury was not a piano-maker, however, notwithstanding this patent, which was the first taken out by a resident of Albany, and therefore has no further interest for readers.

John Osborn, of Boston, settled in Albany in 1829, where he went into partnership with G. King, but stayed in that city only about nine months, when he came to New York and began business on Chambers Street. Osborn seems to have been of a restless disposition, for he was constantly changing his place of business in Boston and elsewhere. He is said to have been of a sensitively exacting nature, which is somewhat indicative of the ability he evinced throughout his life as a pianoforte improver, for he was one of the most nervously progressive men of his time. This condition of temperament ultimately ended in insanity and suicide, as shown in a New York chapter.

John H. Quackenbush, an early maker, made pianofortes as far back as 1834, but his connection with the business was very short. Little is known of his history past that date.

Thomas Clemence and Francis Burns were well-known names in Albany annals. These were engaged in business in 1834 as Clemence & Burns. In 1835 they separated.

James H. Grovensteen, until recently a well-known New York figure in the sphere of the trade, made his appearance in Albany about 1839. His name does not appear in the directory of the city until long after 1840, but it is generally asserted that he was in business there in 1838. Grovensteen had originally learned his art and trade in New York, but moved to Albany about the date indicated, thinking it a sure field for development. After some years' experience he returned to New York some time before 1847, and began business on Grand Street.

Mr. A. C. James, of the present firm of James & Holmstrom, New York, is, to a small degree, a pupil of Grovensteen's Albany shop, where he worked for a short time in his apprentice days. He went into the factory of Boardman & Gray after leaving Grovensteen, where he acquired a thorough knowledge and training as a pianomaker. Mr. James was a member of the concern Marshall, James & Traver in later years. This firm made a very excellent instrument known principally outside of New York City. This was succeeded by Marshall & Wendel, a name well known at this date.

Two names worthy of mention in annals of pioneer piano-making in Albany are George Gomph, who was a maker on State Street, in 1838, and P. Reed, who seems to have won a good reputation as an improver.

Boardman & Gray is a pre-eminent house in Albany pianoforte history. This firm has for half a century maintained a leading place in the sense of moral uprightness, as well as from the art and trade standpoints. William G. Boardman, the author of the business, was a native of Albany, where he was born in 1800. His entry into the piano trade was purely accidental. Mr. Boardman was educated for mercantile pursuits, but having through friendship indorsed a piano firm, he was thrown in possession of all their stock-in-trade after their failure in 1835. Boardman having incidentally obtained an insight into the opportunities for development the business afforded a capitalist, engaged James A. Gray, his future partner, Mr. Henry Hazelton, and others, subsequently to come from New York to work in his shop.

Mr. Gray was born in New York City in 1815. He received a good education, and, in 1831, while yet a boy, succeeded in becoming apprenticed to Firth & Hall. Young Gray soon evinced such decided ability in his craft that he was put at tuning and toning, at which branches he became very expert. His first start in business was made in Binghamton, N. Y., where he went to superintend a factory for a Mr. Pratt, but soon returned to New York. His reputation now travelled ahead of him to Albany in time to reach the ears of Boardman, who immediately made a bid for his services. In two years after arriving in Albany Mr. Gray, then comparatively young in years, became the partner of his employer, out of which compact originated the firm of Boardman & Gray. William Boardman was identified to a large degree with the success attained by the house during its career, while J. A. Gray was identified to an equally large degree with the development of the instruments put forth by the concern. Mr. Boardman died, January 25th, 1881, at the age of eighty-one, but for many years before his death he had retired, the responsibility of the whole business resting on Mr. Gray meanwhile.

James A. Gray visited England in 1850 with several instruments of his own make. In these he exhibited his patented " Dolce Compana" effect, which has since been discarded. Boardman & Gray's American pianos were curiously tested by many of the leading English musicians of the time, and created marked surprise. About this year there was a general idea prevailing throughout Europe that art constructively was almost unknown in America, and pianoforte-making has always ranked so high in England that the decided artistic merit of the Boardman & Gray American piano of the period excited considerably more attention than under other circumstances. The exhibition of Chickering pianofortes at the great World's Fair in the following year added to this feeling, and triumphed over it by winning the respect of the most eminent English musical people to the American principles of construction shown in these instruments.

Mr. Gray realized little only honor from his invasion of England. This feat is claimed to have been the first attempt at importing American pianos into England, but Stewart in 1826 preceded the former in this direction, while there is a remote probability remaining that Hawkins exported several of his " portable upright grands" to England in 1800 and 1801, to his father in Manchester.

James A. Gray was a prolific inventor and an improver in a most decided degree. The most remarkable patented improvements he introduced were his " insulated iron rim and frame," the " corrugated sounding-board," and " Dolce Compana" effect, but aside from specialties of this nature the development of the Boardman & Gray pianoforte has always been kept in line with the best results achieved at the hands of other inventors elsewhere.

In 1877 he took his son William J. Gray into partnership, after he had piloted him through a thorough course of shop training so as to fit him for the practical side of the business. The Boardman & Gray house at the date of the recent death of James A. Gray was composed of James A. Gray, W. J. Gray, W. H. Currier, and W. W. Whitney.

From some correspondence which took place with Mr. Gray, relative to early phases of piano history, a short time ago, I give the following in reference to Albany, just as written :

" Since 1836 the following firms have made pianos in Albany : Meacham & Company, J. P. Cole, F. P. Burns, Hazelton, Lyon & Talbot—see H. Hazelton, of Hazelton Brothers—Myron W. Decker, now of New York—see Decker—Balentine & Barheirdt, and Marshall, James & Traver, succeeded by Marshall & Wendel. If anything more of importance occurs to me I will write you." This was dated September 20th, 1889. He wrote no more on the subject. On December 11th he passed away at the age of seventy-four, leaving behind him an estimable record as a man and a citizen.

W. R. Furgang, of Albany, was granted a patent on April 20th, 1852, for altering the disposition of the raised black keys in connection with the keyboard surface, so as to bring all the keys, " natural" and " accidental," almost to the same level. Furgang's keyboard scheme can hardly be done justice to in a few words, however. This system won many sentimental supporters, and it evoked much notice in 1853, but led to nothing.

Mr. Henry Hazelton, mentioned in various points of reference elsewhere, went to Albany from New York after completing his apprenticeship in Stodart & Dubois' shop in company with Mr. J. A. Gray, and for a short time worked in partnership with Lyon & Talbot, as pointed out in Mr. Gray's letter. He returned presently to his native city, however. Talbot in later years went to Baltimore while Lyon is still in Albany.

A. C. James manufactured in Albany up to 1871, when he changed his residence to New York, where he assumed a responsible position in connection with the Bradbury pianos.

Myron A. Decker, of Decker & Son, was for a time a resident of the capital city, where he began his career as a manufacturer in 1856, and consequently holds its annals in high esteem. Daniel Gray, another well-known figure in Albany, at one time, especially during the "forties," was a brother of James A. Gray and equally eminent as a skilled piano-maker in past years. J. P. Cole made instruments of some repute since 1850 in Albany and deserves some mention as an old maker. Another Albany concern, at present in existence, which cannot be excluded from these paragraphs, is McCammon & Company, which dates its existence from 1835.

In the northern part of New York State various cities began to produce pianofortes before 1820. I find, for instance, that one Morrison made musical instruments and pianos in Buffalo in 1811. He was a Scotchman and hailed from Glasgow originally. The first makers of any particular significance, however, were Kurtzman and D. Benson & Company. Benson & Company were in business in 1842 and made very reputable instruments about that period. I find that Benson & Company carried off the "gold medal" for the best piano at the New York Mechanics' Institute in 1850, and won at the time

JAMES A. GRAY.

high encomiums from the " Committee on Musical Instruments." C. Kurtzman was making pianos before 1850,
and was known up to a recent period as a good maker
of popular-priced instruments. The business to-day is
carried on by Kurtzman & Company, made up of L. S.
Kurtzman, A. Cordes, and Adolph Guger.

Lafayette Louis, another Buffalonian, took out a patent in 1863 for a combination of the reed organ and piano
after Coleman's methods, which had a short term of life.
In Rochester pianos were made as early as 1809 by
George Cartwright, who was in business up to 1813,
when he left the city. After 1840 Michael Miller began
business in a modest way. One of his improvements in
key-adjustment was patented in 1851. This related to
an ingenious and complicated scheme for placing the
keys so as to produce greater elasticity in touch, but it
never survived. Frederick Starr and Dwight Gibbons
started some time during 1850. Gibbons was granted a
patent in 1855 for a peculiar design in an iron frame,
which was later applied by Starr, but this, too, went
into disuse in the course of time.

Pianofortes were first made in the charming city of
Troy about 1840. In later years G. H. Hulskamp became a marked figure in the piano business. He was a
most persistent inventor and improver, mostly, however,
in the mechanics, not in the acoustics of the piano, and
in this connection took out a large number of patents.
Hulskamp was well known throughout the State of New
York, and was regarded with much respect in the metropolis subsequently, where he lived.

In Utica—another of the pretty cities that have sprung
up in the Mohawk country—I find that pianofortes were

made in 1841 by Luther Phileo, who was, like Hulskamp, a German maker. In 1846 he patented an improvement in the French square action, more remarkable as an indication of the inventor's ingenuity and desire to progress than for practical worth. One point of particular note in his patent and drawings is a method of self-adjustment for regulating the escapement of the hammer, which looks very feasible and striking in text. That it has not become known and accepted, however, tends to show that Phileo's scheme was impracticable. Wise, of Baltimore, anticipated several of Phileo's ideas in the direction of producing a self-escaping " jack" movement, however, as far back as 1838. The invention of a scheme to produce this result was a jealous point of contention between makers of pianos in the " forties" and upward, which brought forth many technical ideas and patents approximating to Phileo's and Wise's so-called improvements.

The progress of musical art in this country has grown up in close relationship to the production and spread of pianofortes, and, I may add, organs. A peculiar phase of musical development is shown in the fact that whereever piano-makers concentrated, musical art seems to have followed by some order of phenomena. It will be applicable, therefore, in this section to show that even in 1835 the people of Albany were capable of appreciating and contributing to the art of music, and surpassed all other cities in the State outside New York. In 1831 the Albany Sacred Music Society was founded, and in the *American Musical Journal* for April, 1835, I find a report of a musical programme having been rendered in that city which gave many of the best selections from Handel's

and Haydn's oratorios, including solos, duets, and cho-
ruses, in which forty trained voices assisted, aided by an
efficient orchestra. In the May issue of the same musical periodical a report appears from Albany also, which
reads : " The New York Italian Opera Company made
a visit to this city and gave a few performances at the
theatres. The first was on April 6th, when Rossini's
' L'Assedio di Corinto ' was performed ; this was followed
by ' Mosé in Egitto,' ' L'Inganno Felice,' and the second
act of ' Eduardo e Cristina.' The two first works were
repeated twice. The company also performed during
their stay Mozart's ' Requiem,' and a selection from
' Mosé ' in St. Paul's Chapel."

CHAPTER XII.

New York.

NEW YORK, following the excellent example set by
Philadelphia in 1824, established the Mechanics' Institute system of annual exhibitions in the early part of
1830. Accordingly, the first exhibition was a carefully-
prepared and advertised event, in which the projectors
tried to excel Philadelphia by exciting the desire of
manufacturers of all kinds, artists, and inventors to be
represented. In regard to musical instrument-makers
the first committee set aside a gold medal at each exhibition for the " best upright or cabinet piano," another
for the " best horizontal or square," and a third for the
" best grand pianoforte."

In the first exhibition, held in the building now occupied by " Castle Garden," I find that the following
pianoforte-makers exhibited at this event with these
results : William Geib, 170 Broadway, for a grand

upright pianoforte, first premium ; R. & W. Nunns, first premium for the best square. These were the gold medallists. Among the other exhibitors of instruments were Charles Sackmeister, a square, Dubois & Stodart, two squares, and Geib, a two-stringed square. All of the above were New York manufacturers at that date.

Passing over the next exhibitions, for an instant, I find the subjoined pronunciamento in relation to the financial aspect of the piano trade, as well as the advantage to society resulting from musical art, among the official papers of the Institute for 1836. It is as follows : "There is no branch of the fine arts more worthy of cultivation with us than music. It will soften our asperities of character and render us more and more attached to social intercourse and enjoyment. In our opinion this, among all classes, is the strongest temperance measure that can be 'got up.' Now good music can only be cultivated when good instruments can be procured at moderate prices. In this view of the case Messrs. Torp & Love doubly deserved the *gold medal* awarded them. While on this subject we have a suggestion to make to all of our manufacturers of musical instruments. Let them expend in addition one-half as much on the interior of pianos—upon that part which gives the instrument its character—as they throw away on unnecessary ornamentation on the exterior, ornamentation causing positive injury to tone and durability. The *best* pianos we have seen, though made of the finest wood and well finished, were invariably plain. A much better piano could be made for $250 under these conditions than many that sell for $500 as handsome pieces of furniture." The reference put forward in the foregoing, relating to the word "temperance," was a thrust at the great movement, in favor of this reform, going on at the period in New York among the working population. Torp & Love, mentioned in this quotation, were makers of cheap pianos in that year, and are given elsewhere.

Going back to Dubois, I find that he did not retire from the piano business after his separation from Mr. George Bacon. He subsequently, through various intervals, appears as "Dubois & Company," and in 1845 with Warriner. Dubois & Warriner went out of business in 1851. However, the name of Dubois had little significance in connection with manufacturing after his separation from Bacon, the latter retaining the bulk of the business and prestige meanwhile. The name of Warriner was, however, known in connection with the New York piano trade up to 1862.

In 1821 Robert and William Nunns arrived from London, and went to work in the shop of Kearsing & Sons, Broome Street. The Nunns brothers left no traces in London by which their origin or history could be ascertained, as far as I can find out, and seem to have been unknown there. It is clear that they were journeymen, however, and owe their future eminence in the trade to the circumstance that the newer and freer conditions of American life helped to bring out their latent ability.

In 1824 Robert & William Nunns started in business at 96 Broadway, and soon eclipsed all the New York manufacturers then making pianofortes. This was a notable house truly. They initiated a radical departure immediately after starting into the trade by introducing the present French action in their instruments, then in a rather imperfect state, however, and, in fact, anticipated in detail very important improvements in actions afterward patented by Erard in Paris. A member of the family, John F. Nunns, was granted a patent for a square action on May 5th, 1831, which takes in many of these improvements. In most houses the old English hopper and fly action was in use, and not until about 1850 was it generally discontinued in New York, although several makers in Boston and Philadelphia had for years used various modifications of the French " rocker" principle for regulating purposes, applied in different ways in combination with the English, French, and special patent actions. The Chickerings and Gilberts, of Boston, however, stuck all along to a peculiar variation of the English action, well known to practical piano-makers even now. The Chickerings, even up to a recent period, continued to use that action, improved somewhat, meantime, and many critics have styled them antiquated and so forth, in consequence. A little experience with the " wearing" possibilities of this action-principle will, however, show that when the hammer-centres and flanges become worn and shaky, the interposition of the under-hammer or " hopper" between the jack and the hammer-heel, gives a better and firmer quality to the tone produced than would be possible in the French-action arrangement in badly made actions.

One of the best " scales" ever seen up to 1827 in New York was furnished the Nunns by Charles S. Sackmeister, who showed its value to them in an instrument he had just finished at his house. Robert and William Nunns, who had the reputation of being singularly honorable, instead of devising some scheme and getting the " scale" copied, purchased it from Sackmeister, and it became a most valuable innovation. In a few years it was common property among New York and Philadelphia piano-makers. Before this year the Nunns' and others proceeded very "gingerly" about altering the position and scale of the bridges, length of strings, and other standard features of the instrument as it was then made. Sackmeister started out in a revolutionistic manner by placing No. 10 wire where No. 8 formerly was in the upper treble register, graduating the increased thickness of his wire down to the bottom strings, and placing his bridges in an entirely original range of distance from point to point, so as to correspond with his stringing, with the successful results pointed out. Sackmeister, I learn, drifted around the city drawing "scales" and modelling improvements for piano-makers, who realized largely by his skill and gave him little credit. Germans were scarcely tolerated in those days, and had a hard time to get along, therefore Sackmeister, like Gutwaldt, was kept down by force of circumstances.

Sackmeister patented a down-striking action on May 17th, 1830, that won him considerable notoriety. Apart from this he was noted for many years prior to this date as a most progressive maker and inventor.

Returning to the Nunns brothers, I find that John F. Nunns, another of that family, had a separate place at 57 Orchard Street for several years between 1832 and 1836.

Robert & William Nunns did business from 1824 up to 1833, in which year they had their warerooms at 137 Broadway, when John Clark came over from England and was taken into partnership, the firm becoming Nunns, Clark & Company. In this year their advertisement was to be found on the files of the *Sun*, and reads like this : " Robert Nunns, Clark & Company (formerly R. & W. Nunns) respectfully inform their friends and the public that they have always on hand an assortment of cabinet, square, and horizontal grand pianofortes from their manufactory, at their warerooms, 137 Broadway, two doors north of the City Hotel." William Nunns withdrew from business relations with his brother meantime and began manufacturing for himself. In some time he became associated with J. & C. Fischer, thus giving birth to Nunns & Fischer, which passed into J. & C. Fischer after 1840, owing to the withdrawal of Nunns, who again began business on his own account.

Nunns, Clark & Company became Nunns & Clark in 1838, and continued to lead as piano-makers until 1858, when their star faded. They dropped out of business after this date. While very much is written and spoken about Nunns & Clark, they have never been identified with any reforms or innovations in piano structure or acoustics after 1840, such as we associate with Steinway & Sons, Knabe & Company, Chickering & Sons, Loud Brothers, Hazelton Brothers, and other old firms in existence before the " sixties." They simply made average pianos after stereotyped principles first produced by other makers, employed good men, and paid good prices. I must, however, note one important fact subjoined.

In 1851 Nunns & Clark purchased the hammer-covering invention patented by Rudolph Kreter for a trifle, and thereby were the first to use the present improved method of hammer-covering, probably, in the world. More improved forms of covering machinery are now in existence owing to the exceptional genius of Mr. Alfred

Dolge, but Kreter was really the initiator of the original machine, which made it possible to cover "a whole set of hammer-heads at one operation," to use the words of Kreter's claim.   Nunns & Clark thereupon introduced felt extensively in their instruments, distributed in several thicknesses through the hammer-range varying from treble to bass as desired.

This is not alone a mere technical incident; on the contrary, the discovery of this method of hammer-covering, in connection with the introduction of felt, more generally marks an era in the acoustic and musical development of the pianoforte as pointed out in reference to Alfred Dolge elsewhere.   Therefore this is why it is given particular notice.   Kreter's patent is No. 9526, and was assigned in advance to Nunns & Clark.   This machine was used as early as 1850 by them.   I find that Kreter's machine passed into the hands of Mr. A. Dolge in 1870 and was sent to Brooks & Company, London.

Toward 1840 Firth & Hall became Firth, Hall & Pond, owing to the accession of Sylvanus B. Pond, of Albany, who since 1827 had been connected with the Meachams in the retail piano trade there.   By this date the firm was known over the Union everywhere, aside from pianos, owing to their extensive publication of instrumental and vocal music.   This popularity, to some degree, helped their piano sales, of course.   In 1847, Firth, Hall & Pond dissolved.   Mr. Hall withdrew, and with his son, James F. Hall, began manufacturing at 239 Broadway.

A new firm, Firth, Pond & Company, was organized, composed of J. Firth, S. B. Pond, T. Firth, and W. A. Pond.   This became a very energetic and pushing house, and soon retrieved the former position held by the old concern. John Mayell, brother-in-law of S. B. Pond, in a short time purchased an interest in the firm, and was added to the company. Another dissolution followed, whereupon John Firth started a new business in connection with his son, as Firth, Son & Company, which was, however, of short duration, as within a few years nearly all the principals passed away. John Firth died in September, 1864, aged seventy-five years.

Mr. Thaddeus Firth, a son of John Firth, who played an important part throughout his father's business career, revived the name of Firth for some time in the metropolitan music trade, but finally sold out to Oliver Ditson & Company, of Boston. Mr. Thaddeus Firth is a respected resident of Maspeth, L. I., at present, where he has a large musical instrument manufactory, and to him the writer is indebted for many of the foregoing facts.

The original firm of Firth & Hall was, after the dissolution referred to, succeeded by W. A. Pond & Company, from which the present house of Pond & Company has descended. S. B. Pond died in 1871, aged seventy-nine years. Hall & Son, another outcome of the old Firth & Hall house, was a well-known firm for many years in New York. Finally James F. Hall withdrew and joined the army. His father continued in business for a few years, but retired ultimately. He died in 1873, having survived his old partner by nine years.

William Hall was born in Sparta, N. Y., and was known as General Hall throughout his life, having been a soldier with John Firth in the War of 1812. John Firth, however, was a sturdy Yorkshire Englishman, with republican tendencies. He was born on October 1st, 1789, and came to this country in 1810. Hall and Firth were relatives, having married two sisters, both daughters of Edward Riley, well known in the music trade before 1840.

In the early part of 1830 John Osborn moved from Albany and began business at 184 Chambers Street. In 1832 he had become quite famous as a maker. In 1833 he took the gold medal at the Mechanics' Institute annual exhibition for the best grand and square pianofortes, "both for tone and workmanship, adjudged to be the best exhibited." In 1834 he also carried off the gold medal of the Institute in the same connection. Osborn was a man of superior intellect and belligerent to a high degree, as a business announcement of his printed in 1833 indicates. In this he asserts that all the foreign-born makers then in New York or Boston had "pilfered American methods of piano-building and acoustic development, without any justice or gratitude, but sneers at native Americans and their abstract intelligence," "which, however," Osborn adds, "has been in the past effective enough to create a nation, and fearless enough to fight for its honor." Osborn was, as I have said, the technical progenitor and early teacher of Jonas Chickering.

In January, 1834, he began the erection of a large shop on Third Avenue and Fourteenth Street, which was afterward occupied by Stodart, Worcester & Dunham, and moved into it in October. He was about this time regarded as the best maker in the city, and his business had increased so rapidly that his former quarters on Chambers Street were found inadequate. He subsequently committed suicide.

In Mr. Hazelton's memoirs he refers to Osborn in this manner, at the same time evidently not knowing of his previous career : " Between 1832 and 1833 a new man by the name of John Osborn came into the trade. He made very decided improvements in the construction and mechanism of square pianos, and at the competitions at our local fairs he astonished all the older makers. He was a very decided step in advance. Unfortunately he became deranged, and committed suicide by throwing himself out of a window on Fourteenth Street. At Osborn's death his business was bought by Stodart, Worcester & Dunham."

Few of the old makers in New York who were acquainted with Osborn knew where he had come from or his history, so I am informed. In Boston Osborn's career and fate were not known either, even to many persons likely to be much interested in his history. After tracing Osborn from Boston to Albany, and later to New York, a communication was sent to Mr. George H. Chickering, Boston, asking for information on the subject among other matters. This is an extract from Mr. Chickering's reply : " From Mr. Edwin Brown I learned that, without doubt, John Osborn really met his death, as you supposed, from falling out of a window in New York. Osborn was a passionate, excitable man, and is supposed to have become insane from excitement caused by building a factory."

In this letter Mr. Chickering refers to the author's researches regarding James Stewart, as follows : " James Stewart came from Baltimore to Boston, as you supposed. He was a Scotchman. He was associated in business with my father under the firm name of Stewart

& Chickering.   I have a piano here at the factory that was made and sold to B. B. Leeds, Boston, August 15th, 1823.   Stewart left here and went to London and was appointed foreman of Collard & Collard's.   My father met him there in 1851.''

The foregoing citation may be found admissible in this chapter, owing to the circumstance that it occurs in Mr. Chickering's missive, and is a corroboration of the author on some points.

Bridgeland & Jardine began to make pianos in the early part of 1832 at 451 Broadway, John Jardine, the latter, being the practical partner.   Mr. Jardine was an uncle of Mr. Edward Jardine, the present head of Jardine & Sons, the celebrated organ-builders.   He was an excellent tuner and thoroughly educated in all details of piano construction, mechanical and otherwise, besides being an improver of a pronounced type.   Evidence of this is shown in the fact that Bridgeland & Jardine exhibited a square piano having '' the bass strings crossing over the treble,'' in 1833, which was to all appearances the first attempt at an ''overstrung'' square ever made on this continent.   Moreover, this antedates the accomplishment of overstringing in Europe by two years, according to accepted data on the latter point.   In 1833 Bridgeland & Jardine also exhibited a grand at the Mechanics' Institute.   In 1835 they were at 378 Bleecker Street, and exhibited two instruments that won much attention.   One was a *notable* exhibit, being a '' seven-octave grand piano possessed of a superior tone, and a six-octave square,'' both being granted the diploma of the Institute. Otto Torp & Company, Broadway, were the retail agents for these instruments in this year.   John Jardine went

out of manufacturing in 1838, according to a communication from Mr. Edward Jardine, his nephew. To quote
an extract : " Mr. John Jardine made pianos on Broadway, a few doors below Grand Street, and was engaged
in the business from 1832 up to 1838. In 1833 he made
two pianos with overstrung bass, one of which was sold
to a gentleman whose name was lost, but who owned
the property at the corner of Grand Street and Broadway. The other was bought by Mr. Lewis Webb, who
took it to Greenwich, Conn.''

Regarding Jardine's overstrung squares Mr. Gray, of
Albany, recently wrote : " I tuned what seemed an experimental overstrung piano in 1838, made previously by
Jardine, of New York. It was in the shape of a table,
and was owned by Dr. Kip of this city.''

After 1838 Mr. John Jardine maintained a transient
connection with piano-making, but never again became
actively identified with the trade. Meantime Mr. George
Jardine, his brother, made pianos past 1840 for many
years. The brothers came from England about the same
period, and in their lifetime played a prominent part in
the development of the pianoforte art business in New
York.

John Abbott, a graduate from the shop of R. & W.
Nunns, began business at 66 Walker Street, in 1832, and
became very successful immediately from the standpoint
of making reputable instruments, but went out of the
trade in the course of a few years. In 1835 John Abbott
took the gold medal at the Mechanics' Institute for a
pianoforte which won special mention. In 1836 he moved
to 267 Bowery. Abbott exhibited a grand in this year
which won the second premium at the Mechanics' In-

stitute. This clever piano-maker is yet living, and is a member of a family whose connection with the trade has been of long standing. James Abbott, of Abbott & Sons, action-makers, of Fort Lee, N. J., is his brother, and was connected with him in 1833, when he began business on Walker Street, and is the youngest of the Abbott family of piano-makers, which was made up of five brothers in all, four of whom are living. William died in 1889. Four of them learned their business with Nunns & Nunns.

G. & H. Barmore appeared for the first time in 1832 at 120 Barrow Street. The Barmores in after years attained some reputation as makers of popular-priced instruments, and were in business past 1850. In 1836, soon after starting, they exhibited a square at the Mechanics' Institute and got a diploma for merit, which was an honorary testimonial granted to makers just to assuage jealousies arising from competition. They are mentioned yet further in other exhibitions, with successful results invariably.

Geib & Walker, 23 Maiden Lane—composed of William Geib and Daniel Walker—were very well known past 1830 as piano manufacturers, also as music publishers and importers of miscellaneous musical instruments. Daniel Walker took out a patent on June 19th, 1838, for a pianoforte wrest-pin, which was introduced into the Geib & Walker instruments. This was an anticipation of a method of tightening strings similar to the screw method of tightening hair in the violin-bow, now practised by some piano manufacturers, and created considerable notice at the time. Geib & Walker exhibited this mode of tuning at the Mechanics' Institute, in 1838, in a square, and made a favorable impression on

JOHN B. DUNHAM.

JOHN FIRTH.

the committee. The modern application of metal in pianos, notwithstanding that Walker and Fissore's schemes of mechanical screw tuning-pins failed, makes it entirely possible for makers to reintroduce some of these methods as a substitute for wooden pin-blocks. A strong belief in mechanical screw tuning processes yet exists everywhere. Geib & Walker separated in 1841. Walker opened later at 441 Broadway. Walker & Company in time appeared and led up to many titular changes from time to time, when the name dropped out of existence.

Among the other smaller makers, who appeared in New York from 1830 up to 1840, were Torp & Love, Peter Provost, G. V. Briggs, Tallman & Randal, Wake & Glen, Carmeyer, and others of lesser note, such as Dederer, Gruss, and Fox.

Torp & Love took the gold medal in 1836 at the Mechanics' Institute, and are spoken of specially in the committee's report quoted at the opening of this chapter. They carried on business in this year at 465 Broadway. Love was the practical man of the two. Torp & Love again captured the gold medal for the best square in 1837, while Peter Provost took the second premium.

Torp & Company were the agents for the Jardine piano in 1835, and it was in December of this year that Love was taken in and the manufacture of instruments followed. Love dropped out in 1838, when P. Unger, another practical piano-maker, took his place. Torp & Unger were exhibitors in the Mechanics' Institute in 1838, and continued in business at 465 Broadway for several years after this date. Unger afterward opened a key-making concern.

Peter Provost opened on Canal Street in 1835 and carried on a modest business for a number of years, when he drifted into being a journeyman. Charles Carmeyer began on Walker Street in 1837, and was well known past 1850 as a maker of cheap instruments.

Tallman & Randal had a small shop on White Street in 1838. Tallman separated from the latter in a few years and moved to William Street, between Frankfort and Pearl streets, where Mr. Hazelton remembers seeing his place. Gilbert V. Briggs was at 42 Fourth Avenue in 1839, manufacturing at this number and street up to 1851, when he dropped out of business. Briggs was a maker of some note. He was no relative, however, of C. C. Briggs, of Briggs & Company, Boston, and is said to have learned his business in the shop of Nunns & Clark. Wake & Glen were small makers in 1840 on Canal Street. They ultimately separated and were known in the trade in after years in connection with action and key-making. Levi Dederer had a little shop in 1836 at 67 Bayard Street. Francis Gruss began as far back as 1833 at 13 Grand Street, in which year Joseph Fox had a repairing and small manufacturing place at 307 Bowery. They were known in an insignificant way up to 1845, and are remembered by old piano-makers as journeymen subsequently. Significant names, such as Dunham, Stodart & Worcester, Thomas Loud, and others, are carried forward.

CHAPTER XIII.

Boston.

IT is curious to note how cities only a comparatively short distance apart, like New York, Boston, and Philadelphia, maintained peculiar technical conceptions and customs in relation to pianoforte construction considerably at variance upon special points some years ago. Boston, for instance, originated the use of iron plates cast solid, through Alpheus Babcock and Jonas Chickering, and these were copied and used, with special modifications, by other early manufacturers in that city, at a time when New York and Philadelphia makers refused to see the superior advantages contained in that system. Moreover, on the other hand, some Boston piano-makers maintained the use of an action inferior to that in use in New York and Philadelphia, and refused to be convinced of what was afterward made simple to their children. It is very hard to account for these peculiarities of judgment and taste.

In the excellent sketch of pianoforte-making in this country, from the historical point of view, printed by Messrs. Steinway & Sons in 1876, in a publication referred to elsewhere, I find the subjoined remarks, which go to illustrate these facts. Going on to show the influence of the introduction of the improved iron plate in the pianoforte, after alluding to Conrad Meyer's invention, Steinway & Sons say : " The introduction of this full iron frame was aided, to a great extent, by the excellence of the quality of American iron, and the perfection which the art of casting had already attained at that period. The fact was indisputable that pianos thus made stood better in tune than those previously constructed, but one great defect was their thin, nasal character of tone. For these salient reasons the new invention soon had quite as many opponents as admirers, so that until the year 1855 a large majority of the American manufacturers made no attempt to use it.

" Its opponents were especially numerous in New York, where prior to this year, as can be authentically proved, not one of the prominent makers used the full iron frame in the construction of their instruments. All the pianofortes manufactured in Boston at that time had a full cast-iron frame, the wrest-plank bridge being a portion of the same. Across the acute edge of this iron bridge the exceedingly thin strings were laid, and the action used in these pianos was without exception what is styled the English action. In New York, on the contrary, the instruments made were provided with a small cast-iron hitch-pin plate and the French action, and they differed from the Boston pianos in possessing a fuller and more powerful, though at the same time less 'singing,' quality of tone.''

In the foregoing citation we find an estimate of the condition of things, about 1850, in New York and Boston, in regard to the use of the iron plate and the French action in those cities.

Boston seems to have been peculiarly identified with the introduction of iron above all other places on this continent. Not alone need I mention Babcock's and Chickering's innovations, but to these can be added Gilbert's upright iron frame, illustrated in these pages, and other variations of the complete iron-plate principle introduced by other Boston makers more recently.

To go back for a moment, I find that John Cutts Smith was granted a patent for a tuning-key on November 14th, 1838, which was probably the first contrivance to closely anticipate the present lever hammer. Before and past 1838 the wrest-pins were manipulated by a T-hammer, and Smith's invention was possibly the first American invention introduced to show the disadvantages of the old method.

The old concern of Brown & Hallet, which came in before 1840, occupies a peculiar place in these annals, because it has indirectly been a precursor of the present concerns of Hallet & Cumston, Hallet & Davis, Woodward & Brown, and Henry F. Miller & Sons, as recapitulated.

Brown & Hallet was made up of Mr. Edwin Brown, an apprentice-graduate of the Chickering shop, and Mr. Russell Hallet, who furnished the financial backing. Toward 1842 the piano of their make enjoyed a good reputation from the standpoint of being reasonable in price, which was at the time a decided boon to musical people throughout the New England States, who could not afford a Chickering instrument or another of the standard " makes."

Brown & Hallet began piano-making in Boston as early as 1835. Edwin Brown, of this firm, in 1838 patented a method for " damping" the strings of pianos so as to produce the effects made possible by a shifting action, which limited the action of the hammer to striking one string, as instruments were then made. Added to this a " harmonic" effect was produced by Brown's contrivance, that made it of much interest at the time. I discover that in 1840 the " Committee on Art Exhibitions" at the Franklin Institute Fair cordially bestowed the highest honors upon Brown & Hallet, Boston, for a small six-octave piano exhibited. There were twenty-one instruments on view from the different important makers in New York and elsewhere, but the official report says, in reference to the Brown & Hallet piano under notice : " It is the smallest piano in the collection, having only a keyboard of six octaves, but the tone is superior to all others. The patent soft pedal it contains is a very pleasing and effective innovation, and entirely avoids the necessity of shifting the action to produce similar results."

On January 27th, 1843, Edwin Brown patented a grand action of a very complicated nature, designed to insure more perfect repetition, and taking in some principles of the French grand action, which was used by Chickering & Sons subsequently. It accomplished some good, moreover, for it contained several minor points in which many action-improvements of later years were anticipated. Edwin Brown late in this year retired and became a department foreman in the Chickering shop, which position he held for many years, and is at present alive at the venerable age of eighty-four, and highly esteemed.

Hallet, Davis & Company, a new concern, immediately succeeded Brown & Hallet, being composed of Russell Hallet, of the latter combination, George H. Davis, who was known up to 1879 in musical and trade circles as the presiding genius of the present popular firm of Hallet & Davis, and Henry Allen. In some years Mr. Davis withdrew and formed a partnership with F. B. Hallet, when Hallet, Davis & Company again appeared under slightly different conditions.

On Mr. Davis' withdrawal Hallet & Allen came into existence, being made up of Russell Hallet and Henry Allen. This firm, after a short period, took into partnership William Cumston, a very practical piano-maker, who had built up a very excellent record as an inventor previously. I find a patent to his credit issued in 1839, which relates to a damper improvement in squares. Another curious change occurred toward 1850. About this time Henry Allen withdrew and formed a combine with Edwin Brown, when the Brown & Allen piano appeared. Meanwhile, after another range of experience as a manufacturer, Edwin Brown broke partnership and again went into Chickering's shop. It was in Brown & Allen's that Mr. Henry F. Miller, Sr., the founder of Miller & Sons, gained his first insight into the business with which he was so intimately associated up to the period of his death.

Hallet & Cumston was formed on the withdrawal of Allen, as pointed out, and so the old house has come down to the present day unchanged in title. The Hallet & Cumston pianoforte for over forty years has grown and progressed with the times, but has always been a popular-priced instrument and limited to these conditions. Mr. James Cumston, son of the late Mr. W. Cumston, controls the present firm, and is practically conversant with all the details of his business, mercantile and mechanical. The Hallet & Cumston instrument evidently fills its own sphere in popular life, but aside from the present aspects of the concern, or its product, the historical position of Hallet & Cumston claims attention.

The present well-known house of Woodward & Brown dates its existence from 1843. Mr. Isaac Woodward, the father of this concern, was born in Roxbury, N. H., on June 10th, 1810, in which place he received his education. Like Dunham, the Gilberts, and other well-known American piano-makers of repute, he began his career by learning cabinet-making at Keene, in his native State, while still a mere youth. He came to Boston in pursuit of more congenial opportunities for advancement in his craft when yet a young man, and found his way into the case-making department of Brown & Hallet, where he acquired a thorough knowledge of piano-making in a few years in the old-style sense of thoroughness. In 1843 Mr. Isaac Woodward began business as Woodward & Company, and with John Brown, a fellow-workman, and a member of the family of Mr. Edwin Brown, of Brown & Hallet, he formed a business partnership in 1845 and continued his career as a manufacturer up to the period of his death, which took place in 1883.

I notice many patents recorded in relation to improvements in the pianoforte credited to Mr. Isaac Woodward and various persons connected with the Woodward & Brown concern, from 1843 to this date, all of which possessed some utility and value. Being a living house, there is no necessity for analyzing the present character of the Woodward & Brown instrument, as most readers doubtless know its place in the general category. The most distinguishing personal characteristic of Mr. Isaac Woodward, in connection with his calling, was his love for music. He was one of the oldest members of the famous Handel and Haydn Society of Boston, referred to, and devoted himself assiduously to its art interests during his membership. He died at Brookline, on March 10th, 1883, of Bright's disease, generally mourned. The business of this very old and respected concern then passed into the hands of his son, Mr. Arthur S. Woodward, and John P. Brown.

Hallet, Davis & Company, the second firm of that title founded by G. H. Davis, as indicated, grew into a prosperous house, and at present exists as Hallet & Davis, having gone through some internal changes meanwhile since the date of its initiation. George H. Davis was, like Isaac Woodward, a native of New Hampshire. During an early residence in Boston he acquired a knowledge of the piano business, and while yet a young man became a manufacturer under the circumstances I have exemplified previously. The Hallet, Davis & Company piano became a standard instrument as early as 1851, when it vied with such well-known instruments as those bearing the inscription of Nunns & Clark and Hall & Sons, New York, T. Gilbert & Company, Boston, and

Conrad Meyer, of Philadelphia.   I find that a Hallet, Davis & Company grand was awarded the gold medal at the New York Mechanics' Institute exhibition of 1853. Its many points of excellence elicited warm commendation at the hands of the committee, which included such distinguished persons as Henry C. Watson, whose portrait ornaments these pages, and W. Vincent Wallace, the Irish composer, then a resident of New York.

Hallet & Davis at present claim a variety of improvements patented and unpatented, among the former being their "suspension agraffe bridge," for insuring a more rigid upward bearing, and consequently a better quality of resonance and tone-production in the extreme treble register.   Their "grand action" and "movable keyboard" are among their other specialties.   The present house is an incorporated company.   The principal stockholders are G. Cook, W. D. Cook, E. N. Kimball, with E. Davis as factory superintendent.

Mr. George H. Davis died on December 1st, 1879.

Edwin Fobes, said to have been a pupil of Timothy Gilbert's, began manufacturing in 1843, and became identified with popular-priced pianos very largely.   In 1853 he took out a patent for an improved vertical or upright piano of a peculiar kind.   In this there was a full metal plate reaching to the extreme top of the case, over which the strings stretched.   Meanwhile the wrest-pins were driven down into the top of the case perpendicularly. The strings rested on rollers, and in tuning the angle was therefore avoided.   Fobes' scheme created some attention when produced and is worthy of mention here.

W. Bourne & Company seem to have played a large part in the early civilization of Ohio, for it is recorded

that William Bourne, the father of this well-known concern, went West and began the manufacture of pianos in
Dayton, in that State, in 1837. The city had a population of close on one thousand people when this remarkable experiment was tried. It is hardly necessary to say
that this early art pioneer failed to build up a business in
a centre where the plough, the pick, and brick and mortar
usurped the place of art luxuries, according to natural law.

Mr. Bourne moved to Cincinnati about 1840, and was
employed in a piano shop in that city in a leading capacity. In 1842 he came to Boston, and after some time became a department foreman in the Chickering factory,
which position he left to start in a personal establishment in 1846, in which year W. Bourne & Company
appeared. W. Bourne & Company have made many
notable improvements in their instruments during the
past thirty years, keeping pace throughout with the leading inventions brought forward in piano structure and
" scaling" within that period. They claim to have
brought out an original form of the circular scale in
1851, previously invented by Jonas Chickering, but this
is not patented, therefore it is outside the pale of the
historian to consider. Another invention of this house
relates to an ingenious application of the square-action
damper. Several patents have been taken out during
past years of a general character, in connection with the
mechanics and structure of the pianoforte, by this firm,
which goes in a brief way to indicate the progressiveness
of the Bourne & Company concern.

In the New York Mechanics' Institute fairs of 1847 and
upward, a Boston firm, Hewes & Company, had instruments on exhibition and occasionally won awards.

George Hewes, the head of this firm, was in business before 1840 on Washington Street, and in 1843 Hewes & Company consisted of the latter, Richard C. Marsh, and Nathaniel W. Tileston, of Dorchester, Mass. The Hewes & Company square pianos invariably contained a form of the Chickering whole cast plate when exhibited in New York in 1847 and 1852, but made so as. not to infringe upon the patent rights of the latter inventor. All the Boston makers of the period followed out the same lines precisely as pointed out.

Hewes & Company passed away like hundreds of other firms, and have no more interest outside of historical reference for readers. The Patent Office holds copies of patents issued in relation to those instruments which will probably be examined curiously in after years. These patents, however, are not sufficiently startling in any way to merit space.

Among the other makers in Boston about 1850 were A. W. Ladd—in which shop Mr. C. C. Briggs, Sr., of Briggs & Company, served his apprenticeship—Edwin Fobes, L. Matt, J. Munroe, S. Brooks, Daniel Morris, and a few lesser people. The six last-named aimed at providing a popular-priced instrument mainly, which is always an entirely laudable and worthy mission. Daniel Morris, of all these persons, is yet in being in the trade. The others have passed away as manufacturers, although successors in some cases have maintained the line up to the present time. These instances are not sufficiently important to particularize.

Vose & Sons came into existence in 1851 in Boston, and therefore bear the distinction of being very old piano-makers. J. W. Vose, the founder and senior member of this firm, is a native of Milton, Mass., the birthplace of Crehore, where he was born in 1818. He served an old-fashioned apprentice course in Milton and Boston, first learning cabinet making. At twenty, he became a piano-maker. Later he acquired a varied experience in various Boston shops, subsequently founding his business in the year indicated. The Vose & Sons piano of to-day contains all the standard improvements, besides specialities originated by the firm. It is a popular instrument, and has a large following of admirers in the musical profession throughout the States. The firm of Vose & Sons is made up of Mr. J. W. Vose, the founder, Mr. Willard A. Vose, born in 1852, Mr. Irving B. Vose, born in 1850, and Mr. Julien W. Vose, born in 1859, all practical piano-makers, and graduates of good educational institutions in Boston.

The Emerson Piano Company, at present in a flourishing state of existence, date the first year of their business back to 1849.

William P. Emerson, the original of the concern, now deceased, possessed a remarkable share of the world's brains, and demonstrated his capacity for business by building up a large trade in a few years for his instruments. In 1854 C. C. Briggs, Sr., of Briggs & Company, entered the Emerson shop and immediately rose to be foreman. The first improvements of distinct value were introduced from this date forward by Mr. Briggs, who became in a large measure identified with the musical status of the Emerson piano during his connection with that shop. In 1861 Mr. Briggs entered into partnership with George M. Guild, whereupon the firm of George M. Guild & Company was formed.

After a long stay in connection with Guild the partnership was dissolved.   Mr. Briggs now entered into business with his son, C. C. Briggs, Jr., at 1125 Washington Street.   After several years of steady application to the commercial and musical phases of their business, Briggs & Company had to move to the more commodious building, at 5 and 7 Appleton Street, specially erected for their use.

Briggs & Company were among the first to develop the resources of the upright for general use.

C. C. Briggs, Sr., is an expert scale draughtsman, and many of his acoustic discoveries in relation to upright scales are well known among the practical piano-makers in Boston.   The present Briggs concern is made up of C. C. Briggs, Jr., and C. C. Briggs, Sr.

The George M. Guild piano, first made in 1861, as pointed out, is another instrument well known throughout the sphere of the American music trade.   Numerous patents have been taken out up to date for improvements of a mechanical nature, some of which possess utility. Mr. Guild is said to be thoroughly practical in most respects.   His instruments appeal to the masses, being ostensibly sold to the trade at figures under those of the admittedly leading and pioneer firms, but nevertheless has its place in our history.   Among the inventions worth mention, which have been the product of Mr. George M. Guild's faculties, are his stringing and tuning scheme, and his sounding-board and back arrangement, which is avowedly an adaptation of an old theory to more modern conditions.   Other firms, moreover, use special modifications of this method of sounding-board placement.   But aside from particular inventions of this sort, the Guild piano is for its price and grade up to the times in most respects, being constructed by competent workmen and of good material.

The house of Henry F. Miller & Sons has been so much identified with the progress of musical art in Boston and throughout the New England States, aside from the character of their instruments, that special emphasis is given to this attribute of the concern throughout this sketch. The father of this firm, Henry F. Miller, Sr., was born in Providence, R. I., on September 4th, 1825. Unlike many of his business associates in after life, he had the advantages of a good education in his youth, his father being a prominent and wealthy jeweler of Providence. Having shown strong traits· of musical precocity in childhood, he was placed under the care of a very clever Polish pianist and musician living in Providence, and soon attained a degree of artistic proficiency. The organ came next.

In due time we find him presiding as organist in the First Universalist Church, and later in life in the First Baptist Church in his native city. Mr. Miller's musical genius did not prevent him from looking after material things, however, for after graduating from school he worked at practical watch-making and the jewelry business generally, in his father's store. This education of the fine mechanical perceptions was invaluable to the future founder of Miller & Sons in later years, a fact he never failed to allude to, as I am informed.

Mr. Miller's transition from the domain of musical art into that of practical piano-making was easy and natural. It occurred, owing to the fact that he was called·upon at odd times, as a musician, to decide upon the merit of some

make of piano, and in this way he became interested in
the business and well known to makers in Boston through
correspondence.   Thus it is that we find him at twenty-
five receiving an offer to go to Boston and connect himself with Brown & Allen.   Having previously shown the
associations and tendencies of this old concern, it is apparent that Mr. Miller went into a good school, which
came right down from Crehore collaterally.

Taking up every advantage the situation afforded, and
equipped with trained mechanical instincts of a high
order, Mr. Miller's acquisition of technical knowledge in
relation to pianoforte construction was only a natural
progression of " cause and effect."   After a large experience of over twelve years in various channels of the
pianoforte business, which included five years with W. P.
Emerson, Mr. Miller began the manufacture of the
" H. F. Miller & Sons" instrument.   In 1863, right in the
heart of that " panicky" period when the Civil War was
being fought out, he left the employ of Emerson, where
he held a very responsible position, and embarked in
business in association with Mr. N. M. Lowe and Mr.
J. H. Gibson, at present the eminent superintendent of
the Miller factory.   Soon after starting Mr. Lowe sold
his interest to Mr. Miller, who in a few years bought up
Mr. Gibson's interest, thus becoming the sole owner of
the concern.

The latter meanwhile has been intimately connected
with the progress of the Miller & Sons piano ever since
its initiation, and is responsible for many of the characteristics of these excellent instruments, to the improvement of which H. F. Miiler, Sr., and many of his sons
have equally contributed.

HENRY F. MILLER.

It is outside the province of this work to follow up and point out the business and art methods by which the Miller & Sons pianoforte arrived at its present status, but I cannot help laying special stress, in a sense of sincere gratulation, upon the fact that, like the very best and leading houses in this country, the Miller & Sons pianoforte has come upward to success hand in hand with musical art of the highest type. And in the business career of this remarkable house, it is impossible not to note the high moral methods by which its policy has been governed, and the marked integrity of those responsible for its government. This prevails even in the shop, where the true spirit of republican institutions is seen manifested in the comfortable and contented appearance of the workmen, and their devotion to the house which employs them as equals and men and pays them according to honorable standards. In this respect Miller & Sons rank with Mr. Alfred Dolge and other philanthropic members of the trade, which are too numerous, happily, to be given space here.

Mr. Miller died on August 14th, 1884, at Wakefield, Mass. His five sons—Henry F., Walker H., James C., Edwin C., and William T. Miller—now constitute the firm of H. F. Miller & Sons.

Each of these has been trained to fill some special line of work in relation to the progress of the business commercially and practically, and this harmony of different elements has conduced toward the success enjoyed by the house. As in the case of Miller & Sons, the plane of eminence attained and maintained by many leading firms throughout the country, may be traced to conditions similar with the above.

CHAPTER XIV.

NEW YORK.

THOMAS LOUD, SR.—HIS ORIGIN—STODART, WORCESTER &
DUNHAM—THEIR SUBSEQUENT CAREER—OSBORN'S SHOP—
A. H. GALE & COMPANY—HAINES BROTHERS—LINDEMAN—
LINDEN & FRITZ—PETHICK—MINOR MAKERS.

THOMAS LOUD, SR., whom I have claimed in Chapter
III. to be the first known pianoforte-maker to originate
overstringing, settled in New York probably as early as
1816. In 1822 he had a small repairing and making shop,
at 102 Canal Street, which he occupied for several years,
but moved to Walker Street in 1828, and later, between
1831 and 1833, he was on Broadway near Grand Street.
Mr. Henry Hazelton remembers Loud's place on Broadway perfectly well. In order to emphasize his national
origin as a piano-maker, the latter had over his store the
sign, "Thomas Loud, pianoforte-maker from London."
Other old pioneer piano-makers of New York remember
Loud distinctly on this account, but he was never known
to any of them as a maker of significance.

Thomas Loud, Sr., as he was styled, died in February,
1834, at 52 Vandam Street. His relationship to the Loud
family of Philadelphia is a somewhat interesting question

that I have naturally sought to unravel. On corresponding with one of the family in Philadelphia with this object, a response was received saying that the above Loud was actually the father of the Philadelphia piano-makers, and that my suppositions were correct in this respect. It was furthermore elicited from this source that Thomas C. Loud, the younger, was born in Philadelphia on July 12th, 1812, and was, therefore, American. The " Loud brothers"—Joseph, John, and Philologus— were uncles of the foregoing.

Thomas Loud, Jr., the father of Thomas C., and probably son of the London Thomas Loud, must therefore have been in Philadelphia as early as 1811. Whether the brothers came over from London separately or collectively before 1824 is not clear either.

Mr. W. Whitelock, of the Maryland Historical Society, however, has written to the effect that the Loud brothers were sons, as he supposed, " of a clergyman from Maidstone, England." On further interrogation he replied as follows : " I do not *know* that the emigrant Loud was a clergyman. Perhaps I got the idea from the fact that he wrote ' Loud on Infant Baptism.' I do know he came from Maidstone, Kent, however."

Leaving the matter in this form, I have discovered that Loud made piccolo uprights on Walker Street, probably between 1828 and 1830, in which an overstrung scale was used. One of these peculiar old uprights stood in a piano wareroom on East Fourteenth Street several years ago, having been taken in exchange as part payment for a new instrument, and the sketch presented in these pages was made at the time. The importance of the discovery has been found out since that period.

Loud, moreover, used a peculiar form of upright action that has some interest to the technical reader. Thomas Loud's application of the stringing principle referred to may have been purely experimental, but this cannot detract from the historical significance of the circumstance. Coupled with John Jardine's overstrung square, made in 1833, the credit of producing overstrung pianos belongs therefore primarily to America.

Aside from Mr. J. A. Gray's references to the Jardine piano, he has written further upon overstringing in these words : " Previous to Mr. Jardine's instruments I had heard of overstrung pianos being made in New York by one Herrick." Hiram Herrick was probably meant.

This Herrick, I find, was in business in 1838 on Canal Street. In 1839 he was granted patent No. 1379 for a "square" action. He afterward was superintendent of several prominent factories, but died recently in Brooklyn. Isaac Clark, of Cincinnati, O., whose patent of March 2d, 1836, I have spoken of in a previous chapter, words it partially in this way : " Metal frame with sounding-board slung on, also *peculiar* position of the strings, the treble being nearly at right angles with the bass and crossed, etc."

Loud never entered any of the exhibitions in New York or Philadelphia, or created much notice, being a maker employing only a few men, and principally engaged in repairing instruments up to his death.

About 1836 the formation of the important firm of Stodart, Worcester & Dunham brought to the surface of historical development the names of Adam Stodart, Horatio Worcester, and John B. Dunham for the first time. This combination purchased the plant of John

Osborn's business after his death, and began to make pianos in the same factory, on Third Avenue and Fourteenth Street, built by the unfortunate and clever Boston maker. This building became an historic landmark in after years in the trade, and was used as a piano construction shop up to 1880, when it was torn down. In the interim it was used by the firm indicated, next Worcester, later by Pirsson, whose " double grands" won him some fleeting glory, also by Dunham & Sons, followed by Decker & Son, who occupied it from 1868 up to 1880.

Adam Stodart, of the firm of Stodart, Worcester & Dunham, was a nephew of Robert Stodart. His later connection with the piano business in New York was of a marked character. J. B. Dunham, who became an interesting figure in the realm of the trade subsequently, was born in 1799. He served an apprentice course at cabinet-making, and after travelling extensively in the South and working in Charleston for some time, Dunham settled in New York in 1834, where he got employment in the factory of Nunns, Clark & Company as a case-maker. This illustrates his entry into piano-making. Horatio Worcester was a native of Albany. It is asserted that through his acquaintance with John Osborn, while in that city, he was induced to come to New York, and worked in Osborn's shop in some department at the time of the latter's death. This seems probable, although it is generally believed that Worcester was a carpenter, with no knowledge of piano-making previous to joining Stodart and Dunham.

After a short time in collaboration Stodart, Worcester & Dunham dissolved, whereupon Stodart and Dunham joined forces and began manufacturing as Stodart & Dunham with most successful results for many years. In 1849 Stodart withdrew, thus leaving Dunham alone. Dunham's instruments became very widely known in the course of time and his business consequently assumed large proportions. He added many valuable innovations, patented and unpatented, in the course of his career, among them being his "boudoir grand." In 1867 the business carried along by J. B. Dunham became Dunham & Sons, owing to the accession of members of his family.

Worcester meantime had started on his own account. He, like his former partners, Stodart and Dunham, soon acquired a respectable position among the manufacturers. The H. Worcester pianoforte was a well-known instrument up to a recent period. Worcester, in the course of his career, contributed many improvements and ideas to the construction of the pianoforte. He was evidently the ruling spirit in the first enterprise outlined, and practical to some large extent. I find in Watson's *Musical Times* for 1848 a series of advertisements from pianoforte establishments, among which is Worcester's "card," in which he says : "H. Worcester offers for sale a large assortment of choice pianofortes *from six to seven octaves*, in elegant mahogany and rosewood cases, all of which are manufactured under his own supervision."

"Stodart & Dunham, pianoforte manufacturers, 361 Broadway," also appears. "Thomas H. Chambers (formerly conductor of Dubois & Stodart), pianoforte manufacturer, 385 Broadway," looms up in the same issue of this early trade journal, and furnishes a partial key as to his relations with Dubois & Stodart formerly.

John B. Dunham, Horatio Worcester, and Adam
Stodart, each built up a large business after becoming
separated, the latter particularly. His output in 1856
was supposed to have reached twenty instruments a
week, while Dunham averaged twelve and Worcester
about eight. Popular trade tradition gives confirmation
to these figures. Worcester maintained his business all
along since 1836 up to the time of his recent death, on a
very successful plane, although from 1864 upward his
business got gradually crowded out by younger enterprises and more modern facilities. Stodart carried on his
business from 1849 upward under various associations.
At one time the house was Stodart & Company, then
Stodart & Morris, until the name went out of the trade
prior to 1870, when Mr. D. R. Stanford, a respected
member of the music trade, succeeded to the business
and continued the manufacture of the Stodart piano for
some time. The Stodart piano has been out of existence
for many years, Mr. Stanford finding it impossible to
resuscitate interest in a name that, though once eminent,
had gone down with time into oblivion, as far as the
public were concerned. John B. Dunham died, February 9th, 1873, having outlived his former partners only
a few years, leaving the business in the hands of his sons.
The concern, after passing through some changes since
that year, is still in the trade, but under new conditions.
The Dunham & Sons piano is yet known in the wholesale
trade, and is circulated as a popular-priced instrument. Napoleon J. Haines claims that Dunham made
the first overstrung pianoforte in this country. He
said recently : " I was a ' finisher' and ' regulator' in
the factory of J. B. Dunham in 1843. Between 1843 and

1846 I regulated and finished over one hundred of these instruments. Frank (Mr. Haines' brother) overstrung lots of them. From that time on the overstrung system superseded the flat scale with most of the makers.'' Mr. N. J. Haines and Mr. Francis Haines, constituting the firm of Haines Brothers, as it was originally, were both eminently practical piano-makers, as shown later on, and had gone through their apprentice career in Gale & Company's previous to this experience in Dunham's shop, which is told in their personal sketch.

Mr. Haines' statement on the introduction of overstringing has been often commented upon. Having given John Jardine and Thomas Loud credit for the first known use of this significant system of string adjustment, it must be pointed out that the attempts of these makers were experimental mainly. Therefore Mr. Haines' claim regarding Dunham is acceptable, to the extent that the application of overstringing to squares was probably first carried to a stable and permanent issue in Dunham's shop, but it is from the first source that all modern efforts must have necessarily sprung.

The New York Pianoforte Manufacturing Company began business some time between 1837 and 1838. This was the first attempt at establishing a piano manufacturing business upon co-operative lines ever attempted in the United States, and I believe that it can be furthermore asserted, with a strong show of probability, that this was the first large organization of practical workmen ever brought together in this country upon a co-operative basis ; a fact worthy the attention of writers dealing with the history of industrial development in America. Haines Brothers—Mr. Napoleon J. Haines and Mr.

Wм. B. Bradbury.

George Jardine.

Francis Haines, recently deceased—began a remarkable career in this shop, where they were apprentices in 1839. This is Mr. Haines' personal statement to Mr. John C. Freund : " My brother Frank and I were both apprenticed in 1839 to the New York Pianoforte Manufacturing Company, which concern had been started a few years previously by some twenty of the best workmen of Nunns & Clark, who unquestionably made the best pianos in New York at the time."

These " twenty workmen" undoubtedly made very excellent pianos in their time, as I find mention of their instruments in the exhibitions of 1839 and 1840 of a complimentary nature. In October, 1840, this company took a second premium for a six and one-half octave square at the Franklin Institute, Philadelphia. Immediately after that date they went out of existence nominally. Like all such attempts to get a number of people with different qualities of education, taste, and character into the same harness, chaos came, and presently the firmest and most dominant mind came out uppermost and assumed the management of the business under new basic conditions. This was A. H. Gale, a practical piano-maker and one of the workmen active in the concern. The name of " New York Pianoforte Manufacturing Company" now changed to A. H. Gale & Company. The Haines Brothers continued to serve out their apprenticeship in this shop. Their time in the former concern was so limited on account of the change involved, that Haines Brothers always practically associated their apprentice course with the name of A. H. Gale. Gale & Company soon built up a large wholesale business. The Gale & Company piano was a familiar feature of the trade for upward of thirty years, but like other concerns that practised too conservative methods, A. H. Gale & Company disappeared from sight prior to 1870.

Passing over a variety of makers in business in a small way before 1840, the name of William Lindeman comes to the surface. The present house of Lindeman & Sons, one of the best known of the older firms, began business in New York as early as 1835. About this year William Lindeman began the manufacture of pianos on William Street in a modest manner. Mr. Lindeman was born in Dresden, Saxony, and had already learned the details of his business before arriving in the United States. Lindeman exhibited a square in 1847 at the Mechanics' Institute which won extensive notice for its merit.

Handicapped at first by ignorance of the English language, it doubtless took Mr. Lindeman many years to overcome this great disability, which proved a serious drawback meanwhile. In considering the great achievements of the German element in the sphere of the piano trade in this country, considerable allowance must be made for them on this account, and equally extra credit must be given them for rising to prominence under such a disadvantage.

Lindeman was the pioneer German manufacturer in New York practically, although Sackmeister and Gutwaldt preceded him, because he built up a reputable and lasting business. Previous to 1840 German piano-makers were treated with gross injustice everywhere, and every effort made to obtain a footing in New York as manufacturers seemed to have resulted in failure, until Lindeman the elder broke through these barriers of unrepublican intolerance. The German fraternity in

New York, therefore, owe the house of Lindeman & Sons much respect and esteem. Although the Lindeman piano was known as a progressive instrument since 1850 in musical and trade circles, no distinctly important innovation was brought forward by this maker until 1860, when Lindeman's cycloid piano was produced, for which a patent, No. 29,502, was secured on August 9th of that year by William Lindeman.

This proved the precursor of the "bijou grand," to some extent. It was put forward as a compromise between the concert grand and the square piano, and created much notice in musical circles at the time, and arrived at some popularity afterward. Owing to the patent, the neat and elegant shape of this instrument never met with general adoption. Several attempts were made within recent years by small makers to imitate the Lindeman cycloid, but so far, the well-known leading firms with which all improvements of moment originate, have not attempted to overlook Lindeman's patent, otherwise there would be a general adoption of the cycloid piano as a standard instrument. Prior to 1860 Mr. Henry Lindeman, the eldest son of Mr. William Lindeman, was taken into partnership, when the concern became Lindeman & Son, and within a more recent period Lindeman & Sons, owing to the accession of a younger member of the family. Since 1865, when the termination of the war restored American commercial progress to its normal plane, Lindeman & Sons have grown up to a very eminent place among piano manufacturers. They have always aimed to make instruments of an artistic grade, and their efforts have deservedly won emphatic recognition at the hands of the musical press and impartial connoisseurs in a standard sense.   A higher tribute could hardly be paid to the character of this honored old concern in limited space.   The elder Linde-man died on December 24th, 1875.   Henry Lindeman & Sons subsequently appeared as successors to the business.

Mr. Henry Lindeman, Sr., present head of the busi-ness, is a New Yorker, having been born in the city August 3d, 1838, and bears a high reputation, both as a practical piano-maker and business man.

In speaking of the sufferings endured by the Ger-mans in early years, it should be mentioned that the journeymen piano-makers of that nationality were also made the object of some dislike by their British and American fellow-workmen back in 1830, or even earlier. In 1834 this ended in a general strike throughout the trade in New York, followed by the organization of the first piano-makers' trade society formed in this country. Thanks to the courtesy of Mr. Henry Hazelton, who has in his possession a book fixing prices issued by the society, I am enabled to give the preamble to this inter-esting work, which is of some historical significance in these pages.   It is as follows :

" The social principle of man, reasonably exercised for any laudable object, must be for his individual and social advantage, whether on a large or small scale. This principle is generally acknowledged ; and in these United States it is claimed as the birthright of every in-dividual to associate for all honorable and lawful pur-poses.   The journeymen pianoforte-makers, of the city of New York, believe it necessary and expedient to form themselves into a society, for the better regulating and equalizing their prices."

Another firm started in 1840, viz., Linden & Fritz. Both of these were practical piano-makers and Germans, with some experience in New York shops. They made very good instruments in their time. They began at 115 Walker Street, and toward 1846 their factory was on Broadway near Broome Street, to where they moved on the removal of Roux, a prominent cabinet-maker, well known to fashionable New York early in the "forties." Linden was formerly employed in the shop of Dubois, Bacon & Chambers as a key-maker, while Fritz worked in the same place as a case-maker. They disappeared out of business after 1857. Grow & Christopher, another concern built up by two practical workmen, began business in 1841. They made very good instruments and were known in the trade up to 1857, when they disappeared from notice. Meanwhile none of these instruments, made by the two foregoing concerns, appeared at local exhibitions during these years, and little can be learned of them.

John Pethick, Mount Morris, N. Y., was granted a patent on February 12th, 1836, for "improvements in the grand action invented by Pape, of Paris." Pethick later moved down-town and carried on business in connection with one Hancock on Bleecker Street. He later appears in the directory alone, and was known as a small maker up to 1860.

CHAPTER XV.

Philadelphia, etc.

SOME RANDOM REMARKS ON EXHIBITIONS—STATE FAIRS—
MEYER—SCHOMACKER & COMPANY—MR. GRAY'S ELECTRO
GOLD STRING PATENT — PHILADELPHIA PIANO-MAKERS
IN THE SOUTH—NEW ORLEANS—SAVANNAH, GA.—MINOR
REMARKS—PITTSBURG, PA.

BESIDES the Franklin Institute annual exhibitions—held
regularly in Philadelphia from 1824 upward—and the
New York Mechanics', and later the American Institute
Exhibitions, these events became very general in the
shape of State fairs toward 1850. Maryland, New York,
Connecticut, and Massachusetts were principally identified with these exhibitions. While agriculture and its
concomitants were a leading feature generally, as at the
present time, pianofortes and musical instruments were
very largely catalogued from year to year, in addition
to other exhibits of a general nature. Massachusetts
had, moreover, a Mechanics' Association, which gave
premiums at regular annual exhibitions before 1845 to
piano-makers. Mr. Jonas Chickering was prominently
identified with this excellent institution. Nothing of
interest occurred at these latter events historical enough

to merit special reference, beyond that Boston makers principally competed for honors.

Among the Philadelphia firms that won special distinctions at various exhibitions in Boston, New York, and elsewhere, besides those previously named, Schomacker must be quoted. Conrad Meyer was another believer in competition of this character. This very eminent piano-maker, whose name figures in reference to Babcock's plate frequently, died in 1881 in Philadelphia, after a residence of over fifty years in that city. His business passed into the hands of his sons, who still manufacture reputable pianos carrying that time-honored name. Meyer made very excellent instruments in his time, and won many distinguished honors throughout his career.

In 1838 the present firm of Schomacker & Company came into existence. Bosert & Schomacker was the original title. The former was an American and a practical piano-maker, while Mr. Schomacker was also thoroughly practical. The latter was born in Germany in 1800, and learned piano-making in his native city subsequently. He landed in this country in 1837, and in the year denominated entered into business in partnership with Bosert, as I have outlined. I find Bosert & Schomacker winning recognition at State and institute fairs immediately after starting in piano manufacturing.

After 1842 Mr. Bosert retired, when the Schomacker Piano Company was formed, which has come down to the present date through various external changes as a familiar firm in the trade in this country. Schomacker & Company have been very progressive throughout all these years, and still maintain an advanced commercial plane. In Philadelphia, once the leading city in the piano manufacturing art business, they stand pre-eminent.

In 1864 the business of the firm was organized into a stock company, with a large capital, under its present title. Colonel H. W. Gray, who had previous experience in the former firm, became an officer in this business organization, and has been its president for many years. Mr. J. H. Schomacker, the founder of this concern, died in Philadelphia in 1875, while Mr. H. C. Schomacker, secretary of the company, maintains this familiar name in connection with the business. H. W. Gray is a native of Pennsylvania, having been born at Ephrata, Lancaster County, in that State, on June 3d, 1830.

Many patents have been taken out from 1842—in which year Patent 2,595, for a novel stringing system and action improvement, was granted to Bosert & Schomacker —up to date, of general utility in piano-making, by Schomacker & Company. Colonel H. W. Gray's method of electro-plating piano strings in gold, patented in 1876, is, however, regarded by this firm as their greatest specialty. The introduction of this system in the Schomacker & Company pianos has for over thirteen years created some comment. As it is protected by a United States patent, nobody has attempted to copy the principle. Without attempting in any way to discuss the originality or the opposite of Mr. Gray's patent, coating strings with metallic alloys is admittedly old, having been anticipated in this country by Mr. H. J. Newton, of New York, in 1851, while Patent No. 34,640 was granted to Martin Miller in 1862 for a method of electro-plating steel or other wire with gold, silver, or other metals. In justice, however, to Mr. H. W. Gray, it must be added that his process differs materially from those enumerated, and is in practical use, while the others were merely theoretical patents. As regards the originality of this plating idea, the president of the Schomacker Company—Mr. Gray—admits that coating strings had been tried previously, but not wrapped strings.

Bosert, after leaving Mr. Schomacker, continued in business personally and was known for many years as a small maker in Philadelphia.

Blasius & Son is the name of another Philadelphia firm, well known as makers of popular-priced pianos. They succeeded to the old business founded by C. F. Albrecht—mentioned elsewhere—several years ago, and therefore have some claim on the writer's notice.

I find that many Philadelphia piano-makers settled in various cities in the Southern States, and founded small piano-making concerns as early as 1830, exclusive of Charleston or Baltimore already treated on. For instance, one G. Kingley settled in New Orleans in 1830 and made pianos for several years. Kingley learned his trade in Loud Brothers' shop. The first maker of pianos that attained any note in New Orleans before 1850 was J. Piffaut, whose patent in relation to a vertical piano, granted in 1853, is truly a marvel of eccentricity. Notwithstanding this he is said to have made good instruments in his time. Philadelphians claim Piffaut, but it is evident that he was a native of New Orleans or a French piano-maker, judging from his name.

In Savannah, Ga., Moses Coborn, said to have also come from Philadelphia, was making pianos in 1840, and for several years past that date. Richmond, Va., and other Southern cities had also small piano shops before 1840, nearly all the piano-makers connected with these concerns being from the " Quaker City," so old piano-men say, with a slight flavoring of New York workmen. Baltimore, meantime, had not advanced far enough in those years to be able to spare pioneers, which accounts for the condition of things outlined.

Coming back to Pennsylvania the subjoined communication in reference to early manufacturing and piano dealing in the important city of Pittsburg in that State, written by the old firm of Henry Kleber & Brother, will be found interesting. In reply to the writer's queries they say : " The first regular piano and music store in Pittsburg was opened by W. C. Peters, an Englishman and clarionetist in a Canadian British military band, about 1823. In 1830 he sold out to Smith & Mellor. The American pianos then sold were made by Hiskey of Baltimore, Md. Later on those of Sherr and Scho-macker, Philadelphia, were used. In our city pianos were then made by Fred Blume and Goodall & Warren, both short lived. A piano exhibited by us now was made by Charles McDonnell in Pittsburg long before our existence. Our own firm, H. Kleber & Brother, was the *second* regular piano and music store opened in Pittsburg, and we sold the Chickering, Nunns & Clark, Dunham, and the Carhart & Needham organs ; also the grand pianos of Erard and Herz of Paris, and of Streicher of Vienna. We took up the 'Steinway' in 1856, and have been their agents ever since.''

CHAPTER XVI.

New York.

AMERICA AT THE LONDON WORLD'S FAIR—STATISTICS ON
PIANO MANUFACTURING FOR 1851—LIGHTE & NEWTON—
BRADBURY—MODERN OLD HOUSES—HAZELTON BROTHERS
—HAINES BROTHERS—INCIDENTAL REFERENCES.

THE year 1851 beheld the United States pianoforte
manufacturers represented at the great London World's
Fair, for the first time in the history of European exhibitions. Among the American makers who sent instruments to London was Jonas Chickering, who went
to England personally, in company with Mr. C. Frank
Chickering, then a very young man, to superintend his
exhibit. These instruments carried off the highest
honors. An editorial in the London *Times* at the
period paid high tribute to the American pianos shown,
while making very little of the American exhibits in
general, by declaring that the excellence of the former
redeemed the drawbacks of the latter, to a great extent.
The other piano-makers represented in London were
Meyer, Philadelphia ; Nunns & Clark and Heers & Pirsson, New York ; and Gilbert & Company, Boston. One
Wood, of Virginia, took a money award of $250 for a

piano-violin, which attracted considerable attention, while the Goodyears, of rubber fame, exhibited a rubber flute that won honorable mention. Heers & Pirsson's "double-grand" also won much notice, owing to its features of originality.

I find that the Commissioner of Patents writes, in his report for 1852, concerning musical instruments, after commenting upon the number of patents issued, as follows, among other remarks : " The aim of our piano manufacturers has been to improve the tone and structure of their instruments, without at the same time enhancing their price, and it is hoped that these efforts may tend to increase the facilities for musical education in our country. The manufacture of the piano alone, in the consequent prosperity of the last few years, has become an important branch of industry in our large cities. It is safe to estimate the number of pianos made in this year in the United States at *nine thousand*, at the aggregate value of $2,100,000, and that their fabrication gave employment to nineteen hundred hands, at the aggregate wages of $72,000 per month."

The foregoing is a most interesting and valuable statistical item coming from a Government source, and is as a ray of light falling on a dark corner of the history of American art industrial development.

Looking backward from this year we can distinctly trace between the year 1840 and the period intimated, a great evolution in the character and growth of the piano business in New York. Multitudinous small shops had sprung up in the interval, some of them being the precursors of many large and prosperous firms now in existence, ·while the majority of them seemed to drag

along a fitful life until driven out of being by the competition of large manufacturing firms toward 1855. In
addition to the small makers already enumerated may
be added John Ruck, who was a clever inventor,
Henry Ackley & Company, Thomas Doyle, John Harper,
Jesse Davis, W. T. Reed, Peter Van Baun, Randolph
Kreter, and numerous others. Many of these names
were known up to recent years in various connections.

Between 1840 and 1851 Lighte & Newton, Hugh Hardman, J. & C. Fischer, Hazelton & Brothers, J. A. Grovesteen, and Haines Brothers appeared.

F. C. Lighte began business about 1848 at 22 Canal
Street. In a few years he formed a copartnership with
W. H. Newton, at present alive, but outside the piano
business, when Lighte & Newton appeared. This firm
made excellent instruments, and brought forth many
improvements. F. C. Lighte was a steady patron of the
Patent Office and an inventor of some moment. Lighte
& Newton in 1853 was augmented by Mr. W. B. Bradbury, the distinguished pianist and teacher, when the
firm Lighte, Newton & Bradbury was formed. Subsequently Mr. W. H. Newton withdrew, when Lighte &
Bradbury carried on business with some success until
1861, when William B. Bradbury appeared as the manufacturer of the " Bradbury" piano.

In later years F. C. Lighte formed a combine with Mr.
Louis Ernst. The Lighte & Ernst pianoforte, the result
of this collaboration, has been a very popular instrument
up to 1885, when the last member of the firm, Mr. Ernst,
died. The latter was an extremely genial and highly
respected member of the piano trade in New York
Twenty years ago he enjoyed some reputation as a

teacher of the pianoforte, and was a skilled musician and theorist.   F. C. Lighte was the practical member of the firm, and in the Lighte & Ernst instruments many excellent improvements and modifications of modern innovations appeared from time to time, of which he was the author.   The latter died in 1879.   Both of the foregoing truly deserve a place in these records.

John Buttikofer, another maker, alive at this date, who began business past 1840, had built up quite a reputation among the musicians in the metropolis about 1851, and is credited with having made excellent grands as early as 1845, which were the " talk of the town'' at the period, so to speak.   Within more recent years he was known as a small manufacturer of very reputable pianos.   Mr. Buttikofer is at present in business in an unpretentious way in this city.   This clever maker is a native of Switzerland.   He landed in the United States in 1839, just half a century ago.   Previous to coming here he worked in Brussels, Paris, and London.   In Paris he held an important position in the shop of Pape, where he acquired much of the skill as a piano-maker which he displayed in this city in later years.

Pirsson's innovations in piano structure were the topic of discussion among piano-makers in New York past 1850 for several years.   As I have remarked, one of his " double-grands'' was seen in London in 1851.   Pirsson took out Patent No. 7568, in 1850, for this peculiar form of piano, which had been tried in Europe as early as 1783 by one Swartz, of Munich, a spinet-maker.   Pirsson, however, reproduced the spirit of the idea with more modern conditions, and there is yet an impression prevailing that, with the present development of the piano proper, Pirsson's principle might be carried to an issue of some permanent value, although instruments made on these lines would cost considerably more to manufacture. Pirsson was known as a small New York piano-maker up to 1866. After that year his name disappeared. For a time Pirsson used a mechanical screw tuning-pin invention that was another source of comment in the "forties." I find that a square of Pirsson's having these pins carried off the gold medal at the Mechanics' Institute in 1847. A piano of J. A. Grovesteen's exhibited on this occasion was acknowledged to be equal to Pirsson's, but the latter's tuning-pin principle was the decisive point of superiority.

The origin of the firm of J. & C. Fischer has already been sketched out. The almost unexampled success of this house as large manufacturers of popular priced, though otherwise good, pianos, apart from their long standing in the New York music trade, deserves some historical consideration. Beginning almost half a century ago in collaboration with William Nunns, one of the most original piano-makers of his time, their start in business was certainly auspicious and noteworthy. The growth of J. & C. Fischer into a front place, as regards wealth and output, has been so steady and uniform that few piano-makers until within recent years realized their importance. Within a late period an effort has been made to raise the art standing of these instruments. which may result in a large measure of success if persevered with.

J. & C Fischer have brought forth some meritorious improvements in piano mechanics and structure during the past forty years, that have served to popularize their pianos, many of them patented, while they have at the same time adopted all standard ideas of merit from time to time. The management of the Fischer business is at present in the hands of Mr. C. S. Fischer and his sons, who number five—all practical piano-makers. Each of the latter presides over some special department in the wholesale and retail department, recently made a specialty of, which accounts for the successful perpetuation of such a large concern. Mr. J. Fischer retired from the firm in 1873 with a handsome competence, Mr. C. S. Fischer thereupon assuming the sole position as senior, the business being continued up to the present time under the old title.

The firm of Hazelton Brothers began business in 1850. Mr. Henry Hazelton, the senior member and founder of this old and respected house, is mentioned frequently elsewhere in relation to Albany, and as an authority for many incidental facts in relation to piano-making in New York past 1830. It may be remarked, as an evidence of the vigorous and potent quality of Mr. Hazelton's mind, that in all instances where a comparison was made with authentic data and reliable sources of information, the statements of the latter were invariably found to be correct. Moreover, in speaking generally of past and present houses, Mr. Hazelton is noted for being entirely devoid of personal, sectarian, or race prejudice of any kind, which fact illustrates the personal characteristics which he impressed so vividly upon the business he has ruled for so many years. Such men are the glory of democratic institutions. The production of citizens like Jonas Chickering, James A. Gray, Henry F. Miller, Henry Hazelton, and Americans of that character, amply

HENRY HAZELTON.

compensates for the imperfections noticeable on the surface of every-day politics. Republican government cannot be a failure when it brings forth men of that calibre,
whose lives reflect fraternity, honor, usefulness, and the
courage which looks kings in the face without a tinge of
superstitious cowardice, as man to man. This is the
spirit incontrovertibly of our national institutions.

Mr. Henry Hazelton was born in New York in 1816,
and in 1831 he was apprenticed in an old-style legal
manner to Dubois & Stodart for seven years, during
which period he was supposed to be initiated into the
art and mysteries of pianoforte making, from case-making
upward.

In this shop he gradually acquired a thorough knowledge of the best methods then practised in piano construction, both artistic and mechanical. Moreover, he
had the advantage of working by the side of many of
the best workmen that arrived in this country, from 1831
up to 1838, from England and Germany, thus getting
an insight into European progress in piano-making incidentally. In 1834, during the course of Mr. Hazelton's
apprenticeship, he witnessed the first strike of piano-
makers—which resulted from the society just formed—
ever known before that year in the United States. This
upheaval occurred in Dubois & Stodart's shop, owing to
the employment of German workmen, and spread
throughout the trade ; but matters were speedily readjusted on a new wage basis.

The first venture of moment in the business life of Mr.
Hazelton, after becoming a recognized piano-maker—a
trade then ranking very high in status—was his removal
to Albany. On May 9th, 1838, in company with James

A. Gray and a half dozen other young piano-makers of marked ability, he left New York and entered the shop of William G. Boardman, in a few days following where he was noted as a finished workman during his stay in that concern. He subsequently engaged in the manufacture of Hazelton pianos in that city, and in some time took as a partner Mr. A. G. Lyon, then Talbot, thus creating the firm name of Hazelton, Lyon & Talbot, which was in existence for some time. The hopes of Mr. Hazelton, like many others who believed in the steady growth of Albany into eminence as a manufacturing and art centre, not becoming to a satisfactory extent realized, we find him arriving in New York toward the end of 1841, glad to look once more upon the streets of our historic city, for typical New Yorkers love their town almost as the London cockney loves the sound of Bow Bells.

Mr. Henry Hazelton was not alone among his family as a piano-maker, however, at this date, and in 1850 the firm of F. & H. Hazelton was started, composed of Frederick and Henry, the former being also practical. Mr. John Hazelton, another brother, was in a short time admitted into the firm, when the title was changed into Hazelton Brothers. This was a happy and lucky combination, as the almost immediate prosperity of the firm indicated.

Hazelton Brothers were among the first piano manufacturers in New York to adopt the full iron frame and the enlarged square case of the Boston school past 1850. The addition of the French square "rocker" action to these important developments in case-bracing and structure was the key almost to the subsequent character of the square piano of our day, and Hazelton & Brothers must be credited with having been among the first to rise to the situation in New York. But aside from following out or adopting special technical principles, Mr. Henry Hazelton, Mr. Frederick, and Mr. John Hazelton always paid the "acoustics" of piano construction particular attention, and in their first squares many excellent "scales" were introduced which became copied very generally throughout the trade. In fact, Hazelton Brothers have made this all-important department of piano technology a special study, hence it is why we find very few patents recorded to them in the National Patent Office, because, unless in the matter of very radical departures in "scaling" and stringing methods, it is impossible, almost, to send a working model of a new scale on paper or otherwise to Washington in such a legal form as to insure an inventor protection from plagiarists. I find that Hazelton Brothers, 219 Centre Street, exhibited a seven-octave rosewood square at the Crystal Palace World's Fair, in 1853, that won a high award and considerable praise from the judges.

From this year up to 1876, when they exhibited with most flattering results at the great Centennial Exhibition, their progress toward success had been assured. The present status of Hazelton Brothers has been won by the most honorable business methods—though never conservative, as they have always been liberal and unostentatious supporters of musical art and artists—backed up by the invariably absolute merit of their instruments, for which they have built up an unimpeachable record as first-class pianos in every sense, from the æsthetical, musical, and mechanical standpoints. And what is remarkable, none of their business compeers envy them in the least.   As employers Hazelton Brothers' forty years historical connection with American piano-making, reveals a high moral faculty for treating other men according to the spirit of Christianity and justice, a peculiar point I cannot help emphasizing above mere business details.   In 1883 their warerooms and factory were burned down, which were replaced by the present handsome building in the same year.

Hazelton Brothers have always been manufacturers of grands, the instruments of their make being regarded as "leaders" at this period in some cities of the South and West.   In the development of the upright this old firm has also been always active, and the various " scales" in use in their different " styles" at present are said to be excellent developments in this department of piano-construction, and due to the genius of Mr. Henry Hazelton.   Regarding the personal history of the firm, Mr. Frederick Hazelton, I find, retired several years ago. At present Mr. Henry Hazelton, Mr. John Hazelton, and Mr. Samuel Hazelton, their nephew, constitute Hazelton Brothers.   The latter has been a member of the house since 1881, and is an expert and practised craftsman, apart from being trained in the commercial methods necessary in the wholesale and retail piano business.

Haines Brothers, composed of Mr. Napoleon J. Haines and Mr. Francis W. Haines originally, started business as N. J. Haines & Co. in 1851 at 116 Third Avenue.   Mr. N. J. Haines, who has ever been the presiding and ruling genius of the house, was born in London, England, in 1824.   He arrived in the United States when a mere lad of eight with his brother Francis.   In 1839 the two brothers entered the shop of the New York Piano Manufacturing Company, as I have already exemplified in a past chapter, which concern became A. H. Gale & Company subsequently, owing to the break-up of the former. In these shops they served out an apprenticeship course at piano-making, meanwhile going through every branch. Haines Brothers gained a reputation as skilful apprentices while yet in that stage of evolution, which qualities they in a few years exhibited as regular workmen, and later brought into the service of their own business with such manifest results. After completing their regular time in the shop of Gale & Company, both worked practically at the bench up to the time of their start in business, which proved an eventful and lucky speculation for all concerned.

Mr. N. J. Haines is a great believer in independence of character, and is fond of relating a personal example. It seems that his father, who had arrived previously in New York, sent for the youthful N. J. Haines and his brother Francis, and gave the steward thirty dollars to take care of the lads on the voyage out from London, particularly so as to secure them good food. Young Napoleon J. was aware of the fact, and on putting to sea found out at the first meal that the steward had evidently forgotten his promises. Accordingly at the second meal the future financier and piano-maker took the " hard tack'' and black coffee offered him and pitched them overboard. He followed this emphatic protest up with a " junior" declaration of independence that startled the steward and frightened him almost out of his boots. Amid the general clamor the captain arrived on the scene, heard the whole story, patted young Haines warmly under the chin, and threatened the steward with all sorts of maritime deaths unless he attended from that out to the comfort of the future American citizens. It is needless to say that they were well taken care of for the remainder of the voyage. This was all won by Mr. Haines' young spirit.

To any one conversant with the life of Mr. N. J. Haines and the personal characteristics it indicates, it is easy to trace the transition of the eminent piano manufacturer and financier from the bench to the position he now occupies. Such men are born to rise above other individuals in the " struggle for existence," and it can be no surprise when they reach their predestined plane ; but we must not fail to note the genius and attributes of such exceptional people.

Ordinarily persons are apt to think of Mr. N. J. Haines as an old and leading member of the piano business, but they either forget or do not know that in politico-economic science, finance, and other spheres of intellectual activity he is equally at home.

As shown, Haines Brothers began the erection of their factory at Second Avenue and Twenty-second Street— from which they recently moved—in 1856, moving into it subsequently. I find in the New York *Musical Review* for December 2d, 1854, the subjoined article on Haines Brothers, which is very suggestive : " Three years ago the two Haines Brothers began business at the rate of one piano in two weeks. Their business has kept increasing to such an extent that they now turn out one piano a day, an increase in their business and capital of over twelve hundred per cent. in three years. They are now about to erect one of the largest factories in New

York. As a stimulus to honest industry it may be well to ask why this house has met with such wonderful success when so many houses are creeping along in embarrassment ? 1. Because the principals are practical workmen. 2. Because they are men of integrity, and supply every instrument well made down to every point of detail. 3. They may be found in their factory personally working or superintending the making of every essential part of their instruments." The foregoing serves clearly to show the standing of Haines Brothers thirty-five years ago, and is worth a whole volume of modern history.

Many stories are in circulation by way of illustrating Mr. N. J. Haines' peculiar faculty for estimating the origin and progress of industrial and commercial panics, and the practical use he has frequently put this knowledge to. One instance has it that, in 1863, during the war depression, Mr. Haines purchased a large stock of felt, key ivory, tuning-pins, and other imported material, and got a "corner" upon the whole American piano trade, that would have ended in a local panic in that quarter, had he not generously been satisfied with a reasonable margin on his speculation, and thus relieved all necessities and allowed the piano trade to proceed on its normal course. He, however, cleared $30,000 by this transaction.

Mr. Haines' significant connection with the Union Dime Savings Bank, as its president, which position he held for seven years, is a marked instance of the integrity of the venerable piano-maker, and an evidence of the great trust generally placed in his financial capacity and fitness for this responsible position. In addition to this trust Mr. Haines has been the vice-president and chair-

man of the bank for terms of seven years in each instance, making twenty-one years in all as president,
vice-president, and chairman. The first book issued by
the bank was taken out by Mr. Haines' son John on May
18th, 1859, a fact that was duly honored by the bank in
1874, when they presented Mr. Haines with book No.
100,001, handsomely bound in elaborate style, on November 14th of that year, to further emphasize their appreciation of his vast services. It is said that when Mr.
Haines severed his connection with this institution $30,-
000,000 had been handled under his management. In
1873 Mr. Haines was associated with President Grant
and the leading financiers of the city in their efforts to
tide over the panic of that year, in which scheme the
Federal Government was indirectly represented, which is
another indication of the confidence placed in his intelligence and capacity.

Haines Brothers introduced many improvements in
their instruments from 1851 upward, keeping in line with
all standard innovations in case-extension and keyboard
compass, besides using the present accepted system
of overstringing on the full iron frame at a very remote
period when the straight scale was in general use. Mr.
N. J. Haines claims to have made a double overstrung
square grand in 1853, the credit of which he gives to
William Nunns, a fact that cannot be overlooked. He
further claims to have made overstrung squares in 1852,
and used "overstringing in three tiers in 1853."

Upon the subject of recent patented improvements
Mr. N. J. Haines holds heterodox convictions, believing
that with the introduction and perfecting of the full iron
plate system, and the increase of compass to seven one-

Napoleon J. Haines.

third octaves, together with the general acceptance of " overstringing," and all other details, no important changes have been wrought in recent years in piano construction. Yet we need only place one of Haines Brothers' modern uprights or grands by the side of their first pianos, or even instruments made twenty years ago, to be convinced that, while modern piano-makers are not bringing forward improvements in " leaps and bounds," a subtle progress and development is still taking place in the general character of tone, as well as in the better adaptability of instruments to keep in tune and stay well up to pitch. And the Haines Brothers piano of to-day is keeping pace with all upward tendencies.

To indicate Mr. N. J. Haines' inventive faculty as a piano-maker, Patent No. 24,119 is illustrated in these pages. This was taken out in 1859 and furnishes a very excellent scheme for regulating self-escapement in a square action among other points. This is, however, only one of Mr. Haines' innovations, the majority being in acoustics.

In recent years the upright has received special attention from Haines Brothers. They were the first in the trade to cease the manufacture of squares, Mr. N. J. Haines, with his characteristic foresight, having predicted the present popularity of this instrument as early as 1870. By way of indicating the standing of the " Haines" upright, I need only point to the well-known endorsement of these instruments penned in 1883 by no less a personage than the celebrated diva, Madame Patti.

Mr. Francis W. Haines died on September 18th, 1887, after a useful life, both as a piano-maker and private citizen, at the age of sixty-five. Since his death the house has made no change in the firm name, the head being Mr. N. J. Haines. He is assisted at present by his sons, Mr. N. J. Haines, Jr., and Mr. William Haines, both thoroughly trained in all departments of the business, mechanical and commercial, and thoroughly in sympathy with the progress of musical art. The present Haines Brothers' producing shop is situated on the Southern Boulevard in this city. It covers an immense space of ground, and is one of the best-equipped factories in the country. The historical development of this remarkable house is concisely shown in the foregoing climax.

Before closing this chapter mention must be made of the Van Winkles. These makers sprang into note between 1845 and 1855, and were well known as makers of excellent pianos in the interregnum. In 1849 D. J. Van Winkle, then at 92 West Sixteenth Street, took the Institute gold medal for the best instrument, and attained some status past this date. Many of the old makers now known worked here.

CHAPTER XVII.

New York.

THE year 1853 marks an era in the development of the American pianoforte. This year saw the successful inauguration of the international World's Fair at the Crystal Palace, New York, a building set up in imitation of the London Crystal Palace, in which the World's Fair of 1851 was held. It also marks the founding of the great American house of Steinway & Sons, out of which so many significant developments in the more recent phases of pianoforte improvement have sprung.

At the Crystal Palace Exhibition, in 1853, American piano-makers saw, for the first time, an interesting collection of instruments contributed by European manufacturers, grands and uprights, mostly, which was in itself not only an incentive to higher technical aims and art results in piano-making, but it helped further to show American makers the difference between the instruments made here and abroad, together with the general points of inferiority and superiority as they were noted on both sides. This was actually an education to a large extent. Great Britain made a very small showing on the occasion, the English houses being represented by William Stodart, Golden Square, London.

Germany was represented by nineteen makers of musical instruments, and out of these only one piano-making firm sent an exhibit. Belgium sent one upright piano and a mechanical table piano from the factory of Matthew Lacroix, of Verviers. France was largely and well represented by a numerous contingent of eminent manufacturers, viz., Detir, Debain, Musard, Sholtus, and Pleyel. The first-named sent two uprights, one with overstringing. Debain also had two uprights. The other three makers had only one instrument each on exhibition. Switzerland sent over three instruments from Zurich shops, two by Hüni & Hubert and one from the factory of Sprecher. Even Holland had its representative piano manufacturer on exhibition in the person of Paling, of Rotterdam, who exhibited an upright. Austria, Russia, Spain, and Italy sent nothing in the shape of pianos, and indeed little exhibits of any sort.

Among the domestic piano manufacturers who exhibited instruments at this Fair were Grovesteen, Hazelton Brothers, Lighte & Newton, McDonald, Holden, Bassford, Hall & Sons, Hallet & Davis, Boston, T. Gilbert & Sons, Boston, and Schomacker, Philadelphia.

Hall & Sons, Lighte & Newton, and Holden exhibited " seven one-quarter octave" squares. A Bassford grand won particular notice on account of the magnificence of the case, and a Schomacker square was likewise specially honored for its superior qualities musically and otherwise. Hazelton Brothers made an excellent record on the occasion with a seven octave square. They had been in business in New York at the time only three years, and had obtained a firm footing in the trade at that early date. Many other important makers exhibited in this year, but the rendition of their names serves no object here.

In March of this year Steinway & Sons was founded, Mr. Henry E. Steinway, and his sons, Charles and Henry, Jr., being the initial members of the firm, augmented, however, after a few years by Mr. William Steinway, the present head of Steinway & Sons, on his becoming twenty-one years of age.

I find Steinway & Sons in the directory for 1854 at 88 Walker Street, formerly occupied by William Nunns & Company, and in 1856 at 84 Walker Street and 91 Mercer Street. They began business, however, originally on Varick Street, in a rear house.

The subsequent rise of the "Steinway" piano into American and international eminence is a too well-accentuated and significant piece of history to call for detailed reference or eulogy here. The results we know ; yet it took energy, perseverance, intellectual and technical capacity, vested in the members of the firm, to enable them to reach this high point of development, especially in the United States, where they had to engage incidentally in friendly rivalry with old established and powerful firms.

Henry Engelhard Steinway was born February 15th, 1797, in Wolfshagen, a romantic hamlet in the Hartz Mountains, a region noted in German legendary song and story.   Wolfshagen is in the Duchy of Brunswick, a German province especially associated in history with military prowess and brave deeds.

Henry E. Steinway was the youngest of a family of twelve children.   At fifteen he was the sole survivor of his family, owing to a series of misfortunes that befell them.   Consistent with the military name of the province, several of Mr. Steinway's brothers perished in the Napoleonic wars of 1806 and 1812, while a terrible catastrophe in 1812 deprived him of his father and three surviving brothers.   Meantime, with the temporary conquest of that portion of Germany by France and the creation of a new kingdom of Westphalia, over which Jerome Bonaparte held brief reign, the personal property of the Steinway family had been confiscated and disposed of.   These confiscations were never made good by the provincial government in after years, so that young Steinway had to start out in life with little capital only his native genius and personal worth, all of which he found an opportunity to develop to such advantage in this country in later years.   In 1815 he joined the Brunswickers in the call to arms against the usurpations of Napoleon, and after Waterloo had brought back peace he still served in the army up to twenty-two, when he applied for and was granted an honorable discharge.   His early musical tendencies, his first transition from cabinet-making to organ-building, at Goslar, and subsequently his removal to Seesen, where he married happily and ultimately engaged in pianoforte-making, are already well written up elsewhere in biographical history and need no recital.   In that city C. F. Theodore Steinway, his first son, was born on November 26th,

1825. In August, 1839, Mr. Henry E. Steinway exhibited one grand, one three-stringed, and one two-
stringed square piano at the state fair of Brunswick,
where he won the prize medal, bestowed personally by
Albert Methfessel, the composer, who presided as chairman of the jury on the occasion. Three years prior to this
Mr. William Steinway, at present the only surviving
son of Mr. Henry E. Steinway, was born, the date being
March 5th, 1836. He was the fourth son and sixth child
born to his father. His brother Charles, one of the elder
members, was born in 1829, and was ten years old at this
date, while Henry Steinway, Jr., was eight years old,
having been born in 1831. The elder Steinway now
entered largely into manufacturing and prospered.

Theodore, Charles, Henry, Jr., and William Steinway,
therefore, grew up in the atmosphere of the pianoforte
art business, the two former becoming thoroughly
experienced in their craft before coming to this country in later years, while William had all his mechanical, inventive, and musical faculties largely developed
by this early association with the business in advance.
Meanwhile he attended one of the most excellent schools
in Seesen, where he acquired a knowledge of various
languages in addition to a first-class education, yet ex-
celling in instrumental music, for which he possessed
positive ability, being able, moreover, to tune a grand
piano for concert at the age of fourteen years.

Mr. Henry E. Steinway came to this country with his
family in 1850, upon the solicitation of his son Charles,
who arrived in New York previously, in 1849, and had
seen the better opportunities for advancement afforded
by a new country like the United States. C. F. Theo-

dore, the eldest son, however, was left behind to see after some unfinished business matters connected with Mr. Steinway's former piano manufactory, which was later renewed.

On arriving in New York on June 9th, 1850, the practical members of the Steinway family now consisted of Mr. Henry E. Steinway, Sr., Charles Steinway, and Henry Steinway, Jr., the latter being then aged nineteen, while Charles was twenty-one. Mr. William Steinway at this date was only fourteen. In order to acquire a knowledge of American life and business methods in connection with piano manufacturing, the elder Mr. Steinway determined, very sensibly, to reach the desired end by working in various first-class shops in New York. His sons, Charles and Henry, Jr., were put through the same practical education. William, on his arrival in New York, despite the fact of his musical tendencies and education, became imbued with all the restlessness of American life, and determined to enter some practical vocation. Early associations proved too strong an agent at this juncture, for, despite the chances for success held out to him through adopting the profession of music, he turned instinctively toward the piano business, and was accordingly apprenticed to William Nunns & Company in the summer of 1850, with whom he continued up to the founding of Steinway & Sons in March, 1853.

To turn now to the technical history of the Steinway & Sons piano, I find that the first public indorsement of these instruments, after the foundation of the firm, was the premium awarded them by the Metropolitan Fair held in Washington, D. C., in March, 1854, one year after their start in business, for an exhibit of squares.

Henry E. Steinway.

The first notable piano exhibited by this eminent house was a square, entered in the American Institute Exhibition of 1855. This instrument was awarded the *gold medal* by the committee on the occasion, for superior tone in regard to timbre and volume, combined with several features of novelty in construction described further on.

In this piano the American full metal plate covering the wrest-plank, having a solid front bar, was used. The connecting brace in the treble section was joined to the hitch-pin plate section and the wrest-plank plate in one casting, but elevated above the strings and placed in such a manner as to admit of improved "scaling" conditions and better tone results, while the capacity of the treble section of the plate to resist the "pull" of the strings was considerably enhanced. Bass overstringing—passing over three bridges—was also introduced. The latter were moved in toward the centre of the sounding-board, so as to bring the hitherto dormant section of that medium into sympathetic vibration with the strings as a part of the whole design, which included a new "scale" of great moment and ingeniousness. The outcome was decisive. The musical and technical results achieved are of historical magnitude, because many of these features of construction have since that date become generally adopted throughout this country and Europe.

We can trace numerous other evidences of the technical progressiveness of this house in succeeding years, but 1859 was destined to mark the introduction of some notable innovations in the Steinway & Sons pianos, of great permanent value to the musical world. First, there is the Steinway & Sons method of "agraffe" adjustment, for which Patent No. 26,300 was secured on November 29th of that year, by which a more perfect "bearing" against the upward concussion of the hammers was provided.   On December 20th, a few weeks subsequently, Patent No. 26,532 was taken out by Steinway & Sons for an application of overstringing in grands, in conjunction with a special plate model, illustrated in these pages, which necessitated a radical departure in "scaling" and stringing conditions, of such a nature as to excite widespread attention and comment at the time among old piano manufacturers.   That the results were more than successful simply goes to indicate, in a few words, the revolutionistic genius of the house.   That many of these principles are now in standard adoption goes further to exemplify the far-reaching intellect of the authors.   In the grands made on the lines specified in the patent, the strings were adjusted and "scaled" so as to spread out in fan-shape from the hammer-striking point down to the hitch-pins.   Bass overstringing was also included in the same plan of operation, as shown in the plate figure. The advantages resulting from this dispersion of the strings were manifold, and are too well known to readers to need recapitulation here.   In 1862 this system was applied to uprights.   In squares, to which it was also applied, the strings diverge in the opposite direction, and spread out toward the hammer line, owing to the circular scale.

Among succeeding progressions may be noted Patents No. 32,836 and No. 32,837, for action improvements granted to Henry Steinway, Jr., one of the inventors of the family, and used in the Steinway & Sons pianofortes, also Patent No. 55,385, dated June 5th, 1866, granted to William Steinway, who is also a practical inventor, for a "resonator" based upon an ingenious system of regulating the tension of sounding-boards, which is a noteworthy study in piano acoustics. Passing over many important patents relating to the mechanics of piano construction, all of high utility, recorded by this house from 1866 to 1872, the Steinway & Sons grand duplex scale is specially emphasized as a scientific development in the history of the piano, of deep interest to all scholarly students of the art of piano structure. This "scaling" system was applied with equal success to grands, squares, and uprights, and was the outcome of patient experiment and great elementary knowledge on the part of the originators. This is protected by Patent No. 126,848, issued on May 14th, 1872. Patent No. 127,383, for the Steinway & Sons cupola metal frame, is another significant record in acoustics, approved of by no less a person than the famous Helmholtz.

It would be entirely impossible to classify and discuss all of the patents issued by the National Patent Office, to Steinway & Sons—the majority of which are also protected in European countries—in limited space beyond those given, while at the same time this course would not add anything to the reputation of their world known pianos in which these improvements are practically exemplified and applied. Moreover, they are all recent and practical, therefore of less historical interest to readers —from the standpoint of antiquity—than old innovations and experiments would be. The Steinway & Sons grand action is one exception, and is illustrated elsewhere.

Going back into the personal history of Steinway & Sons, I have to note a great misfortune that fell upon the house in 1865 in the deaths of Mr. Henry Steinway, Jr., and Mr. Charles Steinway, both of whom passed away in the same year. They were the two youngest members of the firm, and their decease was a great blow to the family and a sincere source of grief to the whole piano trade, as well as a decided loss to the art of piano-making, both being eminent inventors. Henry died on March 11th, 1865, in this city, while Charles, the second son of H. E. Steinway, died on the 31st of the same month in Brunswick, Germany, where he was on a visit. Mr. C. F. Theodore, the eldest son, in consequence of these occurrences, sold out his business in Brunswick and joined the New York firm in 1865 as a partner. Steinway & Sons was now composed of H. E. Steinway and his sons, Theodore, William, and Albert. The latter, who was only ten years old when the family arrived in New York, had now reached the age of twenty-five, while Mr. William Steinway, the present head of the firm, was twenty-nine. Reinforced by this element of young intelligence backed up by American training, Steinway & Sons continued to progress on the upward track to their present plane of eminence. Their wholesale business having outgrown in early years the down-town facilities availed of by most makers, we find them located in their present city factory or finishing shop as early as April, 1860. This was extended in 1863, until their buildings covered twenty-six lots, with a street frontage of eight hundred and ninety-two feet. And in ten years all this vast accumulation of trade was won, which is a most remarkable instance of evolution in business life.

With the growth and admission of Mr. William Steinway into the firm, a new element was added, which found its expression in the more emphatic association of the Steinway & Sons piano with metropolitan musical art. In 1866 the present Steinway Hall was erected, and formally inaugurated by a grand concert in which S. B. Mills, Madame Parepa Rosa, and other artists of celebrity, participated. This building, with its concert auditorium in which such excellent acoustic results are remarked by artists, was planned and superintended by H. E. Steinway, then almost seventy years old, assisted by his sons. With the opening of their retail warerooms a city trade grew that has always been a great aid toward building up the art status of the instrument. Past this date the senior Mr. Steinway gradually retired more and more from active business, until death came on February 7th, 1871, after a short illness. Mr. Steinway passed away after a residence of over twenty years in this country, of which he was a devoted citizen, generally mourned. Mr. Albert Steinway, the youngest member of the house, died on May 14th, 1877, after a sudden illness in this city, aged thirty-seven. This was another private affliction of a sad character in the history of this eminent family that won them sincere sympathy from the trade.

The purchase of their Astoria property and the extension of the manufactories to that territory came in due course. Steinway & Sons have built a public bath and fine park for the free use of their workingmen and their families at "Steinway," Long Island City, and have since 1877 maintained a teacher at their expense, teaching music and German *free* at the public school there. Steinway & Sons have now also founded a free circulating library and "Kindergarten" in addition to the above-mentioned educational and other institutions, bearing all expenses thereof.   The extent of these buildings and the general scope of the Steinway & Sons various departments for supplying all the details of materials used in piano structure at this date needs no specific exemplification.   They have also large warerooms, besides a concert hall, in London, and a branch establishment at Hamburg, Germany.   The vast number of premiums, medals, honors, and national distinctions bestowed upon the house and many of its members personally also require only a brief allusion, for all readers are familiar with these details.   The last personal affliction that the firm has endured has been the recent death of Mr. C. F. Theodore Steinway, who died on March 26th, 1889, in Brunswick, Germany.   Mr. Steinway was a member of the Royal Academies of Paris, Berlin, Stockholm, and many other distinguished art societies, and was a practical man of rare acumen in his native sphere, traits which the present head of the house possesses in a large degree.

The members of the firm of Steinway & Sons at this date are, in addition to Mr. William Steinway, the head : Mr. Henry W. T. Steinway, born January 24th, 1856 ; Mr. Charles H. Steinway, born June 3d, 1857 ; Mr. Frederick T. Steinway, born February 9th, 1860 ; Mr. Henry Ziegler, born October 30th, 1857 ; Mr. George A. Steinway, born June 4th, 1865 ; Mr. C. F. Tretbar, and Mr. Nahum Stetson.   The three first named are sons of the late Charles Steinway, all highly educated, besides being practically trained in all departments of piano construction and its acoustics.   Mr. Henry Ziegler is a nephew of Mr. William Steinway, very popular personally, and a specialist of a high type in the realm of piano improvement.   He is also thoroughly practical.   Mr. George A.

Steinway is the eldest son of Mr. William Steinway. Though the youngest member of the firm, he has all the characteristics and qualities necessary for the position, having been carefully educated, while thoroughly schooled at the bench in the different Steinway & Sons factories.

Mr. C. F. Tretbar is a native of Brunswick, Germany, where he was born on February 13th, 1832. Having inherited the strong musical traits for which the natives of the duchy are noted, he in early life adopted the profession of music, in which sphere he shone as a teacher and virtuoso. He has been connected with Steinway & Sons since January, 1865, and is highly esteemed.

Mr. Nahum Stetson was born December 5th, 1856, at Bridgewater, Mass. His connection with Steinway & Sons dates back to 1876 He enjoys the fullest confidence of his *confrères*, and is fitted in every way, by experience and ability, to fill the position he now graces. Behind all these attributes he has hosts of warm friends, which fact speaks for itself.

Little more can be said historically about a firm as " live" and modern as Steinway & Sons. Their immense commercial interests, which embrace two continents ; their great prestige and high moral standing in the sphere of finance ; their great army of skilled, well-paid, and devoted workmen ; their facilities for producing instruments of the greatest art and mechanical excellence ; their generous patronage of American musical art and the musical press, all combined with the individual popularity and character of those comprising the firm, are too well known and too frequently commented on to require tedious recital.

In treating on important firms that figured in the trade from 1853 upward, the names of Raven & Bacon must not be lost sight of.   In 1856 Mr. George Bacon died. He was during his lifetime a very popular manufacturer and passed away generally regretted.   He was succeeded by his son, Mr. Francis Bacon, at present an esteemed member of the metropolitan piano trade.   The firm now became Raven & Bacon.

Under the new order the house continued to prosper, and built up a very excellent reputation as makers of first-class pianos.   Mr. Francis Bacon was an element of progressiveness in the history of this eminent old firm, being specially schooled in piano-making aside from having an excellent education   Raven & Bacon dissolved in 1871, when Mr. Karr, at present superintendent of the F. G. Smith factory, took his place in the firm, which became Bacon & Karr.   In 1880 the latter dropped out, when the Francis Bacon piano appeared.

These instruments are replete with all standard improvements and compare very creditably, from a price standpoint, with most pianos made.   Mr. Bacon's long experience and practical knowledge, no doubt, assists these results.

Among the patents taken out in relation to the Bacon & Raven piano is No. 8320, recorded by Mr George Bacon and Mr. Richard Raven in 1851, which is of some merit.   It relates to an improved metal plate for squares, with a peculiar adjustment of the bridges that is very ingenious, and indicative to some degree of the ability displayed by these makers throughout their useful career.

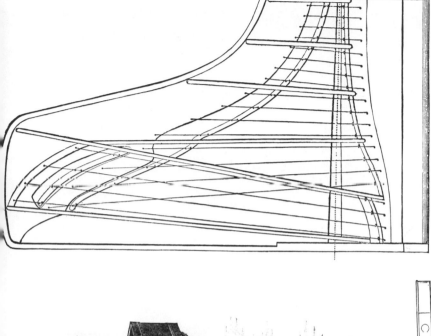

STEINWAY & SONS' OVERSTRUNG SCALE AND DISPOSITION
OF THE STRINGS IN THE FORM OF A FAN.

Patented December 20, 1859.

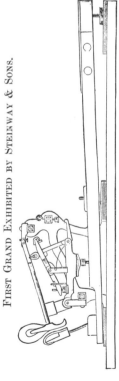

FIRST GRAND EXHIBITED BY STEINWAY & SONS.

STEINWAY & SONS' GRAND REPETITION ACTION, WITH TUBULAR METALLIC
FRAME. *Patented October 20, 1875.*

CHAPTER XVIII.

NEW YORK.

SPENCER B. DRIGGS alighted upon New York like a continental discoverer some time in 1856. In 1855 he lived in Detroit. Here he made some experiments in piano construction and took out United States Patent No. 13,942, on December 18th of that year, for an arched sounding-board held in position by a metallic framing. This was patented in Great Britain on November 1st and created some comment.

Later he arrived in New York and formed the Driggs Piano Company, which manufacturing firm overshadowed all competitors for a short period in specially prepared newspaper space matter and through other advertising methods. Mr. Driggs was convinced that the basis of sounding-board adjustment was practically falsified and he started out to revolutionize that department Hence his entry into the piano business. The latter was no doubt, a very clever man and sincere in his motives but entirely at sea as to the acoustic relationship that exists between the violin and the resonance department of the piano. Mr. Driggs' arched sounding-board scheme was ostensibly an application of the shape of the violin belly to the piano sounding-board, but the latter forgot to calculate the fact that violin bellies are usually carved from blocks of wood, while his method of forcing the sounding-board into a cramped or arched position would, of necessity, destroy the sympathetic resources of the wood fibres by undue compression. But there are yet more serious objections to the Driggs theory, practically, that cannot be discussed.

William Vincent Wallace, the composer, was at some time connected with Driggs as a member of the Driggs Piano Company, which continued for a few years. Presently the latter became connected with a Mr. Tooker, when the Driggs & Tooker piano appeared. Mr. Driggs settled down to an acceptation of standard principles in piano construction toward 1862, and became known as a small maker of some note until about 1870. In the mean time he was an indefatigable inventor and experimentalist, taking out a large number of patents in various departments of piano structure from 1855 up to the time of his death, some of them possessing merit besides originality.

The well-known name of Frederick Mathushek comes in at this juncture. The latter was for a while the interpreter and producer of many of Driggs' innovations. Driggs having plenty of capital, while laboring under the aforesaid impression about his own revolutionary genius, resolved to employ the clever, practical head of Mathushek to put his schemes in operation. Accordingly, Mr. Mathushek was responsible for any little success that attended Driggs' enterprises. Mr. Driggs dropped out of the piano trade some time toward 1870. As regards his inventions they have not survived, which in itself proves their worth. Frederick Mathushek individually had been in business back in 1852, and up to 1857 made the Mathushek piano, until he joined S. B. Driggs, as indicated. After leaving S. B. Driggs he was instrumental in founding the company in New Haven, Conn., at present making the Mathushek & Company piano. In a few years he returned to New York. He subsequently embarked in business on his own account in connection with his son, when the Mathushek & Son piano appeared. In 1879 Mr. Mathushek took out a patent for a method of string adjustment entitled the " equilibre system," which he made a specialty of in connection with his uprights. The principle, however, is but a modification of many old patents referred to, only that it is applied with more modern conditions. Mr. Mathushek is, however, a most noteworthy inventor and piano-maker, and has always been a highly esteemed member of the trade. His personal history, in relation to American piano-making, dates back to 1849, when he landed in this country. He was born at Mannheim, Germany, on June 9th, 1814, and learned the art of piano-making before coming here, meanwhile working in the best shops in Germany, Russia, and Austria. Finally he worked in Pape's, in Paris, and after the Revolution of 1848 came to New York, where he has figured prominently for over forty years.

Among the prominent manufacturers that came to the surface after 1850 was the firm of Scheutze & Ludolff, 85 Varick Street. At the American Institute Fair they were

very close competitors for honors with many of the leading makers, and in 1857 they carried off the gold medal
for the best square.   Lindeman got the second premium
at this event.   In many of the previous exhibitions
Scheutze & Ludolff usually came off second best.   In later
years they attained an important position.

In 1852 the house of Weber was founded.   Albert
Weber, its author, and the genius of its destinies up to
his death, was a Bavarian by birth and was born in 1829.
He landed in this country at the impressionable age
of sixteen.   He learned piano-making in the shop of
Holder, later working in Van Winkle's.   Meanwhile he
mastered the details of the English language with great
avidity, and employed his spare moments so efficiently
that he became a good musician.   Having thus educated
himself in a manifold sense, and indicated his superior
ambition, besides undoubted characteristics for industry,
it is no surprise to find that, with the possession of all
these advantages, natural and self-acquired, he rose up
to a height above other men ordinarily in the same plane
in after years.   Going back to 1869 and looking backward over the space of ten odd years, during which Albert
Weber, Sr., had worked himself into a leading position
as a manufacturer, a most remarkable history is unfolded.

Albert Weber began business on White Street, but later
moved to West Broadway.   In two years after his entry
as a manufacturer he was burned out.   Presently we find
him pluming himself for higher flights, and very soon he
is established in a five-story, marble-faced building on
the corner of Broome and Crosby streets.   His ultimate
prosperity is an almost unexampled instance of self-

creation in the piano business, when we take into account the fact that, unlike most of the other houses, he was almost alone in perfecting the task, having no partner or relative, his son, Albert Weber, Jr., being then a mere schoolboy. And what is more noteworthy, he was a strictly honorable man, the only means resorted to in order to influence his interests being liberal advertising and an aggressive business policy that won him admiration even from his opponents. In 1869 he had invaded the abode of swelldom and opened the present Weber warerooms on Fifth Avenue and Sixteenth Street, which was looked upon with some amazement by the leading people in the piano business at the period. How closely he had prophesied the tendency of the retail piano business was seen almost immediately, when Chickering Hall grew up on the avenue, followed by many of the principal houses.

The progress of the Weber business was checked unquestionably in 1879 when this remarkable individual died, for, as remarked, it all rested on his shoulders. The technical history of the Weber piano is concise, and can be told in a brief paragraph.

Weber made excellent instruments from the start. Satisfied with adopting current improvements, he used the best materials, employed the best workmen, paid them generously, associated his instruments with musical art in a pre-eminent degree, and backed all these conditions up with his own positive genius for getting in on the best side of success, with results pointed out and well known because they are recent and modern.

Mr. Weber passed away on June 25th, 1879, generally regretted, leaving the business in the hands of his son, Albert Weber, Jr.

The latter was born in New York in 1858. He received a finished education backed up by a training as a practical piano-maker, and owing to his father's death was called upon at twenty-one to assume the responsibilities and interests of the large business built up by Mr. Albert Weber, Sr., which was a severe test.

Under the management of Mr. Albert Weber, Jr., many new ideas have been put forth since 1880 of a progressive nature in his instruments. In 1883 we find that he established Weber Hall in the metropolis of the West— Chicago—which undertaking indicates many qualities of energy and push in the present Mr. Weber. Albert Weber was found equal to the large responsibilities thrust upon him by his father's death, and this was his first important move clearly. The Weber house, moreover, claims rightfully to be the first of the New York piano manufacturers to establish a direct branch in Chicago as early as 1880. Mr. Albert Weber, therefore, practically anticipated the future of this city as an important centre for the pianoforte trade. Weber Hall was formally opened in 1883 by a grand concert, in which many eminent artists participated, while the brilliant young pianist, Mme. Madaline Schiller, exhibited the Weber piano in its new home on the occasion.

Albert Weber, Jr., gradually developed many of the paternal traits after his association with the business interests of the house for a few years, and pushed his excellent instruments into many new fields subsequently in the South and West, which gave a vast impetus to the fortunes of his house. He has, moreover, constantly kept the Weber piano before the public gaze throughout in association with the best artists and virtuosi of the period. One of his most progressive moves in this direction was his great tour across the Continent with Sternberg and Wilhelmj.

In 1887 the Weber piano was exhibited at the American Exhibition in London, and won distinguished attention from European musical critics and pianists, while Mr. Weber was made the recipient of many social honors from literary and art circles, owing to the representative position he occupied on that occasion as a leading American piano manufacturer. We find the house of Weber represented at the famous Paris Exposition of last year equally, which was taken as a great compliment by the musical world of Paris as well as by the French press at the time, while the Weber exhibit secured marked attention. The progressive instincts of Mr. Albert Weber are significantly indicated in the foregoing circumstances, and speak for themselves. In connection with the present popular bijou instrument known all over the States by the name "Baby Grand," it is worth recording that Albert Weber, Sr., was the author of this title, which has since become an accepted piece of nomenclature by the trade and musical profession.

Mr. Weber's faith in Chicago as a future New York, which belief he formed in past years, is shown in the fact that he has made preparations to open one of the finest warerooms in that city, in March, at 248 Wabash Avenue, the present Weber Hall being inadequate. Apart from this, Mr. Weber has noted the tendency of the high-class pianoforte business veering in that direction, and he wishes to be first in the field.

As to the musical and art standing of the Weber piano, nothing need be said by way of introduction or endorsement.   It has a national and European reputation of the highest order, and under the expanding and aggressive direction of Mr. Albert Weber, the second, who is necessarily acquiring more experience and force of character from year to year, the house of Weber is destined to win a significant place in American musical and commercial history of the future.   The past history of the house herein sketched is, however, a noteworthy and eminent record as it stands of the ability and commercial genius of one man, Albert Weber, Sr., supplemented by the efforts and significant ability of Albert Weber, Jr.   Like all of the leading houses, the Weber piano has been awarded a large number of exhibition honors that cannot be given here in detail for obvious reasons.   This sketch would be incomplete, indeed, without paying tribute to Mr. Weber's great personal popularity in professional and social circles, while he is highly respected by his employés.   The Weber Factory, one of the most complete in this country in every respect, has for several years been under the eminently practical supervision of Mr. E. Stroud, whose inventions and patents are all applied in the Weber instruments.   Mr. Stroud is entitled to recognition in these annals, and is in every sense an expert and practical superintendent, and devoted to the interests of the house of Weber.

Albert Weber, Sr., had the characteristic foresight to build his manufactory only two blocks away from the warerooms.   It is situated at the corner of Seventeenth Street and Seventh Avenue, and has a street frontage of 400 feet, with a depth of 40 feet.   It is six stories in height, and taken altogether, with its excellent facilities for the production of pianofortes of the highest artistic

Albert Weber, Sr.

grade, it represents truly the technical progress of this worthy and time-honored house.

The firm of George Steck & Company, known throughout as manufacturers of instruments of a very high character, has a record going back to 1857. Mr. George Steck, the founder, began business in this year, and started out with the intention of making only first-class pianos, upon which policy he based all subsequent efforts. Mr. Steck is a thoroughgoing piano-maker of the old school, with strong tendencies toward inventiveness and originality in mechanics and acoustics. Not only has Mr. Steck been a consistent upholder of the policy indicated, but he has in addition been a patient and earnest student all through. Many of his experiments in piano improvement have been very valuable developments indeed. His speciality has been in the region of tone and sound production. All new " scales" and innovations of this character introduced in the Steck & Company piano, from 1857 upward, have been the result of patient experiment and research contributed by Mr. George Steck personally. Among the important patents taken out by the latter, and used from time to time in these pianos, is one of very high utility in relation to the upright brought out in 1870, at a period when this form of piano was yet unpopular. One of his upright " scales" produced in that year is highly spoken of by leading piano-makers, many of the smaller houses having subsequently adopted it. Mr. George Steck has made a particular study of portable instruments, and out of his researches several very noteworthy results have come. One is the Steck bijou upright known as " the little giant" in local parlance. Another is the Steck baby grand. Both are after special " scales" and models apparently. In the former the particular features of originality worthy of comment lie in the circumstance that he has taken the almost obsolete diagonal flat scale and utilized it to very striking advantage, by a very clever use of metal plate bracing. Certainly no European piano-maker has ever produced musical results equal to those exemplified in the Steck bijou upright treated on, and Europe is the home of flat " scaling" at present principally. However, Messrs. Steck & Company have shown in their " little giant" that the flat scale, when combined with the intelligent utilization of metal in small instruments, is capable of being used to very great advantage. Steck & Company's " baby grand," which was brought out as early as 1873, is also a very clever development in portable grands that has long ago won recognition throughout the musical world. In 1881 other significant developments were brought forward in these instruments of much practical worth. Since Mr. Steck's retirement, owing to the remarkable activity of his past life he has found it impossible to remain idle. Meanwhile, he has bent his mind on novel scientific research and experiment, the results of which is " The Pianete," a novel instrument in the form of an upright piano, which is without strings, without sounding-board, without iron frame, and without heavy framework, there being no strain on the case whatever. The instrument weighs about one hundred and seventy-eight pounds, and will never require tuning. It has a full compass of seven and one third octaves. Mr. Steck believes that this instrument will become the popular household piano in the future. The title " Pianete" has been formally adopted and copyrighted. Three patents have been taken out for this instrument, dated June 28th, July 26th, 1887, and March 19th, 1889. A fourth is pending. All these patents have been also extended to France, Germany, and Great Britain. The founder of Steck & Company, Mr. George Steck, is a native of Hesse Cassel, Germany, where he was born on July 19th, 1829. He served an apprenticeship course to Carl Scheel, a well-known piano manufacturer in his native city, and distinguished himself as an expert piano-maker. In 1853 he arrived in New York, and for four years worked in the best shops in the city, until a knowledge of American business methods and the use of the language was gained. In 1857, as designated, Mr. Steck founded his business. He began in this year on Twelfth Street and Third Avenue, right in the heart of the manufacturing centre, and had to move for room in 1859 to Walker Street, another famous trade locality in those years. His next move was to West Thirty-fourth Street, into the present factory. Thus we observe that Steck's rise into success was steady and remarkable in every respect. The progressiveness of Mr. Steck is further illustrated in the circumstance that in 1865 he opened a large retail wareroom on Clinton Place, known as "Steck Hall." In 1871 he entered into occupation of Steck Hall on East Fourteenth Street, which has since that period been known as the home of the Steck piano. Among the most remarkable inventions produced by Mr. Steck was his independent iron frame for uprights, grands, and squares in 1870. In this invention he indicated the skill in utilizing iron in piano structure that he afterward displayed so significantly in his portable bijou uprights and grands. Mr. Steck is one of the most respected men in the piano business, and has not an enemy existing in trade circles. He has earned a large share of practical success in life with these happy results outlined, and his business career has been a practical exemplification of uprightness and good-will to all.

In 1884 Mr. Steck's business was formed into a corporation, over which he presided as president up to January, 1887, when he sold out all his interest, including patents and everything in that connection, and retired into private life.

At present the firm is composed of Mr. George Nembach, Mr. Robert C. Kammerer, and Mr. Fred Dietz ; Mr. Nembach is a native of Saxe-Coburg, Germany. In 1865 he became connected with Mr. Steck's retail business, entering as salesman and bookkeeper. On Mr. Steck's retirement in 1887, Mr. Nembach became chief stockholder in the firm. Mr. Dietz, also a prominent stockholder, at present attends to the manufacturing department, and Mr. Kammerer assists in the correspondence and financial affairs of the house. Both these gentlemen are adequate in every respect.

Among the large makers of popular-priced instruments of good quality mentioned, Gabler & Brother merit a record. The long standing of the name in relation to the honorable craft of piano-making in New York is a further argument in their favor. The initiation of the Gabler business dates as far back as 1854, in which year Mr. Gabler, now deceased, began manufacturing in a modest manner. Having passed through the great panic of 1857, in which year nearly twenty of the small makers in New York were driven out of the trade, his progress from thenceforward was uniform and successful. Many patents have been granted to this firm. The present business is conducted by Mr. Emil Gabler.

The important house of Decker & Son now claims special mention. Mr. Myron A. Decker, the founder of this firm, is largely mixed up with many portions of our historical chapters, and is already familiar to the reader. The founder of Decker & Son was born in Manchester, Ontario County, N. Y., in 1823, and is descended from good American stock of old standing. Living until he had passed his boyhood in the invigorating atmosphere of the Catskill Mountains, he acquired naturally a sturdy and splendid physical development, which has stood him good service throughout his active and eventful life, to which he also owes many of those characteristics of mentality as an inventor in connection with American pianoforte development, for which he is noted.

Having strong sympathies with musical art and the arts generally, cannot one ascribe the fact to being born and bred almost upon the scene idealized and immortalized by Washington Irving's delightful sketch, " Rip Van Winkle," which Mr. George F. Bristow has adapted to national music, and which Mr. Joseph Jefferson has made famous in dramatic form ? There is no spot on this continent, as European travellers remark, so favorable to the cultivation or birth of artistic inspirations and sympathies as Irving's charmed home of Rip Van Winkle, and doubtless Mr. Decker's early tendencies were unconsciously moulded by these surroundings.

In 1844 he arrived in New York, and very appropriately went into the piano shop of Van Winkle, already referred to in a previous chapter, who, as pointed out, oc-

cupied a very eminent place in the trade in his time.
Mr. Decker served four years in Van Winkle's establishment, during which period he went through every department of the business necessary to the education of a
thorough piano-maker of the old school, besides winning
marked notice above his fellows as a skilful and ingenious
workman. The founder of the distinguished firm of Albert
Weber, Mr. Albert Weber, Sr., happened to be a fellow-
workman of Mr. Decker during the latter portion of Mr.
Decker's time in Van Winkle's shop. In 1849 he accepted
an offer to go to Albany to the house of Boardman &
Gray, where he built up a reputation as an adept piano-
maker. A natural desire to secure more scope for his
inventive impulses and individuality as an improver,
soon urged him to establish a business of his own. Accordingly, in 1856, twelve years from the first date of his
apprenticeship, we find him ready to occupy a place in
the Albany directory of the following year as " pianoforte manufacturer."

J. H. Hidley, an eminent Albany dealer, was secured
as the first agent of the " Myron A. Decker" piano, a
position he afterward occupied in relation to Steinway
& Sons. The announcement of J. H. Hidley, printed in
1856, in reference to the Myron A. Decker instrument,
I have read of with a certain amount of curious interest,
even though advertisements of that sort are by no means
unique, simply because it concerned the first days of the
existence of the present respected firm of Decker & Son,
and serves to illustrate the story of its incisive growth
and evolution by a sort of suggestion.

Mr. Decker's instruments soon became widely known
throughout the State of New York and the neighboring

territory. The following honor, bestowed upon the Decker piano in 1858, two years after starting business, is highly treasured as a souvenir testimonial and a talisman of much moment by Decker & Son : " Diploma awarded by the New York State Fair to Myron A. Decker, for Best Piano, at the Syracuse meeting, 1858. B. P. Johnston, Secretary ; H. T. McCoun, President." The foregoing was not the only exhibition honor won at this remote date of the Decker & Son career, but the members of the firm associate it with the history of these early years as a tribute of special interest, and they esteem it as such.

Like many of his old compeers Mr. Decker found Albany disadvantageous for his business from a commercial outlook all along, whereupon he returned to the scene of his first experiences, after ten years' stay in Albany, and began manufacturing in New York on Twenty-second Street near Lexington Avenue. We find him on Broome Street in 1864 located in a larger building, and in 1868 the plant and materials connected with the Decker & Son piano were moved to the historic building which stood on the corner of Fourteenth Street and Third Avenue, built by John Osborn, the first employer of Jonas Chickering, which fact has been traced elsewhere. This site, although unlucky for Osborn, evidently, was regarded as a lucky factory by the trade, and this latter phase was realized in the success which grew up with Decker & Son. They were the last occupants of the building. Meanwhile they occupied No. 2 Union Square as a wareroom for some time, as far back as January, 1868, which fact is verified. The Decker & Son piano, I am assured, was the first instrument sold within the bounds of Union Square. This circumstance is a particular source of pride to the senior partner, Mr. Myron A. Decker, because it makes him the pioneer of all subsequent settlers in that artistic locality, therefore the sentiment is pardonable.

In 1880 they removed from Osborn's old shop to their present factory and warerooms, which cover 1550, 1552, and 1554 Third Avenue, with a large counter extension rearward, but which is entirely inadequate for their output. Therefore on March 1st, 1890, they will occupy a splendid factory specially built by them on One Hundred and Thirty-fifth Street, near the Southern Boulevard, consisting of five stories and basement, which covers an area of 50x100. This building was commenced on October 2d, 1889, and is admirably equipped with improved plant and all facilities favorable to the expeditious production of the Decker & Son piano, as well as combining all that is conducive to the general merit of the instrument as a musical and art product.

The repetition of the foregoing facts outlines in simple perspective the commercial history of a much-respected firm. Throughout those years, from 1856 upward, a few changes have occurred in the composition of those associated with Mr. Decker in the management of the business. At present Mr. Frank C. Decker is the sole partner of his father, a position he has occupied since 1875, when he was formally admitted into the firm. Before that date Mr. J. C. Barnes, a well known salesman, who had twenty-one years' experience in Chickering & Sons' warerooms and elsewhere, was connected for some time with Mr. Myron A. Decker, but the partnership was dissolved after a brief interval.

Mr. Frank C. Decker, the present junior partner, was born thirty-two years ago. He received the privileges of a good education, and in due time turned instinctively toward the technical department of the piano business. In August, 1873, he began a regular course of apprenticeship in his father's factory, commencing at the bench. In a little while he reached tone regulating, and later studied tuning practically, in which acoustic branches he is now regarded as an expert throughout the trade. In most other respects, aside from his native genius as a practical piano-maker, Mr. Frank C Decker is amply equipped to perpetuate with justice the name and character of the Decker & Son piano in future years.

Regarding the development of the Decker & Son piano, the various improvements brought out in the instrument since 1856 have been nearly all left unpatented, being principally in acoustics. In other departments, however, there are such specialities in use in the Decker & Son pianos, as their "composition metal frame" and "improved pin-block" arrangement, both of high utility and entitled to be classed truly as improvements. But above and beyond details of this nature, the art and utilitarian value of the present Decker & Son piano is based largely upon evolution, backed up by the use of intelligent methods and the best materials. In the same sense the present commercial status of the concern has not been the work of a day. It is equally an evolution, but resting on a basis of conscientious endeavor.

The Decker & Son piano has a large following of eminent musicians to-day in New York, and in some outside cities, where the firm is represented by adequate retail houses, these excellent instruments are associated in a marked degree with high-class musical art, and are kept in a leading place. Decker & Son have won a host of encomiums in their time from some of the greatest musicians in this country, and are recognizedly makers of pianofortes of the highest grade. A significant compliment was paid them some time since when the New England Conservatory of Music selected their instruments for use in that admirable institution. The foregoing, in relation to the Decker & Son piano, serves to show its art and musical standing at the present, and completes a sketch of one of the standard firms of the period.

CHAPTER XIX.

New York.

SOME MODERN FIRMS—BEHNING & SON—BRADBURY—F. G. SMITH—THE HOUSE OF DECKER BROTHERS—KRANICH & BACH — NARVESEN—WALTERS—MARSCHALL & MITTAUER —-SOHMER & COMPANY.

AMONG the important firms that came in after 1860 was the eminent house now known as Behning & Son. At the close of 1861 Mr. Henry Behning began business in New York at 196 Elm Street, right in the heart of the war period. Mr. Behning had but just been honorably discharged from service in the Union Army, owing to disability. Previously he had been in active service since the opening of hostilities between the North and South, and finding himself now free to engage in a business enterprise, he entered the sphere of piano manufacturing.

Mr. Behning was born in Hanover, Germany, where he served a rigorous and thorough apprentice course in the shop of Julius Gercke, after which he entered the employ of Helmholtz. Here he became practically conversant with every detail of piano structure, even down to sawing out piano keys out of cows' bones—a primitive custom still prevalent in some German shops. In 1856 he arrived in New York and entered the factory of Lighte, Newton & Bradbury, then a leading firm in the metropolis, where he worked until the panic of the following year—1857—set in and demoralized business so thoroughly that nearly all of the New York shops shut down temporarily.

At this juncture he was offered a position in Bridgeport, Conn., which he accepted. He worked here until the beginning of hostilities between North and South, when he went to the front as a private in the First Connecticut Volunteers, but was released from duty, as shown, after a short interval. Mr. Behning being married at this time, family duties naturally hindered him from returning to the army. He therefore determined to bend his energies toward building up a reputable business and name as a maker of first-class pianos, a laudable ambition that has since then been largely realized. We find him so successful after starting in Elm Street that, after a short period, he moved to 196 Houston Street. Here he formed a partnership, in 1864, with Mr. Klix, when the Behning & Klix piano was first produced. The business now increasing, the firm took, in addition to the above and 196 Bleecker Street, a large building at 21 Minetta Lane. Meantime many developments had been brought forward by Mr. Behning in the tone, character, and structure of these pianos with manifold results ; in the first place followed by an improvement in the intrinsic character of his instruments, further by an increase in business, as indicated.

In 1867 we find Behning & Klix located in a large factory at 427–429 West Forty-second Street, from which period upward their business increased uniformly. In 1873 Mr. Klix withdrew, having sold his interest to Mr. Justus Diehl. The new firm, Behning & Diehl, suffered no change henceforth, but progressed steadily. In June, 1875, they moved to the corner of One Hundred and Twenty-fourth Street and First Avenue, being the first piano manufacturers to settle in Harlem. In 1877 a change occurred, however, in the withdrawal of Mr. Diehl. Mr. Behning having in view his sons, now determined to assume all the business interests and responsibilities. From 1877 to 1880 this continued until the entrance of Mr. Henry Behning, Jr., into the firm. Behning & Son was thus created. This augmentation of young energy and intelligence into the practical force behind the business gave a new stimulus to the fortunes of the firm. The further progress of Behning & Son is exemplified in the circumstance that in May, 1885, they moved to their present large factory at 57 and 59 East One Hundred and Twenty-eighth Street.

Mr. Henry Behning, Jr., is past thirty years of age, having been born in Bridgeport, Conn., November 26th, 1859. At the age of fourteen he entered his father's factory, and there acquired a thorough knowledge of the practical and artistic departments of piano construction, and possesses altogether, in addition to a commercial training, every qualification requisite for the position he occupies in relation to Behning & Son. Mr. Behning, Sr., is fortunate, moreover, in having one of his sons in charge of the bookkeeping, while another of them is superintendent of the technical department. The former, Mr. Albert Behning, was born in New York on September 5th, 1866, and in 1882 became an apprentice and served a four-years' course subsequently at finishing and regulating in the factory. In addition to a graduated course in Packard's Business College, acquired incidentally, he studied music, and officiates as travelling salesman for the firm, besides attending to his regular function as bookkeeper when not out of New York.

Mr. Gustave Behning, the youngest of the brothers, and at present in charge of the factory, is spoken of by the craft as one of the rising lights of the business, owing to the multifarious talents he displays as an inventor, "scale" draughtsman, and general expert. He was born in New York on December 26th, 1868, and, like the other members of the family, was duly put through an apprentice course in the shop, apart from receiving an excellent education. All of the foregoing possess strong musical traits and sympathies, and are prominently associated with the new Harlem Philharmonic Society, of which Mr. Albert Behning is treasurer. This connection indirectly with the atmosphere of art is reflected in the modern tendencies of the Behning & Son pianoforte, which instrument has already won a leading place in several States in the Southwest, and is in the front rank among American pianofortes recognizedly.

The special innovations and improvements originated by Mr. Henry Behning, Sr., and in adoption in the Behning & Son piano, are their compensating "agraffe," for which Patent No. 154,116 was taken out on August 18th, 1874 ; also a patented method of sounding board adjustment, and a concave name-board illustrated elsewhere. The latter improvement is also protected by Patent No. 160,299, the former by Patent 261,523.

The Behning & Son method of sounding-board ad-

justment, exemplified in the Patent shown, has been
adopted for the purpose of increasing the capacity and
timbre of the upper register in upright pianos, which
result accrues visibly from the fact that, unlike the accepted system in practice, the sounding-board does not
cease to vibrate beyond the down line of the wrest-plank
bridge in the Behning upright, as it is extended underneath as near as possible to the tuning-pins. The belly
bridge of the treble section has consequently a greater
extent of sounding-board surface vibrating in sympathy,
which augments the tone considerably, besides improving
the quality.

According to Patent No. 154,116, the "agraffe" here
referred to relates to a clever scheme of string adjustment by means of notches cut into the shoulder of the
"agraffe," in which the strings rest in a peculiar manner
after passing through the bearing holes in front. The
"agraffe," however, is otherwise screwed into the plate
in the accepted fashion. But passing over special features of this nature, we find in these instruments manufactured by Behning & Son every quality requisite in a
first-class piano, besides an individuality of tone that has
made them very popular in musical circles. Glancing
retrospectively at the modest start of Mr. Henry Behning, Sr., in 1861, at 196 Elm Street, the culmination of
an honorable purpose is indicated in the high artistic
standing of the Behning & Son piano, while the present
manufactory and warerooms of the firm—the former
equipped with all improved facilities—furnish, on the
other hand, an illustration of perseverance and honorable
industry justly rewarded. Behning & Son have just produced a unique bijou instrument, which is named the

" General Tom Thumb piano,'' claimed by them to be the smallest ever made for practical purposes. The dimensions are : Height, 2 feet, 4 inches ; width, 2 feet, 2 inches ; depth, 18 inches. It contains a full iron plate, over-stringing, besides a compass of seven and one-third octaves and all the requisites of an upright grand. Mr. Albert Behning has been the originator of this noteworthy development in miniature instruments.

The Bradbury piano came into being in 1861. In this year W. B. Bradbury, as pointed out, took up the position of F. C. Lighte, and began business. From this forward Mr. F. G. Smith, the superintendent of the Bradbury piano, became identified with the progress and status of these instruments, which became very widely known and popular in a few years. In 1867 Mr. F. G. Smith succeeded to Mr. Bradbury's interest and goodwill in the business, and from that year upward has been the sole manufacturer of the instrument bearing that familiar old name. Mr. Smith's two-edged ability, so to speak, technical and commercial, has been cleverly expressed in the promotion of these instruments. In the first place, he has been the author of many improvements of some utility in the Bradbury piano, while, on the other hand, he has all along shaped the business policy of his concern, which he directs entirely, Mr. Karr, the shop superintendent, having complete charge of that department. The Bradbury piano to-day enjoys a fair reputation, and under Mr. Karr is reaching higher in the scale of improvement yearly. Mr. F. G. Smith may be credited here with the distinction of personally directing and controlling more retail branch warerooms than any pianoman in the United States. Some individuals with

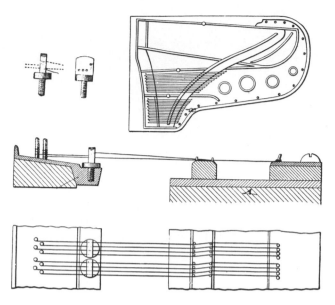

SOHMER & CO.'s REVERBERATION SCALE FOR GRANDS.

Patented March 8, 1887.

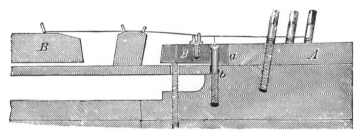

BEHNING & SONS' METHOD OF SOUNDING-BOARD EXTENSION FOR UPRIGHTS.

Patented July 23, 1882.

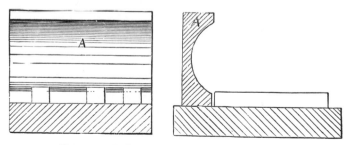

BEHNING & SONS' CONCAVE NAME BOARD.

Patented March, 1875.

ordinary heads think it difficult enough to manage one concern, but Mr. Smith thinks little of undertaking them *per quantum* evidently.

In 1862 the very significant and eminent firm of Decker Brothers came into existence. Mr. David Decker and Mr. John Jacob Decker, the originators of the business, are eminently practical piano-makers. Both were born in Germany, where they learned their craft before coming to these shores. In New York they worked in many of the best shops, and thus became acquainted with American methods very thoroughly previous to starting in business, meantime holding good positions in special capacities in New York factories. Having accumulated a small capital, and being attached to each other's interests, which was in itself an additional point of vantage over other manufacturers, in addition to being both highly skilled craftsmen, it is no surprise to read the story of their subsequent success.

Mr. David Decker is an inventor of marked ability, as the numerous patents recorded in Washington to his credit testify. Mr. John Jacob Decker, head of the house as at present constituted, is also an inventor of distinction and a " scale" draughtsman of considerable ability. The peculiarly fine characteristics of the latter-day Decker Brothers instrument owes much of these qualities to his practical supervision and innovative capacity. Among the patents that have been taken out in relation to the Decker Brothers pianos are No. 25,-393, September 13th, 1859, issued to David Decker ; No. 38,731, June 2d, 1863, to the same inventor ; No. 45,818, June 10th, 1865, and No. 61,612, taken out conjointly by J. J. and D. Decker on January 28th, 1867.

These are all of high utility, although two of them
have been put aside several years ago to make way for
more modern improvements of the same nature.

From 1862 to 1890 Decker Brothers have kept well in
the front rank, and besides originating special improvements, have adopted the best methods as they came into
being elsewhere with many clever modifications, which
is perfectly legitimate, for no one individual can claim
to have produced or developed the piano, and radical
improvements are to an extent ethically the property of
the whole trade.   The familiar illustrations applied so
often throughout to show the rise of other successful
firms apply equally to Decker Brothers.   For instance,
their modest start in business in 1862, culminating in
their present successful position as a large and leading
house devoted to the production of first-class pianos, is a
story easily told.   The conditions necessary to these results are obviously intelligence, perseverance, self-con-
fidence, practical skill, and a sympathy with musical art.
Mr. David Decker retired from business several years
ago, while Mr. John Jacob Decker still retains an active
lead in the firm.

Kranich & Bach came into the sphere of the trade also
in war times, for they began business in 1864.   Mr. H.
Kranich and J. Bach, the originators of this concern,
were both born in Germany, and are practical piano-
makers, each skilled in a special department.   Their first
start in business was unpretentious, but toward 1875
they had become steadily established as manufacturers
of reputable instruments.   Since that period their business has progressed very uniformly.   They have brought
out many detailed improvements, and their pianos appeal

to a large constituency of intelligent patrons, while in some sections of the country they enjoy great popularity among the masses.

Toward 1865 the Narvesen piano was well known as a popular instrument. Conrad Narvesen, the initiator of this piano, was born in Norway, coming to this country at an early age. He began business as early as 1845 in New York. Narvesen, Hangaard & Bergmann were carrying on this old business, in 1880, at 230 and 232 East Thirty-sixth Street, when R. M. Walters purchased their plant and general good-will in August of that year. Since that time Mr. Walters has continued the manufacture of these instruments.

The once well-known firm of Marschall & Mittauer was formed in 1867, and within a short period became noted as makers of excellent instruments. Both of these named were practical, especially Marschall, who was a very prominent inventor in his time. Mittauer, who died in St. Louis some years ago, was a native of Baden, Germany, and was a department foreman in the shop of Lighte & Bradbury previous to joining Marschall. Theodore Marschall was a Bavarian by birth. After arriving in New York, in 1851, he went into business with another piano maker, thus creating Marschall & Locotte, which was of short duration. He afterward occupied the position of superintendent in Lighte & Bradbury's until 1867, as detailed. Marschall & Mittauer were known up to 1871, when Boernhoeft succeeded them, then Hugo Sohmer & Company.

I find that Callenberg & Vaupel, at present in existence, were well known as makers of good moderate-priced instruments as far back as 1864. They, however, began as early as 1858.   Both of the members composing this old concern are practical, and have enjoyed a large experience in the piano business.   Instruments of this class fill a popular want, and are therefore worthy of notice, apart from the fact that Callenberg & Vaupel have been known for thirty years.

The Christy piano was a well-known instrument back in 1865.   Mr. Jacob Christy, the originator of the business that up to a recent period bore his name, entered the trade over thirty years ago, and is in every sense a practical piano-maker.   He built up a very large business meanwhile, and was well known up to a few years ago.   Mr. Christy is at the present time connected with the Colby Piano Company at Erie, Pa.

Among the other piano-making firms that had attained some note toward 1870 as makers of instruments for the masses were C. D. Pease & Company, yet in existence and large manufacturers ; Soebler & Company, Schraidt, Schmidt & Company, Ihne & Son, Ambler & Company, Wing & Son, Ziegler & Company, and other small concerns too numerous to recount.

There are few of our latter-day houses enjoy such popularity as Sohmer & Company.   It is gratifying to be able to trace throughout the growth of this house up to its present plane the fact that their pianos have never been put forth from the standpoint of folding-beds or miscellaneous merchandise, but have always been associated with musical art and the patronage of artists of a high order.   Sohmer & Company is a modern house comparatively, having been founded in 1872, although in reality going back before 1860.

Mr. Hugo Sohmer, its author and head, was born in

the Black Forest, Germany, in 1846. His family were in good circumstances, his father being an eminent physician, and his education therefore was first class. Not only was he put through a good educational system, such as German scholastic methods afford, but he was placed subsequently in the hands of a private tutor, a distinguished scholar and literary man, with whom he finished his studies. Added to these accomplishments, Mr. Sohmer acquired a knowledge of music and the pianoforte in the mean time.

The head of Sohmer & Company must have been, despite his early surroundings and musical temperament, a very practical youth, for we find him at sixteen years of age landing in the new world to seek his fortune, thus following the example of some of the sturdiest citizens this country has seen. In a week after arriving in New York he was working as an apprentice to piano-making in the factory of Schuetze & Ludolf, which was, as pointed out, one of the most significant piano manufacturing houses in New York at the time. Here he learned piano-making through and through, as practised in this country, and had the privilege of working almost side by side with many of the best piano-makers known in New York.

In 1868 Mr. Sohmer paid a temporary visit to Germany, and remained some time. During the interval he travelled in various European capitals and studied piano-making thoroughly anew from the European point of view. 1870 beheld him again back in New York, with a new purpose and aim, which reached the first point of culmination in 1872, when he began manufacturing in conjunction with his present partner, Mr. Josef Kuder, the new firm Sohmer & Company being successors to

J. H. Boernhoeft, who in turn had succeeded the old house of Marschall & Mittauer previously. Sohmer & Company also went into immediate occupation of the factory on Fourteenth Street and Third Avenue formerly used by Marschall & Mittauer, which Boernhoeft had continued in, and which they yet occupy as warerooms and finishing shop combined.

As I said, the start of Mr. Sohmer as a master piano-maker, to use a good old term, was the first culminating point in his ambition ; the next was to make instruments entirely worthy of his name and technical relationship ; and the third and major degree of this ambition was to secure for them the approval of all good artists and authorities in this country. The standing of the Sohmer piano to-day as a musical and art product answers all requirements, and is sufficiently familiar not to need endorsement, while the commercial standing of the firm of Sohmer & Company is so stable and assured that it seems as if all his wishes are already realized. From a few pianos a week, which output was reached within six months after starting, the Sohmer firm gradually developed a business and a name. In 1876 the Centennial Exhibition authorities awarded them high honors in company with many of the oldest houses in the country, which was not without good results.

In 1883 an additional factory was taken on East Twenty-third Street, formerly used by Carhart & Needham, the organ manufacturers, which building was used to its extreme limit up to 1886. Another landmark, so to speak, indicative of progress was set up in this year by Sohmer & Company, for they rented an extension to their building on Fourteenth Street and Third Avenue, while their present extensive shops in Astoria, L. I., were begun, into which they moved all their old plant in addition to special machinery on its completion in 1887. All of the foregoing marks of development speak of the steady growth and extension of the business of this firm, and require no special emphasis.

Mr. Josef Kuder, Mr. Sohmer's partner, is a native of Bohemia, Austria. In his boyhood he went to Vienna, and learned piano-making in the shop of Heintzmann. Here he spent seven years, but hearing of the greater scope afforded talents and industry in the new world, he bade adieu to his native land in 1854, and sailed for New York. His first experience in the metropolis as a piano-maker was in the shop of Steinway & Sons, then on Walker Street. After about a year he entered Lighte, Newton & Bradbury's employ, where he became a department foreman, his specialty being grand and square regulating and finishing ; but owing to the depression and general feeling of inertness that followed the panic of 1857, Mr. Kuder returned to Vienna in 1861, where he re-entered Heintzmann's shop. Like all persons that have lived in the invigorating and independent atmosphere of United States civilization for any time, Mr. Kuder turned his face westward once more and arrived in New York in 1864, having meantime grown tired of work-a-day life in Vienna, where so many hide-bound superstitions and antiquated formalities hold sway, as in all European cities.

He now took a position with Marschall & Mittauer, with whom he continued up to their dissolution in 1871, and continued with Boernhoeft, their successor, up to the time he joined Mr. Sohmer and formed Sohmer & Com-

pany, which firm became in turn the successors to Boernhoeft, as shown.

In conjunction with making first-class instruments,
Sohmer & Company have introduced a number of patented and unpatented improvements from time to time.
Principal among these patents are No. 268,562 and No.
268,563, March 5th, 1882, the first relating to an agraffe
bar for tone augmentation, the second in relation to an
action improvement of considerable utility.   Three other
more important records are illustrated in these pages—
viz., No. 15,250, issued on August 12th, 1884, being a
design for a bijou grand at present in adoption and extremely popular ; Patent No. 358,946, a " reverberation"
scale, taken out on March 8th, 1887, and No. 357,436,
which was granted on February 8th, 1887, for a pianissimo pedal.   They will be recognized by these titles in
the illustrations.

The Sohmer & Company bijou grand was constructed
so as to give a more symmetrical shape and a better appearance to grand pianos.   Unlike the regulation style,
this instrument is semi-circular or cycloid-shaped, with
some points of distinction as shown, and presents a very
pleasing appearance.   Patent No. 358,946, which was
taken out for " certain new and useful improvements in
pianofortes," I have named a reverberation scale, for the
reason that it refers to a system of " scaling" or string
adjustment exemplified in a grand in the drawing given,
where auxiliary strings are arranged in conjunction with
the regular strings for the purpose of giving forth rever-
beratory or sympathetic waves of sound, thus augment-
ing the general tone results of each unison, and consequently the *ensemble* for obvious reasons.   The auxiliary

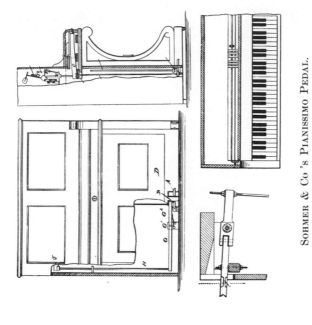

SOHMER & Co.'s PIANISSIMO PEDAL.

Patented February 8, 1887.

SOHMER & Co.'s DESIGN FOR GRAND
PIANO.

Patented August 12, 1884.

string connected with each unison in grands goes through a special hole in the agraffe, and is tuned at the same time as the others. Meanwhile the regulation strings pass through the "bearing" holes in the agraffe lower down, and thence to the tuning-pins. This is applied by Sohmer & Company in a special manner, principally extending from the middle up to the extreme treble register in pianos.

The Sohmer pianissimo pedal, protected by Patent No. 357,436, is an improved attachment for producing refined and artistic *piano* effects in their instruments, and is used in combination with the ordinary soft pedal for these purposes. By an ingenious trap-work and action arrangement, moreover, the hammer line in uprights can be projected to any range of distance from the strings without a diminution of touch control in front with the pleasant consequences outlined, which is invaluable.

In concluding this sketch of Sohmer & Company, the names of Mr. George Reichman and Mr. Charles Fahr, two of their confidential and leading assistants, come uppermost. The former has charge of their retail department, and is a polished and versatile specialist, while Mr. Fahr attends to the financial and business management of the firm, both responsible positions for which they are entirely qualified.

CHAPTER XX.

New York.

THE GREAT CENTENNIAL EXHIBITION—FOREIGN COUNTRIES
REPRESENTED—SOME INCIDENTAL REMARKS—THE MODERN
HOUSE OF CHICKERING & SONS—PATENTS—P. J. GILDE-
MEESTER—THE PAINE EPISODE.

1876, the centennial year of the independence of the
United States, has retrospectively some historical bearing
on the development of the piano. At the great Centennial Exhibition held in Philadelphia in this year, the
principal American pianoforte makers came together for
the second time in national history—the first being the
World's Fair of 1853—and exhibited the products of their
art and skill side by side. Again, as in 1853, foreign
piano-makers were seen arrayed in friendly competition
for honors with native manufacturers, and not a little
benefit was derived on each side from this informal exchange of courtesies. Keen rivalry predominated in the
attitude of many United States makers to each other,
which is, however, the " life and soul " of progress, and
is nothing unusual in commercial life. Curiously enough,
there were about the same number of European manufacturers as Americans exhibited. Among the foreign

countries represented, Germany and France led. The former sent Altenburg & Graue, of Bremen ; Bluthner, of Leipzig ; Schiedmayer and Stalhecker, of Stuttgart ; Ibach & Son, of Barmen ; Schwechten, of Berlin ; Kaps, of Dresden, and E. Seiler, of Liegnitz. France was only one behind. The French makers were all from Paris, which is the centre of the piano business in that country. They were Beunon, Baudet, Brunning, Debain & Company, Focké & Son, C. Gavioli, Jr., and Kriegelstein & Company. Great Britain only sent Brinsmead & Sons, L. W. Collmann, and J. H. Browne, while a few other European countries were indifferently represented by a casual maker here and there. The general .display of pianofortes at the exhibition was very significant in every respect. It showed plainly the superiority and inferiority contained on both sides in European and native pianos in a detailed and analytical sense of comparison, while it served to illustrate the progress made by this country since 1853 in the art of piano-making. This informal convention of European and native makers was, however, characterized by universal good feeling toward the foreign element, while all the strength of competition seems to have reposed between American manufacturers. While many points of excellence worthy of adoption were noted in the pianos of Brinsmead & Sons and Browne, London, Bluthner, Leipzig, and Debain, Paris, American pianomakers in general had reason to feel very proud of their instruments, and the great development reached in the art and craft in this country since 1775, when Behrent announced the first piano in Philadelphia.

While a most courteous and hospitable demeanor was evinced by the judges toward European exhibitors, there was no use trying to conceal the fact that the first-class American pianos exhibited excelled the best instruments of European makers in almost every respect. At the same time, American makers were bound to admit that in point of finish and detail, in regard to construction and ornamentation, many German, French, and English pianos sent across contained points of high excellence. The good that must have necessarily accrued from this competitive convention of piano manufacturers, foreign and native, is shown plainly in the foregoing. The American makers that exhibited at this great commemorative exhibition comprise all the modern and standard firms treated of in these chapters.

This consideration of the Centennial Exhibition serves appropriately as an introduction to the modern history of the internationally famed house of Chickering & Sons.

This eminent firm occupies a unique place in the history of the American pianoforte, for it is at this date the oldest house on this continent, while it has a pre-eminent record in connection with the evolution of the piano and the progress of musical art in the United States, which dates in an unbroken line back to 1823, over a space of sixty-seven years, and yet its prestige has never retrograded in the slightest with the advance of time, and it remains to-day unsurpassed in progressiveness.

The modern aspect of the house as one of the foremost and great leading firms in this country, financially and professionally, has occasionally been lost sight of, by writers who love historic lore. Therefore, while having shown in earlier chapters the historical development of the firm up to the death of Mr. Jonas Chickering in 1853, with a few connecting observations on Mr. C. F. Chickering and Mr. G. H. Chickering, I have reserved for separate treatment the history of Chickering & Sons from that year up to the present time. Upon the death of Mr. Jonas Chickering the task of preserving and perpetuating the honor and fame of the house was bequeathed to his sons, Col. Thomas E., C. Frank, and G. H. Chickering, and, unlike many old pianoforte houses that have gone down into oblivion, the inventive and commercial genius of the Chickering brothers has built up the reputation and stability of the house upon a strong and sure foundation, and made its products known the world over. The first-named—Thomas E. Chickering—whose premature decease in 1871, in Boston, was generally regretted by all classes, was the oldest son of Mr. Jonas Chickering, and one of the original firm of Chickering & Sons. He was a highly qualified member of the house, practically and commercially, having acquired a thorough knowledge of piano-making under his father's care in their factory, commencing at seventeen years of age, after which he devoted himself with assiduity to the commercial aspect of the business. He was admitted into the firm as a partner in 1852 along with his brothers, C. Frank and George H. Chickering, and for upward of nineteen years was largely identified with the progress and career of Chickering & Sons. Meanwhile, Colonel Chickering devoted himself principally throughout to the wholesale department of the business, in Boston. His popularity in musical, literary, and art circles, like his brothers, C. Frank and G. H. Chickering, was very great in his native city and elsewhere, and in connection with the records of the Handel and Haydn Society his name figures prominently, to which may be added the great Boston

Peace Jubilee. This worthy member of a distinguished family of inventors died on February 14th, 1871, in his native city. This was a great bereavement in the private history of Chickering & Sons, by reason of the strong bonds of sympathy uniting the brothers, more than exists usually between members of one family. Mr. C. Frank Chickering, the present senior member of Chickering & Sons, has been its practical and inventive head since the death of his father, in 1853, called him to assume this function. All notable progressions in "scaling," mechanics, and other departments of piano-making that have appeared in the Chickering piano for over thirty-six years have originated with and been produced under the practised and educated eye of this eminent specialist, who continues to be one of the strong factors in modern pianoforte development.

Mr. C. F. Chickering was born in Boston on Jan. 20th, 1827. He received a first-class education, and was duly initiated into the "mysteries" of his father's business under the latter's personal supervision. In 1844, however, he was granted a temporary respite from these duties owing to a slight indisposition, and was sent to India on a trip for the benefit of his health. This fact has some significance, owing to the circumstance that Mr. Chickering took some "Chickering" pianos along, which were disposed of in Calcutta and various stopping-places on the route, where they evoked much praise from European residents, particularly in Calcutta, their construction with the full iron plate making them very acceptable in that climate. On returning Mr. Chickering took a position in his father's business, and finished up his studies, technical and otherwise. As I have remarked in Chapter XVI., Mr. C. F. Chickering visited London in 1851, and while there helped to exhibit the Chickering pianos catalogued at the great World's Fair in that year. His decisive connection with the technical and business progress of Chickering & Sons dates from the beginning of 1853, when, in conjunction with his brothers, he was called upon to assume charge of the great technical sphere left vacant by Mr. Jonas Chickering, who throughout his life had personally invented and introduced all new improvements appearing in his pianos. In this connection Mr. C. F. Chickering has been very progressive and revolutionistic, and has taken out a great number of patents of a thoroughly practical nature showing positive improvements, which are described throughout.

The " circular scale" in squares, which was incontrovertibly the key to the improved method of overstringing now in general adoption, which Mr. Jonas Chickering introduced in 1845, was carried to a high point of development early in 1854 by Mr. C. F. Chickering in two scales, of which old piano-makers speak as the best scales ever produced in this country for pure tone results and uniformity in *timbre*. They were very universally copied. Like the original " circular scale," they were not patented, for the reason—so often referred to elsewhere—that it is impossible to legally protect " scales" or acoustic inventions of that abstract nature by patent. These were among Mr. Chickering's earliest developments in " scaling." About the same year he produced " overstringing" in an upright, which is claimed to have been previously accomplished in 1850 by Mr. Jonas Chickering.

The aim of Messrs. Chickering & Sons has ever been to produce pianofortes in which *quality* of tone is not sacrificed to *quantity*, and throughout their career all improvements brought out by them in the region of " sounds and tones" in their instruments have been conditioned to this artistic end.   Passing over the great commercial and artistic sphere they have filled as leading piano manufacturers, it is impossible to examine the history of this honorable house and not observe throughout the modern epoch of their history a restless, persistent and successful endeavor to associate their pianos with the highest expressions of musical art, and the genius and virtuosity of the best pianists of the century ; while every new development brought forward in the " Chickering" piano, in its mechanics and acoustics, sprang obviously from high scientific and technical knowledge on the part of the initiators.   Conscientious and high-minded endeavor of this nature surely deserves special emphasis !   Numerous patents have been taken out by them in relation to their instruments since 1853   Among the modern patents of Chickering & Sons are No. 32,119, which covered an improvement in squares, the object of which was " to give the square the advantage of an open bottom, similar to that of the grand piano."   Patent No. 121,334, issued on November 28th, 1871, is illustrated elsewhere.   This is a means of applying the circular scale to upright pianos, and is a very significant innovation.   The object is reached, as in the square, by placing the hammers in a curved line.   A corresponding arched form is given to the main rail in the frame, and in addition an arched rail is used for the damper action, with special modifications indicated in the patent.

Patent No. 134,194, December 24th, 1872, and No. 175,336, March 28th, 1876, must be also mentioned.   The

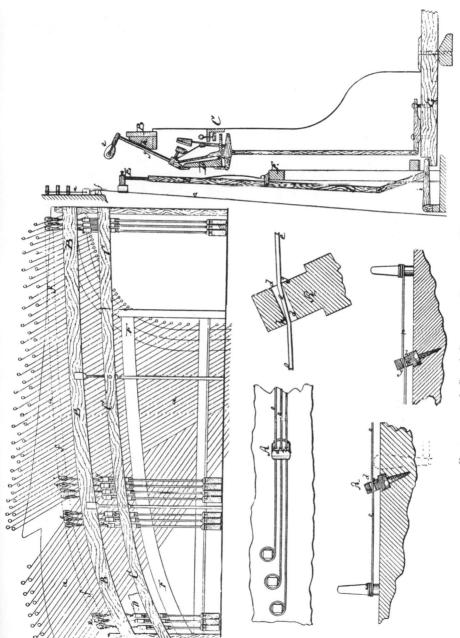

CHICKERING & SONS' CIRCULAR SCALE FOR UPRIGHTS.

Patented November 28, 1871.

first record refers to the well-known Chickering upright
action. The latter is a valuable improvement in the
grand piano frame for the purpose of insuring it
against string tension. Patent No. 177,332, November
20th, 1877, deals with improvements in piano acoustics,
and also relates to metallic string frames. Patent No.
247,887, issued on October 4th, 1881, is a particularly
noteworthy record. This patent deals with a skeleton
metal frame upon which the sounding-board is supported
on isolated or distant points along its edge. The iron
plate is supported by the skeleton frame independent of
the sounding-board. This adjustment of the latter medium tends to increase its effectiveness as a resonance
agency, while the tone results are vastly improved. Another record, Patent No. 330,292, October 5th, 1886, is
another valuable improvement in stringing and plate-
bracing conditions that is illustrated permanently in the
Chickering & Sons pianos. The foregoing emphasize
sufficiently the progressiveness of Chickering & Sons,
while the exemplification given hardly does justice to
the intellectuality of the authors ; but the most valuable
results are demonstrated in the tone, individuality, and
musical character of their instruments. A grand piano
containing an application of the improved plate outlined
in the last patent—which is a significant development
—was exhibited in Boston in 1887. A critical writer on
one of the city papers says of this instrument : " The
difficulty of overcoming the tendency to disrupt that part
of the iron frame bordering on the line of the Agraffes
has seemed insurmountable. That such a serious and
perplexing obstacle has been completely overcome should
be credited to the house of Chickering." The Chicker-

ing upright action at present in use is another development that is largely commented on as equal in results to the grand. In relation to the large number of medals, premiums, and honors bestowed on the Chickering & Sons instruments during past years much could be said. The highest distinction, however, is probably the French Cross of the Legion of Honor, bestowed upon these instruments, which is regarded as priceless in every respect, coming from such a source as the French Government.

To revert to the personal history of another distinguished member of the house : Mr. George H. Chickering was born in Boston on April 18th, 1830, and, like his brothers, received an excellent education up to seventeen, when he was placed in his father's factory, where he was schooled in all departments of practical piano building, subsequently becoming admitted a member of the firm in 1852.

Mr. Chickering, among his other branches, was instructed in the details of hammer-making in grands, and under his father's instruction made many sets of hammer-heads for the celebrated grands used by many great artists. In later years the Chickering & Sons grands used by Thalberg, DeMeyer, Gottschalk, Herz, and other great virtuosi contained hammer sets specially made by Mr. G. H. Chickering, a fact he may take pride in. This talented member of Chickering & Sons has for many years presided over the factory in Boston, which he has governed on behalf of the house with those admirable traits so indicative of the characteristics of the founder. Here the employés are treated with rare thoughtfulness, in the true spirit of our commonwealth, a fact I cannot duly help commending. A great number of employés can be found in this shop who have been there for over thirty years, and from the young apprentice up to the oldest veteran all venerate the history and traditions of the firm they work for, and tender universal respect to Mr. G. H. Chickering. In musical circles his status is indicated by the fact that he was elected president of the Handel & Hayden Society of Boston, after being its vice-president for twenty-nine years. In trade and private circles he is equally esteemed.

In the history of their extensive branch house in New York, since the founding, in 1875, of Chickering Hall, which has exercised a potent influence on musical art, a new individuality has grown up in the person of Mr. P. J. Gildemeester, who has been for several years the confidential business manager of the firm. In April, 1886, the house became a close corporation, in which Mr. Gildemeester became a partner. Mr. Gildemeester was born in New Orleans, La., in 1849, and has been brought up in a musical atmosphere. Among his musical relatives, the famous Louis M. Gottschalk, "the American Chopin," may be numbered. Mr. Gildemeester became known at an early period in his life as an industrious and able member of the piano trade. He entered the firm of Chickering & Sons in January, 1878, as a retail salesman, and was soon promoted to the position of traveller for the wholesale department of the house. His loyalty and devotion to the interests of Chickering & Sons has been duly rewarded by a membership in the firm, and equally with a share in the good-will and esteem of his associates, and he enjoys the fullest confidence of Messrs. Chickering.

Outside of business circles Mr. Gildemeester has few

enemies and a strong host of friends, a circumstance always indicative of personal worth.

The subjoined is without doubt one of the most remarkable episodes on record in relation to the integrity of a business firm or the individuals composing it, and is shown in the fact that for nearly eighteen years Chickering & Sons kept in one of their safes in New York about four hundred thousand dollars in bonds and currency, placed in their keeping by J. H. Paine, known as "Miser Paine," who was a grandson of a signer of the Declaration of Independence. This wealth was tied up in a dirty bandana handkerchief, and was unknown to Paine's friends. When Paine died Mr. C. F. Chickering immediately sent for Paine's lawyer, and revealed the astounding discovery of the miser's wealth. In the mean time, Paine had lived and died in the most abject poverty, and left no clew to this accumulation of the money or its whereabouts. The inference that can be adduced from the foregoing circumstance clearly serves to exemplify the great moral strength and character of the house of Chickering & Sons. Hence the introduction of this dramatic incident. But the principal actor in the drama was Mr. C. F. Chickering.

There is some contrast afforded in the present Chickering & Sons producing factory in Boston, which is said to be the largest factory under one roof on this continent, and the modest shop in which good Jonas Chickering—once styled "upright, square, and grand, like his own pianos"—began business on Common Street in 1823. In this vast manufactory there is an accumulation of the most effective and modern machinery known in piano manufacturing, in addition to every facility for making pianos of the highest excellence. Back of these conditions stand a legion of highly-trained workmen and a staff of eminent foremen, each specially skilled in a separate field. This tells its own tale. And of the house of Chickering & Sons itself what can be said? Clearly the present aspect of the house or the character of the instruments produced by Chickering & Sons require no critical analysis here, even were such a proceeding in order. The firm has existed and come upward to this time through sixty-seven years of national history as an important factor in our civilization ; as the patron and friend of artists and art, and as a sympathetic supporter of musical literature. It has passed unscathed through panics, social revolutions, and the commercial depression of two great wars, and throughout all these years the name of "Chickering" has been and remains an American household word in relation to domestic music and the peaceful joys of home life.

CHAPTER XXI.

New York.

LIKE so many eminent members of the piano-making fraternity, Mr. Henry Behr, senior partner of Behr Brothers and collaborator in the establishment of the firm, is a Grand Army veteran, with a highly honorable record, having done good service during the Civil War in the One Hundred and Sixty-ninth New York Regiment of Volunteers, and meanwhile served one year in General Terry's division of the Army of the Potomac, a distinguished branch of Grant's favorite command. This ought to be a sufficient indication of his patriotism, a worthy aspiration always indicative on either side of bravery, consistency, and uprightness. Mr. Behr is a native of Hamburg, Germany, a city that has given New York many worthy citizens during the past century. Clement Claus, one of the first piano-makers known in this country, was a native of that city, as shown in Chapter V.

Mr. Henry Behr was born in 1848, and arrived in this country at a very early age. He subsequently went into piano-making, and began piano-case manufacturing for the trade in 1875. Mr. Behr is very original and practical in this branch, and is the author of many of the novel designs in case ornamentation and structure that have appeared in recent years, and gone the round of the trade. The well-known Lincrusta designs in closed panels, and quite a number of other improvements, have all been originated by Mr. Behr. Behr Brothers— Mr. Henry Behr and Mr. Edward Behr being the principals—was founded in 1881. They started out by determining to make only instruments of the highest grade, which resolution has been admirably sustained. Added to this, they have been particularly favorable to new improvements, and have always encouraged original experiments in all departments of piano structure. Such firms are the life and pulse of the piano trade. They walk over old hobbies, stir up the dormant energies of antiquated piano-makers, and bring into the atmosphere of the business a spirit of progressiveness that can never fail to be productive of good to art and commercial life.

The practical success of this firm within such a short space of time is almost unparalleled, save in the case of Steinway & Sons and Albert Weber, Sr. Beginning in 1881 necessarily, like all young concerns, with no knowledge of what the future would bring forth, only a sincere reliance on the intelligence and discrimination of the musical public to appreciate the merits of their excellent pianos, they began to manufacture. The success of Behr Brothers is, indeed, a tribute to the intelligence of the people in a large degree, as in this exceedingly utilitarian end of the nineteenth century it takes perseverance and business genius of a high order, in addition to producing instruments of high excellence, to compete successfully with old-established houses in the piano business.

Behr Brothers & Co. have brought forward many innovations in their instruments from time to time since 1881 of a practical nature well known to the profession and the musical press, and all of distinct value. In 1889 their "hammer compensating lever" in grand actions was first produced, for which Patent No. 404,704 was granted on June 4th. This is specially illustrated in one of these pages, and is one of the most noteworthy of modern improvements in grand piano actions. Power and prompt repetition, combined with the least possible expenditure of force at the finger-tips, is considered the desideratum in a piano action and keyboard, and this is what piano manufacturers have been for years aiming at. Behr Brothers & Co. now claim to have reached a height of perfection never before attained in touch and promptness in grand actions by their new " hammer compensating lever." The principal objection, ordinarily, to lightness of touch is the weight of the hammers, which the jacks lift up to throw against the strings. Diminish the weight of the hammers by cutting them, and the power of the blow is sacrificed. Now, without diminishing the power of the hammers by trimming down the heads or resorting to any such expedient, Behr Brothers & Co. have secured the desired ease of touch—and promptness without losing power—by their patented device shown in the drawing reproduced elsewhere. To quote the specification : " This invention is

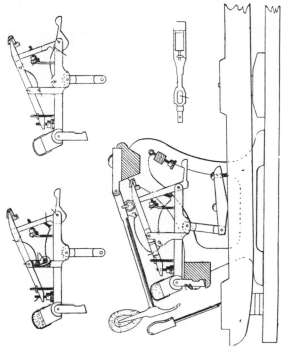

WESSELL, NICKEL & GROSS' IMPROVED GRAND ACTION

Patented July 12, 1887.

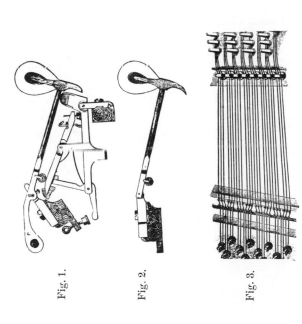

Fig. 1.

Fig. 2.

Fig. 3.

FIG. 1.—BEHR BROTHERS' GRAND PIANO HAMMER WITH COMPENSATING LEVER.

FIG. 2.—ORDINARY HAMMER AND BUTT.

FIG. 3.—BEHR BROTHERS' "STRINGING DEVICE."

All Patented.

designed to overcome the defects mentioned by counter-
balancing the weight of the hammer head by means of a
balancing device applied to the hammer butt, and the
invention consists of a grand piano action in which the
butt of a hammer is extended beyond the pivot and provided with an enlarged eye filled with lead for counter-
balancing the felt head, whereby the heaviest bass hammer can be operated just as easily as the light hammers
in the treble.'' Of course the counterweight is graduated from end to end, so as to offset the weight of the
hammer in front.

One of the first grands with the new action improvement was heard at the New York State Music Teachers'
Convention in Hudson, N. Y., in June, 1889, and, in
conjunction with its tone characteristics, created a decided *furor* among the large gathering of predistinguished
critics present. From among a group of complimentary
musical press notices of this event I select that of the
American Art Journal, which says of this instrument :
'' The new Behr grand is much lighter in its action than it
has hitherto been thought possible to achieve in a piano,
yet the tone is neither shallow, wooden, nor metallic.
Without exertion of power the tone comes pure, limpid,
and wonderfully sweet, with a generous amount of elasticity that renders it prolonged in quality, while the
slightest increase in the power of the pressure upon the
note develops a resonance that seems to broaden the
tone to a superb extent.'' This flattering analysis, combined with numerous other press notices, in addition to
the informal verdict of a large gathering of professional
musicians who tried the new action, must be a source
of some gratification to Behr Brothers & Co.

The foregoing innovation was followed by their new
" Stringing Device," for which Patent No. 416,458 was
issued on December 3d, 1889.   This is also illustrated.
In exemplification I will give the specification in part :
" The object of this invention is to obviate the objections
stated to the present method of stringing pianos, and to
remove the injurious pressure exerted by the strings on
the sounding-board.   The invention consists in stringing
the sounding-board in such a manner that the strings of
one tone are bent in one direction around the straining
pins, while the adjoining strings are bent in the opposite
direction around the straining pins, so that the two groups
converge toward each other."

In Behr Brothers & Co.'s instruments, by this stringing system the sounding-board is relieved of all superfluous pressure, and its fibres are allowed freer scope
to vibrate, thus enhancing the power and quality of
the tone generally.   This result is owing to the fact
that one group of strings—or unison—acts as a counterpoise to the other section, as shown.   This invention has
drawn forth many warm eulogies from the musical press
and technical piano men.

Within a recent period Behr Brothers & Co. secured
the services of Mr. Siegfried Hansing, a well-known
learned authority on piano construction and its acoustics,
and author of the work, " The Pianoforte in Its Acoustic
Relations."   Mr. Hansing is an eminent specialist and
an experienced piano-maker.   He has been in this country since 1884, and is a native of Bückeburg, Germany,
where he was born on June 12th, 1842.   The house became a close corporation on January 1st, 1890, formed of
members of the old firm, with a paid-in capital stock of

four hundred and fifty thousand dollars. The incor-
porators are Mr. Henry Behr, Mr. Edward Behr, Mr.
Emil Hurtzig, Mr. Charles L. Burchard, and Mr. Siegfried Hansing.

Backed up by such an excellent reputation for commercial honor, progressiveness, and first-class instruments replete with valuable improvements—many of
which have not been treated of, owing to space—besides
a splendidly equipped manufactory stocked with the
best plant and all possible facilities for producing pianos
of the highest grade, in addition to ample capital and the
practical heads of Mr. Henry Behr and Mr. Edward Behr,
the firm of Behr Brothers & Co. are bound to rise still
higher in the sphere of the piano trade in the future.

Among the pianofortes that became known toward
1880 in New York as reputable instruments, the James &
Holmstrom piano is entitled to recognition. Mr. A. C.
James, who figures in reference to Albany in that section,
arrived in New York in 1871, under contract with Mr.
F. G. Smith, to superintend the manufacture of his instruments. In 1873 Mr. James formed a partnership
with Mr. Holmstrom, and started in business. Since
that year the James & Holmstrom instrument has come
to be known as a reliable piano in every sense. Like all
makers, they have a following of musical people that
place entire faith in their capability as piano manufacturers, and they do a uniform and satisfactory business.
Both are practical men, and personally much esteemed.

In 1875 Schnabel, Hintz & Lambert began business
at 136 Elm Street, the building in which Behning & Sons
originally started. This firm commenced, like all of the
large houses, on a modest capital, with the intention of

manufacturing only instruments of good grade. The practical member of this firm was Mr. Edmund Schnabel, a very expert and eminently qualified member of the craft. I find that their first pianos created a great deal of notice among musicians, owing to their excellence, having many features of originality introduced by Mr. Schnabel. Among the hundreds of concerns that came into being and then died out in the order of events during those years were many promising makers; but while it is impossible to give them space, an exception must be made in the foregoing instance.

Owing to some cause, Schnabel and Lambert dropped out, and began business in May in the following year as Schnabel & Lambert, the first named being the technical head. They made quite a name in a comparatively short period, and were in business for some years, until through some financial mismanagement they dissolved, meantime honorably settling all debts. In the pianos produced by Schnabel & Lambert, Mr. Schnabel introduced several excellent "scales" that are very significant. In his "overstringing" almost perfect uniformity was reached throughout, and "frogs" and "breaks" were not noticeable under the closest inspection. Mr. Schnabel's knowledge of acoustics and fine musical perceptions of sound and *timbre* assisted him in these results. Aside from the foregoing, many novelties were introduced in case structure and other mechanical departments that have recently been introduced as new in the trade. In 1877 he accepted a position with Wheelock & Company, and has been with them since that year.

Mr. Schnabel was born in Zeitz, Germany, on November 14th, 1850, and comes of a musical and musical

instrument-making family, his father being a piano-
maker. Under the latter's care he studied the business,
and finished with Kahut, Schmitt & Bishop in his native
city. He arrived in New York in 1868, and worked subsequently in such shops as Marschall & Mittauer's, Behning's, and Lighte & Ernst's at various branches, being
thoroughly practical in all departments. He is a thoroughgoing piano-maker, of fine musical instincts and
superior intellectual qualifications, and although he has
not risen up to the height of many of his former compeers, who now rule large firms, his name deserves mention here as one of the "silent workers" in the great
army of piano-makers, whose skill has helped the development of the instrument. His qualifications meanwhile place him far above the mere rank and file of
foremen.

The distinguished house of Conover Brothers, consisting of J. Frank Conover and George H. Conover, was
established in 1870, as dealers in pianos and musical
merchandise, at Kansas City, Mo., and soon acquired a
wide reputation and a large business in high-grade instruments. Ten years later they began the manufacture
of pianos, the senior member returning to New York for
that purpose, while his brother conducted their Western
business. They retailed nearly all of their own production until 1885, when they began offering their pianos to
the trade. Their business grew rapidly, the pianos meeting with general appreciation, and established for themselves a great prestige in a surprisingly short period, so
that to-day the Conover Brothers' pianos are recognized
as a strong factor in the piano trade. In January, 1889,
they sold their Western business, and G. H. Conover

removed to New York to engage permanently with his brother in manufacturing.

Conover Brothers are of Holland extraction, and were born in Mount Morris, Livingston County, N. Y.—J. Frank on January 31st, 1843, and G. H. on June 20th, 1844.   Their father, Garret Conover, believed in giving his boys a practical education more adapted to their bent than farming ; therefore George was sent to Oberlin College, and Frank, possessing a natural talent for music, was thoroughly educated for the musical profession, under the tutorage of a German master named Nothnagel.   Yet his father was anxious that he should prepare himself for the more promising occupation of merchant or manufacturer, and finally arranged with the late Mr. Albeit Weber to personally train him in the art of piano-making. Educated as a musician, skilled as a mechanic, and with an experience as a dealer in handling high-class pianos, Mr. J. Frank Conover is an unusually well-equipped member of the piano trade.

Mr. J. Frank Conover having turned his attention to the improvement of the instruments of the firm with which he is identified, the result was that the general excellence of the Conover piano began to win high encomiums from the musical profession and press.   Their wholesale business grew, and their name became known widely in New York.   Meanwhile, Mr. J. Frank Conover had practically drawn every scale and prepared every pattern and model used in producing the first instruments, which function he fills to-day, in addition to being an inventor of an uncommon type.

It is only ten years ago since Conover Brothers established a manufactory in New York, and within this period they have won popularity and are an aggressive and progressive element in the realm of piano-making.

Within a recent period they have introduced many new improvements in the acoustics and mechanical departments of their instruments, and have developed to a high point of efficacy in this connection a new method of stringing and "scaling," by which they claim to have accomplished a positive reform in overstringing besides improving piano tone quality. I may point out the fact that for many years European makers have hesitated to accept overstringing very generally, owing to the break in tone quality or *timbre* between the under and overstrung sections of the scale, but to all appearances it seems as if the new Conover method of stringing and acoustics illustrated in their upright grand scale on another page is the "missing link" in this respect. The cut given exemplifies the Conover Brothers ingenious "duplex bridge with auxiliary vibrators," for which several patents have been taken out from 1878 up to 1884. These improvements are applied in their grand scale, for the purpose indicated. Messrs. Conover Brothers on request have written to explain the object of these innovations from their standpoint. They say: "Our object is to harmonize the quality of tone in the scale where the steel strings and the wrapped or bass strings meet, which is technically called the transition of the scale. The duplex bridge and auxiliary vibrators adjusted at the end of the understrung and overstrung sections illustrated in the drawings accomplish this result by qualifying and giving to the two sections referred to a uniform quality, aside from giving greater elasticity and vibratory power to the sounding-board. The result is a powerful though refined tone of a charming singing quality." Debain, of Paris, and Pleyel, I may point out, sought to reach this point of uniformity years ago in overstrung scales by tone deflectors placed in proximity to the bass section, so as to refract the sound waves of the bass strings into an approximate line with the underlying section ; but the result was failure in both cases, for the reason that the " cups" used for the purpose imparted to the bass strings a new *timbre* and character.

It has evidently been reserved for Mr. J. Frank Conover to accomplish what so many eminent thinkers and manufacturers have been striving to attain for many years.

For more than two years they have been testing an original method of stringing by the use of a "hollow steel tuning pin." This is shown in two sectional drawings elsewhere. The Conover hollow steel tuning-pin is a hollow pin made so as to fit closely on a stud, the latter being cast permanently in the plate, which is rigidly adjusted on the wrest-plank throughout. The pin has a slot in its side through which the string is carried, and when placed on the stud, and tightened by means of the tuning-hammer, an unyielding and firm grip is given to the pin, both the stud and pin producing this result by frictional sympathy. The effect is, however, apparent to practical readers. While the scheme is plausible, Conover Brothers will not adopt it for general use until they have proved beyond question

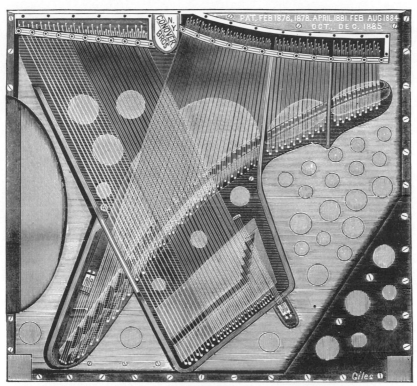

CONOVER BROTHERS' UPRIGHT SCALE, WITH DUPLEX BRIDGES AND AUXILIARY VIBRATORS.

Patented.

Fig. 1. Fig. 2. Fig. 3.

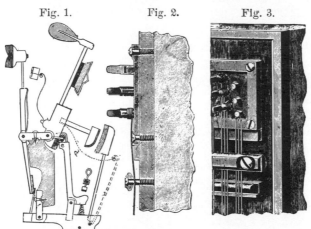

FIG. 1.—CONOVER BROTHERS' REPEATING ACTION. FIGS. 2 AND 3.—CONOVER BROTHERS HOLLOW STEEL TUNING PINS AND STUD PLATE.

Patented.

by actual test whether it is an improvement in every sense, and superior to the general method, so as to warrant the extra cost of its adoption. In this respect they are a conservative firm.

The Conover upright action is yet another specialty that this firm take particular pride in pointing to. Their improvement here consists—as shown in the drawing given—of a small hook centred on the top of the jack. To use Conovers Brothers' language in exemplification. " The improvement consists in removing from the cus· tomary French action the slender tapes and wires to which they are attached and substituting for their use a permanent metal hook centred in the top of the jack, which catches in the slot of the butt and keeps the jack in close proximity to the knuckle, modifying the touch and adding durability to the action.''

Other patented specialities in use in those excellent instruments are a " telescopic lamp bracket'' adjusted on the right-hand end of the piano, which is a most ingenious and useful appliance; also an " automatic music desk,'' which has many admirable characteristics above those in general use. Their " metallic action rail '' is another patented improvement for securing rigidity and precision to the position of the action in connection with the plate and back. The advantages of the foregoing improvements can be easily estimated, and need no detailed explanation.

This progressive house was organized as a stock company under the laws of the State of New York in 1887, and has a large financial backing, with which it intends to promote the name and fortunes of the business in an aggressive manner throughout. It has emphatically

shown in a few years, by experiment and technical endeavor, a desire to add to the development of the piano,
rather than sit still and be content with accepted principles.   In this respect Conover Brothers are entitled to
due recognition.

CHAPTER XXII.

New York.

MODERN MAKERS—THE "ESTEY" PIANOFORTE—KRAKAUER
BROTHERS—WHEELOCK & COMPANY—KROEGER & SONS—
PAUL G. MEHLIN & SONS—HIS INVENTIONS.

AMONG the pianofortes that became known as reputable instruments toward 1876, in addition to those enumerated, may be mentioned the "Arion" piano. This instrument subsequently became extinct, but in its place the Simpson & Company piano appeared, which has since become known as the "Estey," a very excellent instrument, and manufactured under the competent supervision of Mr. Stephen Brambach. The Estey Piano Company was formed in 1885, and succeeded to the plant and interest of the Simpson Piano Company.

Much of the technical and musical merit of these pianos is due to the competency and skill of Mr. Brambach, who is a gentleman of fine musical and mechanical sensibilities, a member of a musical family, the celebrated German composer of that name being his brother, while he himself is one of the best tuners in New York, in which capacity he originally held a leading place in the chief shops in the city. He originates all new ideas in the mechanics and acoustics of the Estey piano, being entirely practical, as remarked. His patents are given in tabulated form elsewhere, and are all devoted to the service of the Estey instrument.

The name of Estey is well known in American musical history in relation to the promotion of the reed organ. Mr. Julius Estey, of the Estey Piano Company, is a son of Mr. Jacob Estey, the well-known organ specialist and manufacturer, and has received a careful training in the commercial and practical spheres of the business in Brattleboro', Vt. The other principals in the Estey Piano Company are Mr. R. Proddow and Mr. J. B. Simpson. In relation to the retail warerooms, Mr. George Whyte occupies the position of salesman, and is a respected member of the trade. In the manufacturing department of the business they are lucky in having in their employ for several years past Mr. Carl Brambach, brother of Mr. Stephen Brambach, one of the most expert and artistic tuners and toners in the country, whose fine perceptions of tone and acute artistic susceptibilities, professionally, have also done much to elevate the tone character of the Estey pianoforte.

Krakauer Brothers, known at present as manufacturers of popular-priced instruments of very excellent character, appeared on Union Square in 1878. Mr. David Krakauer, the practical member of the firm, learned piano-making in this city at Kind & Grube's, and subsequently worked in many of the leading shops. At twenty-one he began business in a modest manner as a small maker, and meanwhile opened a musical instrument store at the upper end of the Bowery. He was joined in partnership by his brothers, David and Daniel, in 1878,

when they leased a small factory and opened retail
warerooms on Union Square.

Their business has since grown to respectable proportions, and they have built an entirely honorable reputation as courteous business men. Mr. Simon Krakauer,
the father of Krakauer Brothers, was at one time a musical artist and teacher of some note. He arrived in New
York in 1853 with his family from his native country,
Germany, and became known as a teacher of music subsequently. Krakauer Brothers are all musical, especially Mr. Daniel Krakauer, who is an accomplished
pianist. Their instrument, for its grade and price, is
very reliable in most respects.

About 1878 the Peek & Son, known in later years
as the makers of the "opera" piano, loomed up as a
good popular-priced instrument, with a large circulation.
Since then the output of Messrs. Peek & Sons, the manufacturers of these pianos, has grown to large proportions.
The origin of the Peek piano dates back to 1851, when
Mr. Peek, the senior member of the firm, a practical
piano-maker, began business in an unpretentious manner.
Since 1878 the present firm has evidently progressed
commercially, and despite the enormous competition existing in their sphere of the trade at this period, they hold
a very respectable place.

Billings & Tremaine, a well-known firm, commanded
a large wholesale business about 1875 as manufacturers
of pianofortes. Mr. W. B. Tremaine, of this connection,
at present holding a leading position in the Æolian Organ Company, was responsible for much of the success
that fell to the lot of this company, being an expert piano
salesman, and a business man of large experience.

This well-known member of the trade is very versatile, and has in more recent years busied himself with improvements in reed organs.   He is also a man of musical attainments.   Mr. Tremaine separated from Billings about 1876, when Billings & Company appeared.   The Billings & Company piano existed up to 1886 as a popular-priced instrument, and was for a long time largely sold.

Rogers & Borst were known in the wholesale trade for several years as manufacturers of reliable instruments previous to 1877.   This was composed of Mr. Philip Rogers and Mr. Charles Borst, the latter being the practical partner.   Mr. Borst at present and since 1877 superintendent of Wheelock & Company is a very progressive piano-maker, and practical in the general sense, being a scale-drawer and inventor in addition to his other acquirements.   Rogers & Borst dissolved in the year 1877.

Francis Conner, whose entry in the sphere of the American piano trade dates back to 1871, had achieved an honorable reputation as early as 1878 as a manufacturer of excellent instruments sold at prices within the reach of the people.   Mr. Conner is a skilful, practical tuner and toner, is equally conversant with all the details of piano structure, and personally superintends every instrument constructed in his factory, and sees that it leaves his shop in the most perfect manner possible. Mr. Conner started out in a modest manner, and by careful and conscientious endeavor, backed by practical knowledge and skill, he has risen to be a large and reputable maker.   His instruments are put forward with no pretensions as to being " the best in the world," but from a price standpoint they are equal to any piano of their grade before the musical public. It may not be amiss to point out that Mr. Conner's business career has been remarkable for fair dealing and uprightness. Recognition of these qualities cannot be out of place in this sketch. Toward the middle of the present year Mr. Conner will move into a more commodious factory from his present quarters in East Forty-first Street. In order to increase the prestige of his pianos in New York, Mr. Conner has leased large warerooms at 4 East Forty-second Street. His business hitherto has been principally wholesale.

William E. Wheelock & Company deserve a large share of recognition as a highly honorable firm devoted to the production of reputable instruments. In 1877 William E. Wheelock & Company began manufacturing on West Twenty-fourth Street, the factory being under the supervision of Mr. Charles Borst. The business almost immediately grew to large proportions, thanks to the executive genius of Mr. Wheelock, who is a gifted young business man and financier, until they were compelled to look around for more room. In 1880 they moved to the building formerly occupied by the " Arion" Company, on East One Hundred and Forty-ninth Street and Third Avenue, Harlem. This building was inadequate, and they immediately erected their present factory, which is one of the best-equipped shops in the country. Within recent years this has been extended still further, and additional extensions are in progress, owing to the rapid increase in their output. Mr. William E. Wheelock, the head of this progressive firm, is a native of New York, his father being Mr. A. M. Wheelock, an eminent and highly respected citizen of Brooklyn, who for years has been the treasurer of the city funds. He received a first-class education and an excellent commercial training previous to becoming identified with the piano business. Those traits of sterling commercial honesty and moral uprightness for which Wheelock & Company have been always distinguished as a business firm are part and parcel of the individuality of the head of the firm, W. E. Wheelock. Competitors all concede this fact aside from business rivalry. Mr. Wheelock has inherited these traits from worthy American forefathers. The name of Charles B. Lawson has an important bearing on this historical sketch. Mr. Lawson is an active partner in the business, and complete reciprocity exists and has always existed between him and Mr. W. E. Wheelock as to the government and policy of the firm since his entrance into the company in 1880. Mr. Lawson is a native of Brooklyn. He received a good education in early life, and after some preliminary mercantile experience went into Wheelock & Company as a confidential bookkeeper, when they began business. He became rapidly conversant with the details of the business, and having a scientific and mechanical bent of mind, acquired an incidental knowledge of various departments of piano structure, and practically learned several to a degree sufficient to be able to judge efficient work from bad work. He has a strong mathematical mind equally, and can calculate with perfect ease every exacting detail familiar to a large piano manufacturer. Wheelock & Company have introduced several improvements which have never been protected by patent, and they are always in line with new progressions. Their instruments hold a very high place in some cities throughout the States, and in territories where pushing agents sell them they command high musical patronage, for much of this success out of New York is due to the efforts and character of agents. In speaking of this firm, I cannot help alluding to their conduct toward their employés, which is characterized by liberality and an American spirit of good-will that always deserves recognition in a material age like ours.

Wheelock & Company have maintained large retail warerooms in New York for over six years, where they have built up an extensive business. Much of their success in this department is due to the ability of Mr. William D. Lazelle, who has been in charge of this branch for over five years, during which period he has built up a large and steadily increasing patronage. On January 1st, 1890, he was admitted as a partner in the retail department. This clever specialist is a native of Brooklyn. He has been brought up from an early period in the retail trade, and has a large reputation in his professional sphere and is highly esteemed in private circles. In connection with the retail warerooms of Wheelock & Company, the name of Mr. E. O. Vidand has a place. This gentleman, up to his death in 1888, had been connected with the business for several years. During his relationship with this department his sturdy sense of fair-dealing, high-bred ideas of business discipline, and courteous attention to the patrons of the house won the retail business of Wheelock & Company in New York many friends. In addition to a New York retail branch they maintain a Chicago warerooms which has been equally a success, and are altogether a truly successful modern firm.

The firm of Henry Kroeger & Sons, composed of the first named, together with Mr. Otto Kroeger and Mr. Henry Kroeger, Jr., became known to the musical public in 1879.   Mr. Kroeger is a practical piano-maker, inventor, and acoustician of eminent and varied experience. His start in piano manufacturing on his own account was conceived and designed with but one fixed ambition, and that was to manufacture only the highest possible grade pianos.   This commendable ambition still rules dominant in Kroeger & Sons.

Mr. Henry Kroeger, Sr., is a native of Germany, where he was born in 1827.   At fifteen he was apprenticed to a leading manufacturer of Hamburg, with whom he finished out his time.   He displayed early ability as a piano-maker, and subsequently after his apprentice days, between 1847 and 1855, worked in many of the leading factories in Hamburg.   In 1855 he arrived at New York, and in time became employed in the factory of Steinway & Sons.   His skill was soon noted by the house, and he was promoted to a very important position in their employ.

There remains very little to be said about the "Kroeger" piano, only that it is in the very front rank, made of the best materials, constructed by excellent workmen, and especially supervised by Mr. H. Kroeger and H. Kroeger, Jr., who is also practical and devoted to the interests of the factory department.   The "Kroeger" piano has very few patented improvements, a fact conceded by Mr. Kroeger, Sr.   Kroeger & Sons' principal patent relates to a Capo d'Astro bar issued in 1886, also an acoustic patent taken out in 1884 for a method of sounding-board adjustment.

The growth of the business of this young firm has been very uniform and steady. They moved into their present factory and warerooms on Second Avenue and Twenty-first Street, owing to want of facilities elsewhere, about two years ago, and they seem destined to become a standard house. Mr. Otto Kroeger, who attends to the retail and commercial interests of the house, is specially singled out for eulogy by persons acquainted with the firm, and much of the success of Kroeger & Sons, in a commercial sense, is credited to his ability and courtesy. This member is also practically conversant with piano building, and taken throughout, the personal capacities of the members are well calculated to ensure success to all concerned.

Coming down to 1884, among the first makers that started in New York in this year were Newby & Evans. In October they began manufacturing. The firm is composed of Mr. Alfred J. Newby and Mr. John Evans. The former is the practical partner. Mr. Newby is a well-known piano-maker. He served his time to Mr. Peter Mixell, his brother-in-law, an old time Albany and later a New York maker. He, too, is a native of Albany, and has charge of this department. Mr. John Evans, the intellectual and business partner, to whose ability so much of their success is due, is a native of Wales, where he was born in 1846. He is a member of good Welsh stock, a race that has given America many of its best citizens, and acquired a first-class education in early life. He first entered the banking business, and for five years held a position in the National Provincial Bank of England, an institution very difficult to get a footing in, and only open to members of good families. He arrived in

New York in 1868, and with his scholastic acquirements and cultivated tastes turned toward journalism. In this department of activity he was successful, both as a writer and publisher. He became connected with Mr. Newby in 1884 with the result intimated. Their quick rise into eminence as makers of reputable instruments sold at popular prices may be judged from the fact that, in 1888, they erected a factory with a capacity of forty instruments per week on One Hundred and Thirty-sixth Street and the Southern Boulevard, and are not yet satisfied with building space.

Mehlin & Sons are entitled to serious notice as a modern firm of only a few years growth. Probably Mr. Paul G. Mehlin, head of Mehlin & Sons, the youngest firm treated at length in these pages, may be ranked among the revolutionistic and progressive piano-makers of our time. He is not one of those pessimists who believe that the "excelsior" notch has already been reached and passed in the making of pianos, those people who give us no hope of further progression in the technical and acoustic regions of the "household orchestra." On the contrary, he thinks, and thinks wisely, too, that there is yet plenty of room for the improver—not for the rule-of-thumb improver and experimentalist, but for those duly qualified by scientific, acoustic, and practical knowledge as piano-makers, backed up by cultivated musical sensibilities, so as to enable them to judge tone results from the standpoint of acoustics and that of the cultivated artist.

Mr. Paul G. Mehlin, like so many of our greatest piano-makers and American art pioneers, is a native of Germany. He was born in Stuttgart on February 28th,

1837. His first mechanical experience was acquired in a first-class cabinet-making establishment in his native city, where art furniture of the finest kind was made a specialty of. Here he served a short apprentice course, which experience has since been invaluable. Having in the background keen musical susceptibilities, he learned to play the piano in the mean time, and later on drifted into the piano shop of Frederick Doerner in Stuttgart, where he went through the regulation education of an old-time piano-maker, from case-making up to expert regulating and toning. Here he studied the first principles of acoustics, as exemplified in piano " scaling" and general tone improvement. Mr. Mehlin arrived in New York in 1854 and entered the establishment of Raven & Bacon, where he whetted and improved his former experience, meantime spending a considerable period in this shop, then celebrated, as I have shown elsewhere. Later he was with Lighte & Bradbury, an equally prominent concern. Mr. Mehlin evidently has other national traits aside from skill in piano-making and the concomitant arts, for we find him in the honorable rôle of soldier-patriot in 1861, at the opening of the Civil War. At this period he gallantly became one of the Twentieth New York Infantry, known as the " Turner Regiment," having volunteered in answer to Lincoln's call for seventy-five thousand men. In two years he came back with the rank of first lieutenant, and now musters among the " veterans" of the craft. The war being over, Mr. Mehlin again turned his mind to peaceful pursuits and entered his old calling. In 1865 he took a position with the Gablers and remained here for sixteen years, during which period he contributed many of his characteristic innovations to these instruments. Not having scope enough for his individuality as an improver in this house, he, in 1881, became partner in a reputable firm that had just started out to manufacture pianofortes, and were earnestly seeking some one who could combine originality and individuality in their instruments.

Two years ago Mr. Mehlin decided upon starting in business for himself, and in conjunction with Mr. H. Paul Mehlin, his eldest son, he formed P. G. Mehlin & Sons.

Mr. Mehlin is an indefatigable inventor. His principal patents are No. 129,727, a metallic agraffe cast in the plate, July 23d, 1872 ; metallic action frame in one piece, No. 190,306, May 1st, 1877 ; Bessemer steel action frame, No. 252,370, January 17th, 1882 ; wrest-block bridge, No. 254,209, February 28th, 1882 ; cylinder top, No. 286,425, October 9th, 1883 ; key-rail finger guard, No. 295,383, March 18th, 1884 ; harmonic scale, No. 311,243, January 27th, 1885 ; mute-bar damper, No. 353,301, November 30th, 1886 ; touch regulator, No 356,759, February 1st, 1889 ; tone reflector, No. 397,121, February 5th, 1889 ; grand fall board, No. 397,121, February 5th, 1889 ; grand scale plate for uprights and grands, No. 403 583, May 21st, 1889.

Out of this formidable list I have selected for illustration Mr. Mehlin's grand scale plate, together with his harmonic scale and touch regulator. The first named is a very clever innovation in upright piano development in a composite sense necessarily, because Mr. Mehlin's system of plate structure and general "scaling" conditions cover a wide territory in mechanics and acoustics. This grand plate scale shown is intended to give the uprights to which it is applied all the characteristics of the horizontal grand, with the advantage of being put into the convenient space of the former. Mr. Mehlin's harmonic scale has an auxiliary fourth string to each three-string unison, as represented in the drawing, damped separately by an ingenious damper action. This string passes over the belly-bridge in the usual manner, and then through an agraffe fixed rigidly in the sounding-board and secured behind by means of a screw nut. The agraffe is so adjusted as to bear down upon the centre of the string, thus dividing its vibratory surface into two halves, so that, for instance, the same length of string tightened to the exact tension of the regular strings in the same group would produce two tones an octave each above the former. This fourth string is intended for harmonic reverberation, each giving forth sound-waves in sympathy with the unison to which it is affixed. The increase in the power and *sustenuto* possibilities of the piano is therefore considerably enhanced, not only in single tones necessarily but throughout, according to principles easily understood. Not only does the latter claim musical results such as I have shown in connection with this scale system, but the additional string, moreover, has a tendency to brace the sounding-board, and thus act as a counterpoise to the pressure of the other strings on the belly-bridge. The principle theoretically has been known for centuries, and is an accepted problem in acoustics. It has been often tried in piano development, which makes Mr. Mehlin's clever application of the thing doubly noteworthy. Of the harmonic scale the *American Art Journal* wrote on May 2d, 1885 : " The harmonic scale has for several years been used by certain manufacturers of grands, but until

Mr. Mehlin invented a method of applying a fourth string and of tuning it so as to cause it to vibrate in sympathy with the regulation strings, it was considered impracticable to use the harmonic principle in upright pianos.   Mr. Mehlin, however, has accomplished this in a very simple and practical manner, and secured for the upright a beautiful sympathetic and singing tone, with an increase of quality as well as power.''

The utilitarian value of Mr. Mehlin's touch regulator is incalculable almost to tuners or regulators, being a simple device, as exemplified, for regulating the position of the key-frame independent of the sinking of the key-board, so as to attain correct touch without resorting to the usual expedients, which consume much time.

Mr. H. Paul Mehlin, Mr. Mehlin's oldest son and partner, is also practical, and in addition has gone through an arduous commercial course, and is eminently equipped to enter upon the duties he now fulfils.   In addition he has personal qualities, aside from the degree they influence success, which has made him very popular in private and in business circles.   Mr. Charles H. Mehlin, the second son of the clever piano-maker under notice, is also trained from the two standpoints shown, having studied piano-making in Stuttgart, Germany, for some time in conjunction with music and acoustics, and is therefore equally well equipped to enter upon a piano-making career.

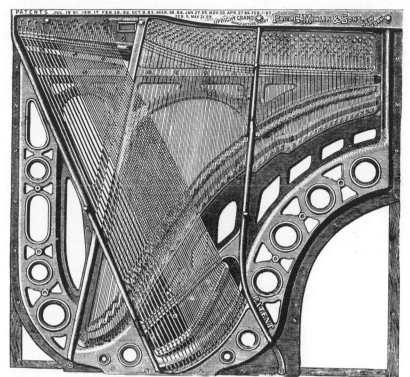

P. G. MEHLIN & SON'S GRAND PLATE AND SCALE FOR UPRIGHTS. *Patented May 25, 1889.*

P. G. MEHLIN & SON'S HARMONIC SCALE. *Patented January 27, 1885.*

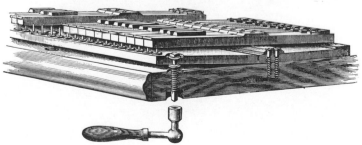

P. G. MEHLIN & SON'S TOUCH REGULATOR. *Patented February 1, 1887.*

CHAPTER XXIII.

Miscellaneous Firms.

KNABE & COMPANY FROM THE MODERN STANDPOINT—
HARDMAN, PECK & COMPANY—IVERS & POND, BOSTON—
THE SMITH AMERICAN PIANO COMPANY—THE STERLING
COMPANY—MASON & HAMLIN—CHICAGO—RANDOM NOTES.

THE house of Knabe & Company is one of the oldest
firms in the United States, with a high standing as manufacturers of first-class pianofortes, and I need not add, an
untarnished record.   It has necessarily a modern history
that calls for recognition in that form.   The standard
and uniform success enjoyed by Knabe & Company for
the past fifty years has been marked with little or
no personal events that call for reference beyond those
enumerated elsewhere.   They have been consistent
throughout that period in maintaining their business
upon a high plane, while their instruments have been
associated with musical art and artists of the best type
throughout.   They have kept in the front rank from the
first, which is yet more significant when the age of the
house is considered.

For over twenty-five years they have been known
prominently in New York business life, where they secured a firm footing after 1865.

The extensive warerooms on Fifth Avenue from which they recently moved were occupied by them since 1873, and with their progress in the metropolis must be mentioned the name of Mr. Herman F. Keidel. The latter was a brother of Mr. Charles Keidel of the firm, and was manager of the Knabe & Company warerooms and large retail trade in New York for many years. His decease, which occurred on February 17th, 1889, at the age of forty-two, under peculiarly sad circumstances, was much regretted, and through his death the house lost a faithful assistant. While it is admissible and proper to encourage young firms that cultivate high aims in their instruments and business conduct by mention and detailed reference to their pianofortes, the Knabe instruments need no specific introduction to readers or members of the pianoforte business. It would also be out of keeping with the character of the work to give a detailed account of the large number of medals, premiums, diplomas, and other honors bestowed upon these instruments beyond a generalized reference.

Among the honors that have fallen to the lot of Knabe & Company in recent years must be mentioned the fact that in 1879 they were selected, as an American firm producing instruments of national excellence, to supply the Japanese Government with a large number of pianofortes —squares and uprights—for use in the public schools in that country. These were the first instruments ever purchased by the Japanese Government, and it is a matter of some consequence in musical history to know that, though England and other European countries supply Japan with most goods usually, the United States was chosen by the Government of that highly-civilized Eastern nation as the place to buy its first pianos. The relation this fact bears to Knabe & Company is also noteworthy. Coming down to 1889, the prestige of the Knabe piano received a decided stimulus from the flattering patronage bestowed upon it by the celebrated conductor and virtuoso, Von Bülow, who used it in his tour throughout this Continent. The publicity and honor accruing from such a significant event it need scarcely be said is a matter of some consequence in the business history of the firm, and must result in great benefit in the future to their interests. The present factories of Knabe & Company, in Baltimore, are among the largest and finest of their kind in the world. Their buildings are situated near the outer section of West and Eutaw streets. The main buildings are 210 feet long on Eutaw Street by 165 feet on West Street, to which are added a building 110 feet long and two wings 40 by 50 feet. A boiler-house 60 by 40 feet may be included in the foregoing. The annex on the opposite side of Eutaw Street is 165 feet long on West Street by 50 feet on Eutaw Street, with a boiler-house 40 by 50 feet. The whole premises, including lumber yards, cover over three acres. The buildings are lighted throughout principally by Edison's incandescent light. Here Knabe & Company manufacture all sections of their pianos—in many cases utilizing special machinery—and employ a large number of skilled department foremen and an army of competent hands. They practically control and manage three warerooms : one in New York, another at 817 Pennsylvania Avenue, Washington, and a third at 22 and 24 East Baltimore Street, Baltimore. In the industrial and art history of the " Monumental City" Knabe &

Company occupy a pre-eminent place, and all Baltimoreans recognize the fact. Readers can mentally contrast the very early days of Baltimore, when Harper, Stewart and Hiskey controlled the trade of the city and the
Southern States, with the present aspect of piano manufacturing there. Certainly the study is fraught with historical interest, and in a book of this character, where
the history of the pianoforte business is treated in detail,
the present standing of Knabe & Company, their immense factory, improved facilities, and all other phases
of their modern status stand out in singular contrast
with the first days of pianoforte-making in Baltimore, as
sketched in a previous section, and completes a prominent chapter in the history of that city, where the name
of William Knabe is entitled to an honored place.

The name of Horace Waters has been before the musical public for over forty years in connection with music
publishing and the retail pianoforte business. At present Horace Waters & Company, of which Mr. Waters is
the principal, are manufacturing pianofortes, and have
been engaged in the business since 1880. Hitherto a lack
of enterprise in advertising and following out progressive business methods in relation to the wholesale department has resulted to their disadvantage. They
control a large retail business, however, in New York.
Mr. T. Leeds Waters, son of Mr. Horace Waters, at present associated with the firm, is a progressive and able
member of the house, and has contributed much to the
business success of the firm. Mr. Horace Waters, in addition to being one of the old-time men connected with the
music trade, enjoys a wide reputation as a temperance
advocate and political reformer.

Mr. Horace Waters, Jr., at present retired, was for some years connected with his father's business. He is a cultivated musician and a gentleman of many estimable traits of character, and is acquainted with all details of piano manufacturing and music publishing, in addition to possessing artistic perceptions of a high order.

The firm of Hardman, Peck & Company dates its existence back to 1842, in which year Mr. Hugh Hardman, at present living, began to manufacture the "Hardman" pianoforte in New York. Passing through many subsequent changes, Mr. Hardman's business went into the hands of Hardman, Dowling & Peck within recent years, when the instruments bearing this name received a new artistic character and standing. Subsequently, Hardman, Peck & Company appeared, the two principals being Mr. John Hardman, son of the founder, and Mr. Leopold Peck. Meanwhile Mr. Hugh Hardman retired from business. Within the past ten years the "Hardman" pianoforte has risen into high favor throughout the States. When Mr. Peck was taken into the firm a new stimulus was given to the commercial fortunes of the business. The latter is a shrewd and aggressive member of the piano trade. The association of the "Hardman" piano during the past five years with music in New York, and the opening of the firm's warerooms on Fifth Avenue, which is fitted up in an elegant and tasteful manner befitting the æsthetic character of the piano business, is ascribed to Mr. Peck's personal judgment and good taste.

Mr. John Hardman died on November 10th, 1889, aged forty-six years. The firm name still remains unchanged. Mr. Hardman was an extremely popular member of the house. He was an excellent tuner and a practical piano-maker all through, as well as an inventor. Many patented improvements used in the " Hardman" piano at this period were originated by the latter, and during recent years he made commendable efforts, in connection with the practical side of the business, to elevate the general character of the instrument. Among the patented improvements used by Hardman, Peck & Company are their " key frame support" and " harp stop."

Mr. S. La Grassa, who has for several years been in charge of their factory, has also introduced many little points of improvement in the " Hardman" piano from time to time, and is an inventor and patentee of some importance. In connection with the retail wareroom department, Mr. W. H. Dutton has been prominent in promoting the firm's success. The latter has also taken out several patents for piano improvements.

Hardman, Peck & Company have a splendidly appointed manufactory, which covers a large area, extending over a block, from Forty-eighth to Forty-ninth streets, also from Eleventh to Twelfth avenues, in New York.

Mr. Peter Duffy, a practical piano-maker of some originality and force of character, began business in 1880 in New York, and soon became known as a maker of good popular-priced pianos. Recently, however, he changed the title of his business to the firm name, the Schubert Piano Company, of which he is principal. The instruments bearing this name are meritorious for their price and character.

Dusinberre & Company is a comparatively new concern. It came into existence in 1884, and is made up entirely of practical workmen of experience and skill. Mr. F. L. Dusinberre, the head of the business, is a graduate of Haines Brothers' shop. He was born in Bradford, N. Y., in 1846, and entered Haines Brothers' employ in 1863 Since that time he has acquired a large and varied experience, and is a thoroughgoing piano-maker in addition to possessing native American business ability. Mr. R. E. Small, Mr. Dusinberre's partner, is a New Yorker, and a practical man also. He attends to the business of superintending the factory and its necessities. Dusinberre & Company only manufacture uprights, and their instruments are, from a price standpoint, excellent and well made in every respect.

The Stuyvesant Piano Company was formed in 1884 for the purpose of making instruments of a grade and price adaptable to popular requirements. Among a number of other New York makers known at present are Weser Brothers, Cable & Son, C. H. Henning, Kohler, Pollock & Company, Harrington & Company, and others.

The Braumueler Piano Company has a recent origin. In connection with this concern Λ. H. Hastings, superintendent, a very clever piano-maker and inventor, may be spoken of. The latter learned the business in Albany many years ago, and subsequently became a tuner, in which capacity and as a dealer he travelled all over South and North America and Cuba. He later came to New York and spent several years in Raven & Bacon's, and another period in Chickering & Sons' New York house as tuner and tone regulator. Mr. Hastings is a prolific inventor. Many of his patents are given in index form among others elsewhere. At present he is in charge of the Braumueler factory. For many years past he has been known extensively as a scale draughtsman and pattern-maker to the trade. Mr. Hastings was born in Malone, N. Y., in 1834, and comes of New England parentage. The historic Jonathan Hastings, through whom the expression "Brother Jonathan," applied in national parlance, originated, was a near ancestor of the clever pianomaker.

Augustus Baus & Company began to manufacture pianos in 1880, and enjoy a very excellent reputation as a courteous business house, and as makers of reputable and meritorious instruments. Up to a couple of years ago this firm was coming rapidly into notice in musical circles in New York and the East generally, but they encountered some business reverses, which resulted from entirely honorable causes familiar in the commercial sphere. They maintained a retail wareroom for several years in the metropolis, but were compelled, owing to causes intimated, to give up their retail department temporarily, and devote themselves to the wholesale trade. Meanwhile the former standard of their pianos has been well maintained, and they are fast regaining their old plane of popularity. Mr. Augustus Baus is a business man of no common order. He has been prominently identified with the firm's growth and fortunes, and is very popular in commercial and private circles. Mr. Baumeister is in charge of the practical department, and is in every respect a qualified superintendent. He is, in addition, a member of Baus & Company.

In relation to very modern houses outside of New York City, aside from those previously given, many well-known makers residing in various cities are referred to in the informal order assigned.

In 1872 William H. Ivers began to manufacture the present Ivers, Pond & Company pianoforte in Boston. In later years he was succeeded by Ivers, Pond & Company, Mr. Ivers meanwhile maintaining a leading interest in the business. The latter is a graduate of the Chickering & Sons factory in Boston, where he was employed for a number of years. Under his management the present "Ivers" piano has become known as a reliable instrument at a fair price. Mr. W. H. Ivers is, I may add, an inventor of some moment, and has patented many improvements since 1872.

Among excellent instruments of modern import are those manufactured by the Smith American Piano Company of Boston. This firm has for many years enjoyed a world-wide reputation as manufacturers of organs. They have been in business over thirty-seven years as reed organ-makers, and during that period have been instrumental in promoting the growth of musical taste in this country in connection with that branch. We can, however, only treat them in relation to pianofortes. In 1884 they began to manufacture the latter instruments, having noted the tendency of popular preference coming around to the piano, in no sense, however, withdrawing their attention from the organ, with which they have been so largely identified.

The Smith American Piano Company have been building up a good reputation since 1884 in this department. Many improvements have been applied and invented by them, but in particular their "Regal Piano" is deserving of more than a cursory allusion. This is a specialty title given one of their instruments, constructed upon novel principles after the designs and patent of Mr. H. W.

Smith of the company. This pianoforte, which was exhibited in August, 1889, created marked notice in New York and Boston at the time, and seems to have grown into high esteem since that date. Mr. Smith, having carefully studied for many years the laws relating to resonance and sympathy in pianos, came to the conclusion that the tone quality of the instrument would be considerably enhanced by insulating the vibratory body of the piano from the case proper. This he accomplished by covering the instrument all over with a soft velvety material that serves the purpose, while it gives to the instrument an artistic finish and charm that must serve decorative art largely in the future.

Mr. Smith, the inventor of this method of tone qualification and piano-case decoration, is a native of Enfield, Mass., where he was born in 1830. He subsequently became an apprentice in the factory of Hill, Ryder & Owen, where he learned piano-making, but later went into organ-making. Mr. David Smith, the father of H. W. Smith, was an inventor of cotton machinery of note, and it is to him we owe the old-fashioned speeder. The inventive genius displayed by Mr. H W. Smith in connection with the organ and piano is, therefore, inherited. In relation to the former he has taken out a great many patents of significance. His " Regal Piano" is his most valuable contribution to the trade Mr. S. D. Smith of the firm is a cousin of the latter, and was born in the same place and in the same year. The latter is also practical. Mr. E. W. Smith, another personality in the business, is a brother of Mr. H. W. Smith, and occupies a commercial position. The Smith American Organ and Piano Company is a close corporation. The officers are

S. D. Smith, President ; H. W. Smith, Vice-President ;
E. W. Smith, Treasurer ; George T. McLaughlin, Secretary. The latter is known in connection with this house
for fourteen years.

The New England Piano Company is another large
Boston firm specially well known. Mr. T. F. Scanlan
is the genius and head of this business.

The B. Shoninger Piano of New Haven, Conn., is a
well-known instrument. This old organ house began
the manufacture of pianos over fifteen years ago, and in
the interval has built up a large trade. Mr. Bernard
Shoninger, the head of this firm, is a native of Bavaria,
Germany. He arrived in this country in 1847, and in
1850 began the manufacture of melodeons in New Haven.
Mr. Simon B. Shoninger, his son, is another member of
the firm, and an able business man. They have New
York warerooms.

The Mathushek Piano Company of New Haven have
been known for over twenty years as makers of reputable
instruments, and enjoy a good share of patronage at this
date. These instruments are popular in New York, where
they are largely sold. In Bridgeport, Conn., Keller
Brothers have a factory. In adjacent manufacturing
cities small shops too numerous to recapitulate are to
be found, all making cheap and in some cases criminally
bad pianofortes.

The Sterling pianoforte of Derby, Conn., is an instrument of an excellent character. The Sterling Company
manufacture organs and pianofortes. Mr. Charles A
Sterling began to make the Sterling organs in 1871, having succeeded to the business of the Birmingham Organ
Company. In 1873 the business was formed into a stock

company. Mr. Sterling died on May 3d, 1887, in his seventy-third year. Mr. Rufus W. Blake, the highly energetic head of the present house, for many years secretary and general manager under the former firm, has been identified to a very large extent with the business of the firm in a manifold sense. They began to manufacture pianos in 1885, and have in five years created a very large business. The "Sterling" organ need only be mentioned as an indication of the firm's progressiveness. Mr. Blake meanwhile is responsible for much of the success enjoyed by the house.

The Mason & Hamlin Organ Company, a firm which requires only a brief introduction, owing to its eminence, began to manufacture pianos in 1883. They made a very courageous step in advance by introducing a patented system of stringing and tuning that was hailed as a piece of radicalism by the trade, while predictions were rife that Mason & Hamlin would discard their method of tuning inside of a year. Contrary to all these surmises, however, they seem to have found it thoroughly satisfactory, and the commercial and artistic results appear to be equally successful, for they enjoy a very enviable reputation already as piano manufacturers. In the Mason & Hamlin system of stringing and tuning, the violin bow principle for tightening hair is the basis, worked out, however, in a very ingenious manner. They claim that by their method pianos are more easily tuned, and are insured against getting out of tune rapidly. The present officers of the Mason & Hamlin Organ and Piano Company are : Mr. Henry Mason, President ; Mr. E. P. Mason, Treasurer ; Mr. H. Thielberg, Secretary ; Mr. A. H. Foucar, Clerk.

In Chicago W. W. Kimball & Company are fast building up a large business as piano manufacturers. C. A.
Smith & Company is another Chicago piano manufacturing firm. Bush & Gerts and W. H. Bush & Company are two other firms in business in the metropolis
of the West. In Detroit, Mich., the Clough & Warren pianos are made. These are reputable pianos in
most respects, and are largely used in the Northwest,
where the Clough & Warren organs are well known.
The "Starr" piano is a standard instrument manufactured in Richmond, Ind., of good repute. Coming to
New York State, the Ahlstrom piano, made by C. A.
Ahlstrom in Jamestown, N. Y., has been known since
1875, and is said to be a meritorious piano at a fair price.

Wegman & Company of Auburn, N. Y., have some
reputation as makers of pianofortes.

The Colby Piano Company of Erie, Pa., began business in 1887.

Mr. C. C. Colby, the senior member of this firm,
is a gentleman of remarkable attainments, scholastic
and otherwise. He is a native of Vermont and is
descended from New England stock of long standing.
His boyhood was passed in Pennsylvania. He settled
in the West in subsequent years, where he was identified
with educational movements of much significance. Mr.
Colby is an excellent classical scholar, in addition to
possessing a splendid English education, all of which have
been of valuable assistance in his career. He is a member of a musical and inventive family, and in boyhood
Mr. Colby explored the technical mysteries of the piano,
and acquired a knowledge of tuning practically, which he
has since found of much service. In the line of inven-

.tion he experimented largely in past years upon some practical method of producing sound in the piano other than strings, and in this line of research he made a tuning-fork piano after familiar principles containing new improvements of note. All of this experience, need it be said, was productive of many good results. The Colby Piano Company manufacture reputable instruments, and are fast winning popularity. They occupy a large and well-equipped factory in Erie, Pa., formerly used by Derick & Felgemaker Organ manufacturers. They have also retail warerooms in Erie, conducted by Mr. C. C. Colby, junior, who is a practical tuner, in addition to having other qualifications necessary for the position he occupies. The success enjoyed by the firm so far has come through the executive ability of Mr. C. C. Colby, the senior member, very largely.

CHAPTER XXIV.

Kindred Branches.

ACTION-MAKING—PREFATORY REMARKS—SOME OLD MAKERS —THE FIRM OF STRAUCH BROS. —ALFRED DOLGE—WESSELL, NICKEL & GROSS—GENERAL REFERENCES.

An historical work of this character would indeed be very incomplete without due recognition of the kindred industries of action-making, key-making, and the manufacture and supply of piano materials generally. Unless in a few leading houses, where special departments can be maintained with advantage, the benefits that accrued to the whole trade from the establishment of separate industries, as indicated, outside of the routine of the piano shops, is incontrovertible, for specialists necessarily can produce better results than manufacturers that aim at doing everything at the same time. A few large firms are, however, excepted, for obvious reasons. As regards action-making, the first manufacturer that appeared in New York, as far as can be learned, was Andrew Brunet, an Alsatian. He opened a shop at 30 Clark Street in 1842, and was located here up to 1856. Later on Francis Bonneau, 176 Centre Street, Andrew Orlander, and Stebbins & Smith appear. Coming to 1856, C. Rogers, Jesse

Davis, Koth, Herter, and Westland were in business. Herter in later years arrived at some prominence. Coming down to more modern years and passing over a host of names we find Bothner and Abbott Brothers, at present in business, well known as action-makers. Bothner began to make actions in 1861, and is yet doing a large and conservative business in New York. The Abbotts, being old piano-makers, are mentioned in that connection elsewhere, but rank very high as reliable action-makers at present. Two examples, however, of notable development in action-making in this country are selected for treatment here. Following out the order invariably maintained in this work, the firm of Strauch Bros. is entitled to mention at this juncture.

The well-known and popular house of Strauch Bros. is an old and prominent firm devoted to action manufacturing. This establishment dates back to 1866—almost a quarter of a century—during which period Strauch Bros. have enjoyed high favor in their department of the piano trade. Mr. Peter D. Strauch, who founded this successful business, is a native of Frankfort-on-the-Main, Germany. He arrived in this country as far back as 1851, being fifteen years old at the time, and shortly after was apprenticed to Mr. F. Frickinger, of Nassau, N. Y., piano and piano action-maker, recently deceased, with whom he served six years. After going through this installation experience, Mr. Strauch continued to work in Frickinger's shop as a journeyman piano-maker, in such confidential relations with his employer as a skilled piano-maker that he was admitted subsequently to partnership.

After a couple of years Mr. Strauch felt that, with his

native capacity as an inventor and knowledge as a piano-maker, the metropolis was the proper field for advancement, and accordingly he withdrew from partnership with Mr. Frickinger and settled in New York, where he gained riper experience in various piano factories in the city.

In 1867 we find him engaged in the manufacture of actions—grand, square, and upright—on West Twenty-fifth Street. In 1868 he was joined by his brother, Mr. William Strauch, when Strauch Bros. was originated. The steady and uniform success that Strauch Bros. enjoyed from their earliest association and promotion of interests may be found illustrated in their change from the original shop on West Twenty-fifth Street in March, 1873, to a larger factory on Fifteenth Street and Tenth Avenue. Later business developed so rapidly that they located their plant and business in a five-story building —50 × 100 feet—at 116 and 118 Gansevoort Street. Here they continued to progress at the same ratio of advancement, until they settled finally in their present factory on Tenth Avenue. This is a splendidly equipped manufactory in every respect. It contains the most improved plant known in relation to this branch of the business, in addition to special machinery originated by Mr. Peter D. Strauch, and has ample facilities for producing an immense quantity of high grade actions from year to year. It embraces an area of 130 feet frontage on Tenth Avenue with a depth of 100 feet, and running through the block in the rear, with 25 feet frontage on Little Twelfth and Thirteenth Streets. This sketch of their material development exemplifies in itself one phase of the history of this very honorable firm. Meanwhile a change occurred in the composition of Strauch Bros. on January 1st, 1887, owing to the withdrawal of Mr. William Strauch, since which period, however, the old firm name has been maintained.

Strauch Bros. have paid much attention to the promotion of upright actions since commencing business, particularly since the Philadelphia Centennial Exhibition, when the large showing of foreign upright pianos seen there excited much interest in this style of instrument. This, it is believed, assisted in some measure to popularize upright pianos in this country. In conjunction with their business generally Strauch Bros. have invented and applied automatic machinery of a most ingenious character for facilitating the production of these actions, as well as for the purpose of improving the quality of the work, for which the most perfect lathes and accessory machinery are ordinarily needed.

Among the improvements introduced by this progressive firm during recent years in the upright action must be mentioned their " metal hammer-butt flange." This flange is adjusted in such a manner in relation to the centre pin upon which the hammer rests and moves, that when tightened it secures a rigid bearing for the hammer-butt, and is also less liable to be affected by atmospheric changes. It is needless to reiterate the fact that in the piano a considerable part of the tone-results, in point of quality, rests upon the stability of the hammer in its bearings. Otherwise a " cracked," unstable, and disagreeable quality of tone is distinguishable, no matter how the piano may be otherwise. An improvement, such as Strauch Bros. flange, is therefore of vital importance, especially in uprights, where, owing to the perpendicular pose of the hammers, all the weight rests upon the hammer-butt flanges. Clearly this is indisputable !

Their "brass damper-block" on this principle is another valuable innovation, consisting of a dowel in a metal band which holds it rigidly in position, and prevents such occurrences as splitting or swelling in that region. Strauch Bros. have also recently taken out among other patents one for "separable springs in grand actions," which covers another point of improvement in relation to better repetition. In connection with these actions Strauch Brothers claim, in conjunction with properly weighted keys and skilful regulating (important factors in showing off the artistic value of any kind of action that are generally overlooked), a degree of lightness and elasticity superior to any made.

Assisting in the functions and promotion of the growing business of Strauch Bros. at this day, and who have since January 1st, 1890, been partners in the firm, are Mr. Albert T. Strauch and Mr. William E. Strauch, two sons of Mr. Peter D. Strauch, both educated and practical young men. Mr. Albert T. Strauch was born in New York in 1865, in due time learning piano action-making ; then went into the commercial department of the establishment, of which he now has charge. Mr. William E. Strauch was born in 1866, and is a practical piano and action-maker, and has control of the manufacturing department. Both of these gentlemen are very popular in trade and social circles. With their practical assistance, added to the experience of Mr. Peter D. Strauch as head of the business, this firm has certainly a very hopeful future ahead.

On the subject of felt-making and the piano supply

trade generally the name of Dolge needs no introduction. In approaching the subject of writing a historical and biographical sketch of Mr. Alfred Dolge, I am impressed with the weight of the task in more senses than one. First, there is so much to write about in relation to his various industries and bearing on the trade in short space, while, in a secondary sense, I feel that I am attempting to sketch out one of the most remarkable citizens and self-made men known in the realm of the piano business. And this can even be carried further. The word "remarkable" is used not to indicate the material status to which Mr. Dolge has risen altogether, but to emphasize the peculiar characteristics he displays as a philanthropic employer of labor, coupled with unostentatiousness in the exemplification of generous deeds.

Mr. Dolge was born in Chemnitz, Saxony, December 22d, 1848. His family having during his early life moved to Leipzig, Mr. Dolge attended one of the excellent schools in that city up to his thirteenth year. At this period he ceased school going and became an apprentice in the shop of A. Dolge & Company, piano manufacturers, of which his father was nominally head and otherwise the principal. Mr. Dolge's transition into practical life at this early age may be ascribed to his splendid physical development, added to his native brightness, which characteristic exhibited itself even in his remote school-days. An evidence of Mr. Dolge's industry and ability is furnished in the circumstance that, in 1865, he was awarded the diploma of merit for progress and application at the Industrial Sunday-school by the Directory appointed by the German Government to superintend and report progress in these institutions.

A youth endowed with the individualistic traits so soon evidenced in Mr. Dolge naturally turned toward this continent, and it is therefore no surprise to note that in 1866 he landed on these shores at the age of seventeen. Mr. Dolge's first American experience as a piano-maker was gained inside the shop of Mr. Frederick Mathushek, where he was employed on his arrival. After a few years he returned to Germany. He soon tired of the old world, however, and although offered a good chance to become a partner in the firm of A. Dolge & Company, in his native city, he forfeited this and every other opportunity, and sailed for New York again, determining to cast his future lot in this country.

Mr. Dolge on returning went to work at piano-making again, but he was not destined by intuition or intelligence to be a mere wage-earner. His first endeavor to rise from the bench now began, for having, during his residence in this country, observed that, unless in a few of the leading houses, many materials, such as felt and toning leather for hammers, used in American pianos could be improved, he realized sufficient capital to order a small supply of superior leather from Germany at first, which he speedily disposed of. He meanwhile continued to work at the bench and kept up his small leather importations, to which Poehlmann's wire was added in due time. This brand of piano stringing wire was little known here only in a few large shops, and Mr. Dolge speedily acquired new customers. These little evidences of success were so complete a testimony of Mr. Dolge's future chances in this field in an enlarged sense, that we find him entirely engaged in 1869 in importing piano materials, having said good-by to his piano-making days forever.   In 1871 he began the manufacture of felt under most discouraging conditions, but still persevered steadily, until the year 1873 brought the first augury of success.

The principal competitors that Mr. Dolge had, in the mean time, in this branch were Smith and Chapuis.

Chapuis produced a fair quality of hammer-felt, and fearing competition, the agent of a German felt manufacturer, who, with a French manufacturer, practically monopolized the American market at that time, bought them out and employed Chapuis in his felt factory in Germany.

Their process of felt-making was most primitive, similar to the old way of making felt hats by hand.

Numerous attempts had been made by various felt makers, but none were successful until, in 1871, when Alfred Dolge started.   In fact, the only patents for piano hammer-felt on record are either granted or assigned to Alfred Dolge, and whatever progress has been made in piano hammer-felt manufacturing dates from the establishment of the Dolge factory.

Almost from the beginning he discarded the old way of making felt by hand, and employed, at least partly, machinery so successfully that he received the highest prize at the World's Exhibition at Vienna, 1873, only two years after he commenced manufacturing, and his felts were acknowledged superior to any other then made.

The first radical change in the manufacturing of piano hammer-felt was successfully introduced by Dolge, in running the web direct from the carding engine to the hardening machine, for which process he was granted a patent at the time.   This process secures a more thorough felting of the different layers of wool, in consequence of which the inner part of a sheet is just as solidly felted together as the outer part, a very important improvement on the old method, whereby only the outer layers were well felted while the centre remained soft, causing the hammer to swell after it had been used a short time.

The next Patent we find is No. 314,810, March 31st, 1885, granted to Dolge, which covers the process of putting a layer of hair mixed with wool on the outer parts of the sheet. This seems to be the only really important progress made in the manufacture of piano felt during the past forty years.

It is a well-known fact that hair or fur is not only softer, but also much more durable than wool, and while almost every felt-maker has produced what is called " hair felt," yet no one but Mr. Dolge, as far as can be seen, has been able to produce a hair felt which has the necessary firmness combined with the indispensable elasticity.

The idea of making felt of fur is admittedly not a novel one, yet Mr. Dolge deserves the credit of finding a process by which hair and wool could be so worked together that it became virtually one, the wool having the necessary fulling properties to give the felt the required firmness ; and the hair or fur being soft and velvety, produces a clear sympathetic tone, which with the ordinary felt can only be temporarily produced by pricking up the upper layers of a hammer.

The next patent which we find on record is No. 363,-217, May 17th, 1887, and is granted to Alfred Dolge for crossing the webs of wool as coming from the carding

machines direct, by which process again the dense connection of the wool fibre is very materially assisted, since
the wool must naturally interlock in all directions, and
instead of being built up by regular thick bats or layers,
the felt made under this patent is built up by thin, cob-
web-like layers crossing each other in right angles as
they come from the carding machine, similar to the cross
layers of veneers of a wrest-plank.

The object of the invention is to secure better wearing
quality for the felt, which seems to be accomplished,
because the strings will more easily cut into a felt wherein
the fibre lies in one direction, exactly on the same principle that an impression is much more easily made along
the grain of the wood than it can be produced on end
wood.

As a natural consequence a hammer made of such felt
cannot be as smoothly sand-papered (the hair will stick
out in all directions), but for that very reason the hammer will last so much longer than the smoothly finished
hammer of the old style of felt, in which the grain of the
felt, so to speak, runs in the same direction as the shape
of the hammer.

Patent No. 364,496, June 7th, 1887, granted again to
Alfred Dolge for an improvement in piano hammer-felt,
by laying alternately with the wool a woollen netting
into the felt for the purpose of interlocking the fibres of
the felt with the meshes of the textile fabric, without
destroying the elasticity of the felt, and consequently the
hammer will retain its original shape even if, as it is
necessary on all overstrung pianos, the hammer is bev-
elled off on two sides.

While the other patents mentioned have proved them-

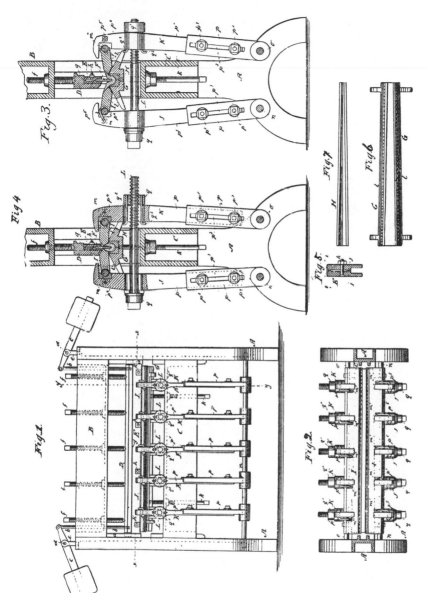

ALFRED DOLGE'S PATENT HAMMER-COVERING MACHINE.

selves positive improvements, and are so acknowledged by the leading manufacturers here and in Europe, no judgment can as yet be passed upon this invention.

The improvement described in Patents Nos. 397,812 and 397,813, granted February 12th, 1889, seems to be destined to revolutionize the whole process of fulling felt, and because of the startling simplicity of these machines it can be understood at the first glance by any one that this most natural process of "setting" the felt, or, more properly speaking, the wool hair, must produce just exactly what every piano manufacturer always desires, a *firm* and *yet elastic tenor and treble*. That these setting machines will eventually make the pressing of the felt superfluous is obvious.

In connection with the felt Mr. Dolge's hammer-press, Patent No. 361,144, April 12th, 1887, which is acknowledged as the most perfect system known, must be specially mentioned. Besides its many other excellent qualities it "draws" the felt instead of simply pressing it onto the wooden mouldings. These Dolge machines are now extensively in use in American as well as in European piano factories. It is illustrated in these pages, and will repay study.

Mr. Dolge, in addition to felt for hammer covering, manufactured rubbing and polishing felts from the beginning, and has carried his skilful appliance of felt to many other purposes outside the piano business. Going back to the story of his material advancement, we find Mr. Dolge, in 1874, a few years after starting, removing his producing factory to Brockett's Bridge, a village about two hundred miles from the metropolis, which now bears the significant name of Dolgeville. Presently, with the new facilities opening up, Mr. Dolge began to manufacture sounding-boards, which branch has grown in recent years to immense proportions. Suffice it that Mr. Dolge's business is to-day practically a supply centre for the music trades of piano and organ building, and is the largest special business of that nature in the world. Dolgeville from one hundred inhabitants has grown up under the magic of Mr. Dolge's wand to seventeen hundred. Here his immense factories, fitted with rare and modern appliances suitable to the numerous industries concerned, are situated. Upward of six hundred hands are here constantly employed, well housed, and generously paid according to Mr. Dolge's methods. The great business success of Mr. Alfred Dolge is too well known to require comment at the hands of the historian. His technical contributions to the American piano trade have been briefly shown, but his position as a factor in the trade is not inconsiderable, and hardly requires reiteration.

A noteworthy fact in connection with the profit-sharing scheme which Mr. Dolge has adopted in relation to his employés is that his life history, theories, and political speeches delivered in this country during the 1888 campaign were pamphleted and published for the section " Participation du Persones dans les Benefices" at the Paris Exposition of 1889, and drew forth warm tributes from leading French statesmen and the press, many of which were re-echoed in German and English papers.

The action-manufacturing house of Wessell, Nickel & Gross is a noteworthy example of the growth of the specializing process treated of in connection with the historical development of the pianoforte on this continent. Starting in 1874, at a period when the piano trade and commerce generally were recovering from the effects of a great business depression caused by the panic of 1873, they rank to day in point of status and finance with the leading piano houses. And this plane has been reached in sixteen years, at a period when the keenest competition prevails in all departments of commercial activity.

The founders of this concern are Mr. Otto Wessell, Mr. Adam Nickel, and Mr. Rudolph Gross, all highly practical action-makers. Mr. Wessell entered the shop of Herter at seventeen years of age, in New York, where he served an apprenticeship course. Here he became an expert and finished workman. In after years he was employed in Steinway & Sons' factory, where he had the opportunity of assisting at the finest work then known in New York, and in addition practically saw and studied the application of the action to the piano, which was a valuable experience not acquired in every action shop. Mr. Nickel and Mr. Gross are natives of Europe. Here they learned action-making, meanwhile working in many of the best shops in the various countries. After arriving in New York they were employed in Steinway & Sons' action shop, where they formed the personal friendship for each other which led to their subsequent successful business start.

The first move of the three partners in establishing their business was to secure the necessary plant and tools. Their beginning was modest and truly after Ben Franklin's own heart, for Mr. Wessell recounts with sturdy satisfaction the fact that during the first year it was his custom to go around to the trade and sell any actions made from week to week, then go back to the bench and repeat the process.   Presently the characteristics of their actions became known to the piano-makers. Regulators and finishers in all the shops that worked upon them began to speak highly of them.   Orders piled up so fast in the office of Wessell, Nickel & Gross in the course of twelve months, that a large number of hands were added and special machinery acquired.   This permitted the partners to devote more time to invention, which leisure was productive of many improvements in special machinery for the manufacture of actions, which have not been published in patents for reasons easily understood, while numerous patents were taken out at an early date for action improvements, four of which are illustrated here.

Upright and grand actions were largely imported in 1874, owing to the fact that hitherto the square piano was the leading instrument, and native action makers with one or two exceptions paid but little attention to the grand and upright action department.   Starting in 1874, when the modern upright had just received its first decisive advance in popularity, owing to the skill of piano firms shown incidentally, Wessel, Nickel & Gross saw the drift of matters, and prophetically issued a circular, in 1875, which read : " We beg to inform our customers and the trade that we are now, and have been since 1874, engaged in making grand repetition and upright piano actions.   As was predicted, the demand for upright pianos has had a steady increase, and will be the popular instrument, as it is and has been in Europe for many years."

Following this we find that, in 1877, Patent No. 188,706 was issued to them on March 20th for improvements in

upright actions. Their principal point of improvement
in this patent consists in the invention of a compound
flange at each end of which the damper and hammer has
its bearing. This flange is exemplified in the drawings.
It is so formed that it rests snugly in the main rail to
which the brackets are attached, as practical readers will
understand, having a transverse groove in its under side
which rests in a tongue cut in the rail. By this method,
it is claimed, the necessity for using two screws is obvi-
ated, while greater stability is given to the hammer and
damper. The advantage to the tone quality of pianos
from greater stability of the hammer and action joints
can be easily estimated, therefore this claim is very valuable. On November 26th, 1878, they took out Patent
No. 210,381 for a pedal-damper, action improvement
(illustrated) for uprights. By their system of adjusting
the damper-lifting bar, rattling on the bearings is entirely
done away with. This is accomplished by a circular
metallic plate bearing to which heavy cloth bushing is
applied, which perfectly insulates the piano from any
jarring in this locality, were such possible, while the
pedal is given an easy elastic foot touch apart from the
trap work springs, and in addition the wooden main rail,
it is claimed, cannot be warped. This is merely a digest
of the points of vantage claimed for this invention.
Their piano damper, Patent No. 295,317, taken out on
March 18th, 1884, is another action improvement applicable to all forms, whereby the damper-block is made
more stable by a set screw, after the manner described
in their specification. This makes it possible to use any
kind of fine straight-grained wood in actions instead
of knotty-grained wood usually selected for these pur-

poses. This is also illustrated. Another illustration is furnished of Wessell, Nickel & Gross' grand repetition action, in which improvements protected by Patent No. 366,360, issued on July 12th, 1887, appear. The novelty and advantage claimed herein consist in their peculiar method of adjusting the springs to the repetition lever and the " jack," by which more easy and prompt repetition is obtained at a considerable saving in " touch" expenditure by the artist. While there are more advantages set forth in the official specification, the foregoing is a concise definition of the invention in the abstract. The drawings can be easily recognized elsewhere by the titles given, and will repay study.

This firm to day employs over five hundred hands which is a further illustration of rapid business advancement on the one hand, while it goes, moreover, to exemplify historically the growth of action-making as a special branch of piano manufacturing in this country.

In regulating such a large output of first-class actions, Wessell, Nickel & Gross have to keep constantly on hand an enormous supply of material of the best quality, which necessitates expert judgment and skill in stocking and selecting, while the plant and special machinery in use in their immense factory furnish in themselves a curiously interesting study for persons interested in the evolution of what deserves to be known as the American piano and the trade as it is to-day. Surely the names of Otto Wessell, Adam Nickel, and Rudolph Gross deserve special distinction in these chapters in relation to the modern aspect of American pianoforte history. And all three are admirable examples of self-made manhood, liberal, upright, personally devoted one to the other, and model citizens of our great commonwealth.

Besides the action makers spoken of in relation to New York, specialists in that department of the piano business sprang up toward 1860 in various parts of Connecticut and other States adjoining New York. In Boston Howe and other smaller makers were known. In Milford, N. H., George L. Darracott made actions about this period. Sylvester Tower, at this time a very large and probably one of the oldest action makers in this country, was firmly established in the year given at Cambridgeport, Mass. Mr. Tower began the manufacture of piano keys, in addition to melodeon and organ keys, in 1853, and later began to make piano actions. The present Tower manufactory in Cambridgeport covers a formidable amount of ground space, and is well fitted out in most respects. Mr. Tower is an old and popular personality in connection with the piano business, and enjoys a good measure of practical success. Comstock, Cheney & Company, Essex, Conn., are very old specialists in the sphere of the piano trade. They have been manufacturing piano keys and actions since 1858, and have a large circle of customers in Boston and New York, and employ a large number of hands.

The present firm of G. W. Severns & Son, Cambridgeport, Mass., has an honorable record going back to a very remote period, and are well-known manufacturers at present. Many other action and key makers have appeared and disappeared from time to time from 1850 in various provincial cities outside of New York and Boston, but it would be impossible to follow them out in this section.

Among those in New York that make hammer covering a special business at present, Schmidt & Company are evidently the oldest. This firm has a record going back to 1856, and has built up a permanent reputation in this business. The members are Messrs. Schmidt and Gerlach, both practical. Charles Pfreimer is another hammer-coverer of note in the metropolitan trade, whose sole business is devoted to that branch.

E. Chapuis, mentioned in relation to Mr. Alfred Dolge, is reputed to have been the first to make hammer felt in the United States. Previous to his arrival in 1854 all felts were imported. The latter was a native of France, and was in business here until 1862, when he returned to Europe. In 1873 he came back to the United States, and began felt-making in Paterson, N. J., where he was joined by Mr. Harvey S. Crane, at present his successor, when Crane & Chapuis was formed, followed by the results intimated. H. S. Crane is yet known as a felt manufacturer.

Regarding the introduction of felt in the pianoforte many misconceptions exist on the matter. It is generally believed that felt was not thought of in this connection until 1840, but this is a fallacy, for John Landreth spoke of a " woolly substance manufactured after the manner of a hat " so early as 1787 in his British pianoforte patent of that year. Alpheus Babcock, while in Philadelphia in 1833, took out a patent anticipating the general use of felt as a substitute for leather hammer covering, while P. F. Fischer, of London, in his patent of May 13th, 1835, spoken of in an early chapter, set forth a method of hammer-felt making in the specification, that clearly intercepted early French felt manufacturers.

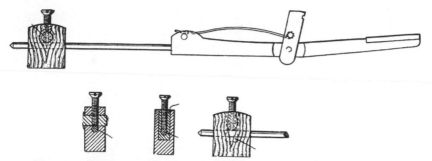

WESSELL, NICKEL & GROSS' DAMPER BLOCK.   *Patented March 18, 1884.*

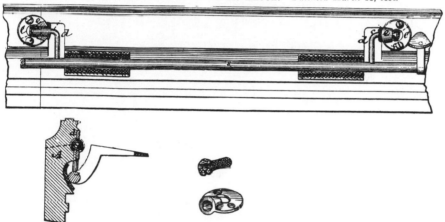

WESSELL, NICKEL & GROSS' IMPROVED UPRIGHT ACTION DAMPER-LIFTING CRANK SHOWING
BEARINGS.   *Patented November 26, 1878.*

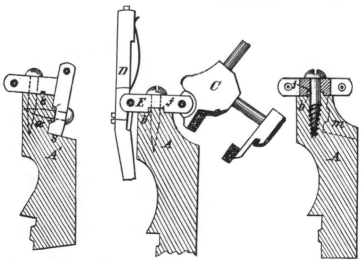

WESSELL, NICKEL & GROSS' IMPROVED UPRIGHT HAMMER FLANGE.   *Patented March 20, 1877.*

There are numerous other firms throughout the country devoted to action and key-making and the piano supply trade in existence, but cannot, however, be treated of here beyond those given in the foregoing order.

CHAPTER XXV.

KINDRED BRANCHES.

THE CASTING OF PIANO PLATES—A CONCOMITANT BRANCH
—DAVENPORT & TREACY—THEIR RAPID ADVANCEMENT—
VARNISH MAKING—HOTOPP & COMPANY.

In line with the special manufacture of actions, keys,
and other concomitant parts of the piano, came the manufacture of iron plates as a distinct branch, now grown
into a department of more than ordinary magnitude.
Previous to the general acceptation of the full iron
plate in New York and other manufacturing centres
outside of Boston, as I have shown in a past chapter, a
small hitch-pin plate, with compensating tubes or other
simple modifications of the iron bracing system, was used.
To prepare these primitive iron structures no special
skill in working or casting iron was required, therefore
it was not until the general adoption of the full solid cast-
iron plate by piano-makers, combined with heavier stringing, that the importance of good castings made by skilful foundry men was realized. In Boston, however, the
Chickerings had developed the principle of whole-cast
plates at a remote period, but previous to about 1860 the
stringing and scaling of pianos was so conditioned by

the use of thinner wire throughout, that the enormous tensional pull known to-day in pianos was not realized. Therefore effective plate casting was not a matter of such vital importance as it has become within the past fifteen years in this country, especially since the upright became popular. At this time Steinway & Sons, Chickering & Sons, Knabe & Company, and all shops doing their own castings fully appreciate this fact, and pay their foundry-work serious attention. And in recent years it has become an accepted acoustic belief in piano structure that not only is it necessary to have immense strength and solidity in iron plate castings, but the quality of the metal, as an aid to increased resonance, is a matter of vast importance.

Unlike actions, keys, and such material parts of the piano, the great mass of manufacturers could not each maintain foundries for the casting of their own plates, and were compelled at an early period to go outside for them. While the small hitch-pin plates and such adaptations of the plate-bracing principle were in use it was not so difficult to procure these sections, as almost any small concern could supply them ; but when the solid cast plates were adopted, followed by the introduction of modern stringing conditions, it then became a matter of some concern to procure the proper castings.

The demand, therefore, in time brought to the surface specialists in foundry work, who catered for the piano trade specially. Among the most important of the first foundry men to become identified with the manufacture of pianos in this country were the Shrivers. Years ago, when they were without competitors of any note, they ranked as the best piano-plate foundry men in the United

States.   They were unquestionably a large factor in improving the quality of plate castings in this country. Thomas Shriver, the father of the firm of T. Shriver & Company, was born near Westminster, Md., on September 2d, 1789.   His education was acquired in a country school presided over by an Irish schoolmaster.   His family being by trade iron workers, his mind turned in that direction subsequently.   In after years he became an engineer, and in designing bridges and similar work soon became conversant with the nature of the metals. He invented the elliptic springs for wagons about 1819, which have since become accepted over the world, and was the author of many subsequent inventions of great moment.   In later years he was owner of an omnibus line in Philadelphia, but the adoption of street cars superseded that mode of conveyance.   He then moved to New York, and in company with his son Walter established a foundry for fine castings and piano plates.   Meanwhile this much-respected citizen passed away, leaving a large family of clever children.   The firm soon became preeminent in the latter department, but within the past ten years new competitors arose, and while the first-named house was conservatively reposing on its past record, other firms appeared and began to take possession of the field by virtue of enterprise, push, and absolute capability.

Prominent among piano-plate founders at this period stand the firm of Davenport & Treacy, whose extraordinary rise into eminence in a comparatively short space of time is unprecedented in trade annals.   This firm is composed of Mr. John Davenport and Mr. Daniel F. Treacy.   The personal history of the former illustrates the origin of the house.

Mr. John Davenport is a native of Stamford, Conn., where he was born in August, 1840. He comes of Revolutionary stock. Mr. Davenport received a careful preliminary education, and entered Yale College subsequently, from which he graduated with high honors. At the age of nineteen he entered the office of the Still Water Iron Works at Stamford in the employ of his father, who was the proprietor. He remained here until 1863, when he withdrew. Meantime he had an interest in the business which he retained up to 1880.

We find, however, that Mr. Davenport was not idle, for in 1863 he went into partnership with a Mr. Betts, and started large machine works under the firm name Davenport & Betts, for the purpose of manufacturing light machinery and tools for boring oil-wells, then in much demand. In 1866 he retired from active business, and for the two following years remained in private life, devoting himself to laying out the grounds and building his present beautiful home on the shores of the Sound. To one of Mr. Davenport's training and ambition inactivity was impossible, and in 1868 he purchased the business of the Brown Scale Works and Foundry, situated on the northeast corner of Third Avenue and Fifty-seventh Street in New York. The manufacture of scales was abandoned in 1872, when the foundry works were moved to Jersey City, and in line with larger and better facilities, a successful foundry and general jobbing business was soon developed. In 1873 a significant event in the personal and commercial history of Mr. Davenport occurred. This was his first meeting with Mr. Daniel F. Treacy, his present partner. In this year the latter was engaged as superintendent of the foundry works controlled by Mr. Davenport, after a few moments' conversation, during which both partners—between whom a steady and unbroken friendship has existed for seventeen years—met for the first time.   Subsequently Mr. Treacy became an equal partner in the business, when the firm of Davenport & Treacy came into being.

Mr. Treacy is a man of remarkable professional and scientific attainments.   He is, first, a practical iron moulder, and in addition possesses a deep knowledge of metallurgy and all scientific and experimental departments related to foundry work and metal working in general.   Many composition metals have been originated by him for bearing purposes, plates, and a variety of objects only capable of being fully appreciated by engineers and metal workers.   As Davenport & Treacy stand to-day the largest producers of refined pianoplates in the world, the assistance of such a man in improving the resistance and resonance quality of pianoplates is invaluable to the trade.

Mr. Treacy was born in the British province of New Brunswick.   In his youth he was apprenticed to the moulding trade in Chatham, N. B.   In exactly three months after his term of apprenticeship had ended Mr. Treacy's family moved to St. Louis, Mo , where he acquired a varied experience in the Corandelet Iron Works in that city.   We next discover him in the Government employ.   His subsequent experience served to make him restless and disinclined to settle down to one occupation or one city.   He now drifted considerably around, working in the best shops in the principal cities, meanwhile having no difficulty in always finding good positions, owing to his skill.   In this way he happened to find

himself in the whaling town of New Bedford, Mass., in
1866. Having been brought up in early life within easy
reach of "old ocean," young sailoring aspirations combined with restlessness induced him to ship on board a
whaling vessel bound on a three years' cruise. Before
the term was completed the ship was disabled and returned to port for repairs, while Mr. Treacy again sailed
on a second voyage, which came near being his last ocean
trip, for the crew were cast away on one of the West Indian islands, from which he emerged safe, however. In
1870 he was back at his old business, and held the position of foreman of the Acushnet Iron Foundry in New
Bedford. He subsequently moved to Brooklyn and
started business, hoping to be able to find scope for his
professional originality as a metal and iron founder ; but
while attending too much to the inventive side, the commercial side suffered, and he was obliged to retire. After
this he entered the employ of Mr. Davenport, as indicated. It is sixteen years ago since this firm began to make
piano-plate castings for the late W. A. Conant. The
latter took the plates unfinished to his shop, where he
drilled and finished them, and supplied the trade. They
held all Conant's work and the trade of his successors
until 1884, when they became direct caterers for the piano
manufacturing houses. They were located at this period
in Jersey City. In this year exactly two hundred and
seventy-five plates were cast, refined, drilled, and finished in their shop.

They now settled down to make a specialty of pianoplates and hardware. With the excellent facilities at their
disposal, assisted by their generous commercial enterprise and a solid backing of sound practical knowledge

of all the requirements necessary to produce the finest grade of plates, to which sixteen years' experience may be added, immediate success followed.   Success is such a handy word, and so often used that it hardly expresses the situation in this case.   The amount of success that has fallen to the lot of this enterprising house in six years may be easily estimated by the fact that from two hundred and seventy-five plates in 1884, their first year, they developed up a patronage so vast that in 1889, as their books indicate, they produced the enormous quantity of sixteen thousand plates, and a correspondingly large output of piano hardware.

Davenport & Treacy, finding their works in Jersey City inadequate for their growing business, in 1887 selected a site in Stamford, Conn., where they erected the present foundry works.   The first move of Davenport & Treacy was to locate their extensive finishing rooms and city offices at 444 and 446 West Sixteenth Street, in New York, but these additions were found of little assistance. Accordingly they determined to secure adequate facilities both for present and future purposes, and selected their present site in Stamford, on which they began their buildings.   This location was chosen after some deliberation, because it places them within easy access of the piano manufacturers by rail and boat.   Their foundry works reach to the water's edge.   Here they have unexceptionable advantages, and employ a steamer specially to ply between New York and Stamford, carrying plates and bringing back the crude iron used in the process of plate casting, as well as material for general purposes. Their buildings have a street frontage of 475 feet, while they cover four acres of ground.   A sectional ground

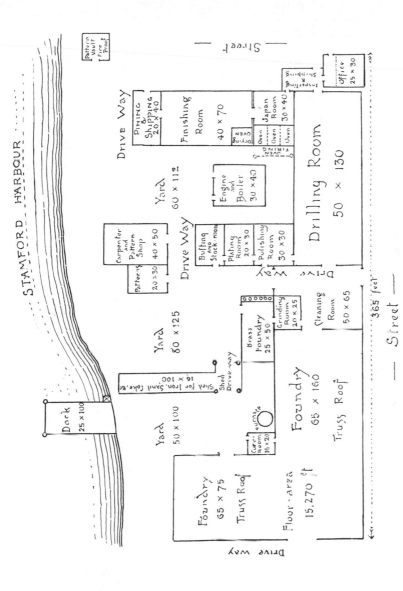

SECTIONAL GROUND PLAN OF DAVENPORT & TREACY'S PIANO-PLATE FOUNDRY, STAMFORD, CONN.

Illustrating the growth of one special branch of the pianoforte business.

plan of this colossal department of piano manufacturing is honored by a page-plate illustration elsewhere. Davenport & Tracey have, moreover, anticipated further progressions by securing ample space in reserve for enlargements, while they have been constantly adding to their stock of plant and outside facilities since 1887. In connection with piano hardware they have improved polishing and nickel-plating machinery for refining and coating brackets, pedal guards, pedal, agraffes, and all work of that character. Apart from piano materials, they produce superior castings in composition metals— brass, copper, and phosphor-bronze—for scientific and general purposes, from one-half ounce up to two thousand pounds. Their foundry also contains ·one of the most complete pulley-moulding machine plants in this country, by which they are enabled to produce any size pulley from eight inches up to one hundred and forty-four inches diameter, with any desired width of face. During past years they have filled large orders from the National Government, and in 1889 they made two hundred thousand pounds of composition castings alone for the National cruisers now in course of construction.

Added to the personal supervision of Mr. Treacy, who looks carefully after the mechanical departments, besides attending to other important duties of the business, Davenport & Treacy employ the most expert foremen in all departments, so as to insure the highest possible results. Under no other conditions could such a vast business be successfully conducted. Mr. Treacy has been a diligent student of the piano for several years from the mechanical standpoint, and incidentally of resonance in plate development, and much of the success that has fallen to the share of the firm as plate founders is due to his ability and personal attention.   Mr. Treacy's skill has enabled the firm to supply plates from mere drawings in themselves apart from models for casting purposes.   In this departure they claim to stand alone.   An important fact in relation to Davenport & Treacy is that they have their iron regularly tested at Stevens' Institute, Hoboken, and are thoroughly in touch with scientific progress in all departments of metallurgy, metal founding and working.   Mr. Treacy, I must add, has figured somewhat in the scientific journals devoted to metallurgy, iron, and foundry work as an original thinker and progressionist.   One of his recent articles on the use of coke *versus* coal in smelting processes commanded much attention, and was copied very generally in England and elsewhere.

In sketching out the history of Davenport & Treacy and their unprecedented rise into an important place in relation to piano manufacturing in this country, a most interesting chapter is unfolded.   Both gentlemen, in addition to possessing high business qualifications, have always taken pains to merit the good-will and esteem of the piano trade and the musical press, and are highly esteemed as private citizens.   Within the domain of their business interests they are highly progressive and liberal. They have succeeded only by honorable methods, and are altogether a firm entitled to eminent esteem and favor, and are no small factor in the statistics of piano history.

American piano manufacturers found it necessary at an early period, owing to climatic influences, to adopt a means of polishing and preserving the surface of pianos

different from the methods in general use throughout
Europe. The introduction of a reference to American
varnish in this section has, therefore, a special meaning, apart from the fact that varnish is a material part
of the stock-in-trade of the piano manufacturer, and has
no small bearing on the appearance of the instrument.
A piano, we must remember, has an æsthetic and artistic
value as a resident of the drawing-room independent of
its musical qualities, and the varnish manufacturer contributes much to the external beauty of the instrument.
Our early manufacturers of pianos found that not only
was it necessary to adopt the means now in use for dec-
orating and securing a comparatively permanent lustre
in their instruments externally, but it was discovered
that every varnish will not produce equal results, and
that it required scientific and subtle knowledge on the
part of varnish manufacturers in order to produce varnishes suitable for the demands of the piano manufacturer, and capable of being handled throughout with
confidence by workmen. Among the first to make varnishes in this country was P. B. Smith of New York,
who was well known in relation to the piano trade as far
back as 1830. Later Tilden & Hulburt appeared. Newark, N. J., became a centre for varnish manufacturing about 1840, when the term "Newark varnishes"
was originated. At present Newark has one of the largest varnish manufacturing establishments in this country, which is maintained through other branches of art
and industry where this article is used, although the
piano trade is also a contributor.

Many well-known varnish houses are known to-day in
relation to piano manufacturing through the musical

press, and require no enumeration here—all good and reliable firms, who supply their article to coach-builders, railroads, and other departments of industry largely. The firm of Hotopp & Company has been known in relation to the piano trade in this country since 1854 as large and reliable makers of varnishes for piano manufacturers' use. Their business at this period is principally supported by the piano trade, and in this connection they claim to occupy a special place in relation to piano manufacturing. To use their exact words, which are taken from a communication sent : " In fact, we are the only varnish-makers who have developed and grown up with the American pianoforte trade. We do a more extensive business with piano-makers in this particular branch than any other varnish houses. By this we do not mean to say that we excel in point of production, as there are more extensive works ; but the trade of most other varnish houses depends largely upon other sources of support, such as the carriage trade and all that. Hence it is why we can and do claim to be a part of the piano art business.''

For the special uses of piano-makers, Hotopp & Company carry a large stock of "aged" varnishes, for which they have won a reputation which goes back to 1854.

Steinway & Sons were for ten consecutive years large customers of Hotopp & Company ; Weber, Steck & Company, the old firm of Lighte & Bradbury, and many other prominent piano-makers of that period were among the first on their books, and to-day they claim to supply every house of prominence with their piano varnishes, and ship a large quantity to Europe to manufacturers of pianofortes for extreme climates. In this respect this old firm occupies a peculiar place. A large number of European pianos going to India, Australia, the British Colonies generally, and imported into the United States from abroad are provided with a substantial coating of the Hotopp & Company's varnish for protective and decorative purposes, as many European manufacturers recognize the necessity of preparing and finishing pianos on the American principle and by the use of American varnish, so as to stand severe climatic conditions. The rise of Hotopp & Company is evidenced by the circumstance that their manufactory in Hoboken, N J., covers 100 by 25 feet on Marshall Street and 100 by 50 feet on First Street, with a frontage of 100 feet facing the West Shore Railroad. Here one can see another incidental illustration of the diversity and range of the industries developed and maintained by the piano business in this country, and Hotopp & Company deserve recognition in this connection, owing to the claims they advance as specialists to the piano trade. This large building is equipped with the most improved plant, and although admittedly not the largest, is second to none in point of facilities for producing the best grade of varnish known.

Much of the success of this firm is due to the fact that those composing it are practically conversant with the theoretical and technical side of their business, as well as the working application of varnish to the piano, its diseases and remedies, and every point of practical value necessary to render them entirely capable and qualified.

The business was founded by Mr. William Hotopp in 1854. Mr. Henry Hotopp, the technical member of the present firm, is a native of Hanover, Germany, where he was born in 1837. He came to this country at an early age, and has been a practical varnish-maker since his eighteenth year. In 1856 he entered the firm, and up to this date has attended to the manufacturing department and superintends the works personally, thus insuring the best results. Another member of the firm, known among piano manufacturers as an attentive and courteous business man, Mr William F. Braun, is also practically acquainted with varnish-making and the precise qualities necessary for piano use. Mr. Braun was born in Jersey City in 1856. In January, 1872, he entered the employ of Hotopp & Company, and by dint of ability and business courtesy worked himself up to the position of head salesman. In November, 1887, his services to the house were generously recognized by a membership and share in the firm. Mr. Braun manages the outside business and attends to the financial department of Hotopp & Company. Many facts given here in relation to varnish have been contributed by this gentleman, as he is thoroughly conversant with the business and everything concerning it.

I need not add that, in achieving artistic results in varnish work in pianos, much depends upon good varnish. Yet a great deal depends upon intelligent workmen, proper methods, and a number of conditions which can only be regulated by practical varnish foremen in piano shops. These are, of course, recognized facts, therefore varnish-makers cannot always be blamed for bad results coming from the latter causes. Hotopp & Company, however, claim to assist perfect results in piano varnish work by their method of manufacture.

The foregoing sketch will, no doubt, be interesting in connection with another section of the supply business, and has a bearing on the modern aspect of piano manu-facturing.

There are several other large houses existing that have for many years been known to the piano trade through the press, but it is a pleasant task to bring into promi-nent notice an old firm that has always filled a modest though not less useful place in the great industry of piano manufacturing.

CHAPTER XXVI.

Musical and Trade Journalism.

In the development of the pianoforte business in this
country, within the past half century in particular, the
musical press has played no insignificant part. American musical journals since 1835, when the *American Musical Journal* was founded, have been largely identified
with the music trades, and in promoting these excellent
factors in musical education by practical support, piano
and organ manufacturers have rendered art culture in the
United States an incalculable benefit. Meanwhile, the
music trades gained dignity and force from a special
press, while a spirit of professional fraternity and mutual
good-will was fostered. Practical benefit was derived,

Henry C. Watson.

however, aside from the sentimental, through the medium of musical journals.

The advantages of newspapers to the purposes of society and business require no elaboration here. I have to deal with special journalism, to which department of literature the musical press belongs. In addition to newspapers, special class journalism is a necessity of the age ; otherwise, according to natural law in sociology, it would not exist and thrive.

With the growth of our nineteenth-century civilization, the intercommunication of the human race by electricity, railways, steamships, a more perfect mail service, and a thousand other phases of progress, the newspaper proper became necessarily devoted to the reflection and circulation of passing events and the multifarious details of life in a generalized and abbreviated form. It was, therefore, discovered soon after the beginning of the century that every important branch of art, science, and industry would be benefited by a special journal devoted to chronicling new improvements in the business and personal affairs of that separate branch. Special journalism began in the art field first, then industries and trades followed suit in time. Now it is considered indispensable and necessary that every trade should have its own organ. Music trade journalism, unlike most other branches of special journalism, is simply an evolution from musical journalism proper, for we can trace the relation of the music trades to musical papers back to the first periodical published in this country. Passing Henry C. Watson's *Musical Chronicle*, founded in 1843—spoken of in his biographical sketch—the *Musical Review*, a weekly, founded by the Mason Brothers in 1853, dealt largely

in trade material.   Here we can find modern music trade
journalism anticipated to a laige extent during several
of the first years of its existence.   Substantial reports of
improvements, personal sketches, and periodical statistics
of manufacturing appeared, while all the standard piano
manufacturers of New York, Boston, Philadelphia, and
Albany advertised.   This journal passed into the hands
of Mr. Theodore Hagen in later years, and continued as
a weekly.   It ceased after the death of this clever musician in 1871.   Meanwhile, the first music trades organ,
having a distinct title, to emphasize its functions was
started in 1875.   In addition to Mr. Hagen and Mason
Brothers, Mr. John S. Dwight, the well-known Boston
musical critic, founded *Dwight's Journal of Music* in that
city in 1851, which had a long lease of existence, and
was incidentally connected with publishing music.   This
was a semi-monthly, and published by the music house
of Oliver Ditson & Company.   Among the early American editors of musical journals and critics associated
more or less with the progress of the piano in this country, the name of Henry C. Watson is entitled to an
important place.   His name has some more direct connection with the pianoforte business at this date, owing to the fact that he founded the *American Art Journal*
in 1863, at present vigorously alive and representing the
best interests of the piano trade under the able and upright editorial management of Mr. Wm. M. Thoms.   Mr.
Watson, moreover, had published since 1843 up to the
time of founding the *Art Journal* several musical papers
in succession, all supported largely by the profession
and advertising patronage of piano manufacturers, and
in the pages of his various musical publications are to be

found able reviews of new improvements appearing in the piano, together with biographical and current notes in relation to kindred subjects. More than this, he officiated as one of the judges at various exhibitions of the American Institute from 1840 up to 1865, and was known as a writer and musical critic of rare acumen in everything that concerned tone production in piano performances.

Henry C. Watson was born in London on November 4th, 1818. His father was chorus master at Covent Garden, and an excellent musician and composer, while his mother was equally gifted ; therefore the musical precocity that Watson exhibited while in his youth was legitimately inherited. He was gifted with a voice of rare sweetness as a boy, and between nine and ten made his first appearance at Covent Garden in " Oberon," in the character of a fairy. He immediately attracted distinguished attention, and became from thenceforward a public favorite. He devoted himself to study as he grew older, yet he was continually before the public, and became intimate with theory and composition while very young. When Watson reached the age of seventeen his voice disappeared. This loss was to him a heavy affliction. Being compelled to turn his talent to account in other directions, he followed up the study of music, and in time essayed composition. Meantime he developed a strong literary and poetic faculty, which he afterward cultivated with such excellent results. At twenty-three he sought these shores. His object was the object of nearly every matured person that has ever landed here from the discovery of the Continent downward—viz., to seek out a new field for self-advancement and for his talents.

When Mr. Watson landed in New York in 1841 he came armed with letters of introduction to the leading literary lights of the metropolis, and in time was in high favor with such celebrities as Bryant, George P. Morris, Parke Benjamin, and Horace Greeley. Under Mr. Benjamin he first found a position in American literature as musical critic of the *New World*, then edited by Horace Greeley and Mr. Benjamin. The scholarly, cultivated, and spirited tone of his criticism, general writings, and poetic effusions soon became the talk of society and literary circles in New York, and there was a widespread demand for the services of his pen. During this period he essayed lyrics for song purposes, and published many songs, which faculty of versatility added to his fame. He subsequently engaged in some journalistic ventures in partnership with many of the well-known lights of literary New York of the past. The *Broadway Journal* was one of these feats. It counted among its editors such a celebrity as Edgar A. Poe. Watson's personal influence drew the advertising patronage of at least eight piano firms to this journal. These periodicals not being sustained by sufficient capital, they necessarily became obsolete.

His first venture in musical journalism was the *Musical Chronicle*, founded in 1843. This brought him into communication with the piano manufacturers, and it was principally through the advertising patronage of Gilbert & Company, Boston, Jonas Chickering, Boston, Stodart & Dunham, Worcester, and Pirsson, New York, Conrad Meyer, Philadelphia, and other piano houses that he was enabled to spread the light of musical literature throughout the country. This was the first musical journal that directly bridged over the line between the pianoforte manufacturers and the musical and artistic world, and the fact deserves recognition. Not for selfish or pecuniary reasons, however, was this union effected, but to benefit both sides, by showing that the progress of musical art and that of the pianoforte as a musical instrument were linked indissolubly, and all his writings were couched in this vein. In the first number of this journal can be found letters from Boston describing the condition of the piano trade there at the time, and personal facts about the principal shops, together with incidental trade notes. When this venture ceased the *American Musical Times* followed, and drew its advertising support from the same source. Next came Watson's *Philharmonic Journal*, then the *American Art Journal*, which has been brought down to the present time, as indicated. As critic of the New York *Tribune* from 1863 to 1866, Mr. Watson's personal influence brought to that paper a patronage of over thirty thousand dollars, a large part of which came from the pianoforte and kindred trades. Chief among the many positions he occupied in New York may be placed the fact that he was the first editor-in-chief of *Frank Leslie's Illustrated Newspaper.*

His connection with American music was pre-eminently significant. He was one of the founders of the Philharmonic Society. He organized the Mendelssohn Union ; he organized the great Mendelssohn Memorial Concert, which was held at Castle Garden, at which over sixteen thousand people were present. He wrote the libretto of "Lurline," Wallace's well-known opera, and was identified with a host of successful projects in relation to American musical art and artists. Up to 1874 he was devoted to the success of his last venture, the

American Art Journal, and from that time forward his health declined. He died on December 4th, 1875, aged fifty seven years, much regretted in professional and social circles, after a residence of thirty·four years in this country. Among H. C. Watson's works he published three hundred songs, piano pieces, glees for mixed voices and part songs for male voices, hymns, Te Deums, and a Romanza for the violin that was famous in its time. He also published the "Ladies' Glee Book," the "Masonic Musical Manual"—being organist of the Grand Lodge of the State of New York—and "Simple Elements of Musical Instruction." Mr. Watson also occupied the position of musical editor of the New York *Albion*, also the *Mirror*, with N. P. Willis and George P. Morris, the author of that universally known song, "Woodman, spare that tree."

Mr. William M. Thoms, whose handsome portrait appears elsewhere, the present editor and publisher of the *American Art Journal*, is the successor of H. C. Watson, and was a *protégé* of that distinguished critic and editor.

Mr. Thoms, whose significant connection with musical journalism and the music trades is a matter of twenty-three years' standing, is a typical New Yorker. His first *entrée* into musical journalism and literature dates from 1867. In this year he joined the *American Art Journal* as a successor to Mr. Alfred Pirsson, son of James Pirsson, the piano manufacturer. He became publisher immediately. Mr. Thoms received his first inspirations in literature from being thrown into the society of some of the leading literary people of the city, who frequented the sanctum of the *Art Journal*, and contributed to its columns. Among the people who influenced his artistic and literary tendencies in these first years of his professional life were Mr. H C. Watson and Mr. Cornelius Matthews, a distinguished writer recently deceased, who drafted the first American international copyright bill. To these two may be appended Henri L. Stuart, a right-hand associate of Horace Greeley, an indefatigable worker and promoter in connection with public enterprises of an industrial and political character, who first introduced the pianoforte into the New York public schools ; "Barry Gray," author of "Cakes and Ale at the Woodbine ;" Charles G. Rosenberg, the poet, painter, and dramatist, and author of "You Have Heard of Them," being a series of personal memoirs of stage celebrities ; Dr. John Savage, the poet ; James McCarroll, the encyclopedist, author of "Madeline and other Poems ;" John W. Watson, of "Beautiful Snow" fame ; Ingersoll Lockwood, who was the United States Minister to Hanover during Lincoln's administration, author of "The Perfect Gentleman," "Legal Don'ts," and the child's classic, "Little Baron Trump ;" Colonel Thomas B. Thorp, the art critic and author of "The First Piano in Arkansas," and A. J. Goodrich, the theorist and author of "Complete Musical Analysis." During his long career, moreover, he has come in close relations with all the well-known people connected with creative and reproductive art. Mr. Thoms became known as a versatile and dignified writer on literary, art, musical, and kindred subjects, and filled a most important post in the management of the *Art Journal* in an unprecedentedly short space of time.

His rapid advance in literature was considerably assisted by a good early education, studious habits, and a splendid vocabulary of acquired information that he had stored away previous to settling down to serious literary work. To these qualifications may be added a thorough knowledge of musical, art, and dramatic forms, and fine æsthetic and artistic perceptions, the latter resulting from his fine temperament, special education, and natural intuitions.

During 1870 and 1871 Mr. Thoms published and edited the *Journal of the Day*, the first daily musical paper ever attempted in the United States, a bright, dignified publication, which met with singular success among cultivated people ; but it was in advance of the times, consequently he ceased its publication after 1871. In 1873 and 1874 he embarked on a new venture, the *Musical Monthly*, a thirty-six page quarto publication edited on a high plane, and devoted to the advancement and uplifting of musical art as a whole, but particularly devoted to the cause of American music and its concomitants. In 1877 he published the *World of Art—Its Eminent Men and Women*, a superb art publication, edited in such a very superior, earnest, and scholarly style that he was warmly congratulated by the best journals in this country and Europe, and commended for his work throughout. In the mean time, his duties in relation to the *American Art Journal* were not discontinued, and after 1877 he gave his whole attention to this publication.

From 1867 upward he has been thrown constantly into the society of piano manufacturers and members of the trade, and learned to recognize all the phases of the business, its history and personalities, as time progressed. This has done much to insure the universally recognized stability and permanence of his publication.

Wm. M. Thoms

About 1876 the *American Art Journal* set aside an enlarged technical department for the purposes of trade matter, after the manner followed out at present. Weekly notes about the movements of agents out of town and manufacturers were introduced, together with specifications and illustrations of new piano and organ patents, statistics of musical instrument exports and imports, portraits of manufacturers, scientific articles upon improvements and construction, and many other general methods at present in adoption in trade journals.

Meanwhile, in the order of events, competitors sprang up, which Mr. Thoms has never been insular enough to regard with feelings of envy, for he is cognizant of the rights and liberties of other citizens, and he is modest enough to be great in this respect.

On April 14th, 1888, the twenty-fifth anniversary edition of the *American Art Journal* appeared and gave considerable impetus to its standing and patronage. The young manufacturers and musicians were brought to recognize the age and character of the paper on this occasion, for a special emphasis was necessarily laid upon its prolonged life and prestige as an organ devoted to the interests of music, artists, and the music trades. In this issue the editor pays a graceful and generous tribute to the founder, Mr. H. C. Watson, in acknowledgment of his personal indebtedness to the deceased. As a tribute to Mr. Watson's services to American art and literature, and in honor of the man personally, I cannot help appending a few sentences, which are distinguished by a high scholarly tone and a characteristic atmosphere of sincerity, while they exemplify the writer's power. " After more than twelve years, Watson's memory lingers like the remembrance of sweet flowers. He was an artist with the lofty temperament and high taste that attach to the artist in the truest sense. He was a poet, with a mind full of the sweet fancies and pure thoughts that inspire one to high literary endeavor and expression. He was a man of affairs in that he was alive to all the rare opportunities of a busy life, and developed and rounded his talents to a degree which was to be attained only by one of high and pure ambition. He seemed never to forget that he had been sent into the world to do good, to increase the happiness and welfare of his fellow-beings, and to hold up to the world the bright and sweet side of life."

Although the veteran of the weekly musical trade press, Mr. Thoms is yet one of the youngest, having reached only his thirty-eighth year.

By his marriage with a distinguished and cultivated lady several years ago, Mr. Thoms received a stimulus to higher efforts in literature and art. Mrs. Clara E. Thoms is an eminent pianist, with a reputation won on two continents. At eight she was starred as a piano prodigy throughout this country. In 1873 she went to Vienna, where she studied piano, harmony, and singing under Proch. In due time she appeared in Austria-Hungary, Germany, and Poland with distinguished success. After a six years' absence abroad she returned home and repeated her successes in her native country, where she has established well-deserved reputation as a virtuoso, artiste, and musician. On her marriage she retired for several years, but returned to professional life in 1887. Since this advent she has won back her old place. Mrs. Clara E. Thoms was born in Minnesota,

and comes on the paternal side of old Revolutionary
stock, one of her ancestors being General Putnam, while
on her mother's side she is descended from a family of
three brothers who came over with Lafayette. Mrs.
Thoms, aside from her musical and artistic genius,
is a lady of fine literary tastes, culture, and general breadth of character. As one of our most distin
guished modern American pianists, she belongs to the
group of eminent virtuosi who have contributed so much
during recent years to raise the character of the American pianoforte.

Mr. W. M. Thoms is assisted in his duties at this date
by Mr. Guido Hecker, a familiar personality in relation
to the *American Art Journal.* Mr. Hecker is a native of
New York, and is a son of Mr. Carl Hecker, the eminent
portrait painter and art teacher. The "Carl Hecker
Art School," of which the latter is director, is a celebrated
institution that has furnished some of the ablest artists
known in the high and the industrial arts in this
country. Mr. Guido Hecker's popularity is widespread
in art and musical circles. He has inherited much of
the family genius, though in a literary direction.

Mr. John C. Freund, at present one of the editors of
the *American Musician,* is another remarkable figure in
this sphere of recent pianoforte and musical history. His
connection with this department of journalism dates back
to 1875, when he founded the *Music Trade Review,* referred to elsewhere, the first weekly with a distinctive
title published in this country devoted to the music
trades. Mr. Freund's early tendencies were literary and
musical to a large degree. Constant association with the
pianoforte as a student, besides a knowledge of mechan-

ics and natural philosophy acquired in his college days, made the literature of the instrument and its manufacture a labor of love, while these acquirements have been eminent qualifications in his professional career as a music trade editor, apart from the standard reputation he enjoys as a critic and feuilletonist.

Mr. Freund's principal fault is said to have hitherto been a magnanimous spirit of lavishness, which all his journalistic ventures have indicated in their general getup and contents. This is a pardonable thing, and at times commendable. The worst sufferer, however, by over-generosity or philanthropy of that unproductive nature is the philanthropist usually. John C. Freund, whose distinguished face graces these pages, was born in London in 1848 of German parents. His father, a most eminent physician, and an authority of note in scientific and medical lines, was an Austrian, who settled in London, where he built up a large practice among the titled classes and aristocracy. He was professionally a philanthropist, for through his personal efforts he raised money to establish the great German Hospital in London, which Germans in London remember as a great deed. At the Crimean War he was one of the principal medical officers in the service of the allied armies. Throughout his life he enjoyed the friendship of many of the most eminent people in Europe. Mr. J. C. Freund's mother, a distinguished lady, whose recent death in 1887 will be remembered, came to London very young, being adopted by her uncle, a noted scholar and linguist in the service of the Foreign Office. This gentleman, Mr. Freund's granduncle, is said to have spoken and written fifteen languages with perfect

ease. He was deputed to accompany Lord Macart-
ney's first embassy to China as interpreter, so as to facilitate intercourse with the natives. Mrs. Amelia Lewis·
Freund, Mr. Freund's mother, inherited much of the
linguistic genius of her uncle, and was known as a lady
of extraordinary accomplishments—which included science—and great strength of character. In music she
equally excelled.

Mr. Freund was a favored mortal in the sense that he
was born, unlike so many others of the race, under the
most favorable conditions, and with the figurative silver
spoon in his mouth, for his father enjoyed a splendid in-
come from his practice. It is no surprise hence to know
that he received an unexceptionable education. He is a
graduate of Oxford and London universities. In his
college days and after he was known as an athlete. He
studied painting under good masters, and became a lawyer. The step from law to journalism is very brief, as
many of the leading London newspaper men are notably
lawyers ; so it is we find Mr. Freund enjoying an early
reputation as editor of the Oxford University magazine,
the *Dark Blue*, in 1870, 1871, and 1873. Tom Hughes, of
"Tom Brown's Schoolboy Days" fame ; Gilbert, the
librettist and satirist ; Charles Reade, and Rossetti were
among the contributors during this period. As a dramatist Mr. Freund is well known. Mr. Henry Labou-
chere, of *Truth*, brought out "The Undergraduate," Mr.
Freund's first play, in 1871, at the Queen's Theatre, London, which the press received very warmly.

In 1872 he arrived in New York, and contributed
subsequently to several leading journals and magazines. He bought out the *Arcadian* in 1873, and en-

gaged a brilliant staff of specialists, such as Mr. Stephen
Fiske, A. C. Wheeler, Montague Marks, and others.
The paper had a great circulation, but in 1875 Mr.
Freund sold it to Mr. George Butler, a nephew of
General Butler. Mr. Freund became known in 1875
as a music trade editor. In this year he started the
Music Trade Review, devoted to the art, its literature,
and the trades. Mr. Louis Engel, at present of Yates'
London *World*, a celebrated musical critic, was engaged
on this journal for some time. In 1878 this became the
Musical Times ; then it developed into the *Musical and
Dramatic Times.* In 1880 Mr. Freund, in consequence of
overwork, withdrew, but in 1881 he had recovered, and
was in the field again with *Music*, which presently became *Music and Drama.* In 1884 *Freund's Weekly* appeared, which subsequently became *Music and Drama.*
Being by instinct a dramatist, and possessing a fine elo-
cutionary, backed up by vocal training, Mr. Freund was
induced to go on the stage. He opened McVicker's
Theatre in Chicago with a new play, '' True Nobility,''
in which he made his *début* in a star part in 1885.
Meanwhile, he was on the stage for two years, playing
leading parts with Mayo and Madame Janish. As a
lecturer, Mr. Freund also shone. In 1886 we find that
his lecture '' Before and Behind the Footlights,'' delivered in Boston, secured no less than sixteen columns
of press notices in that city alone. After this temporary
absence from journalism Mr. Freund returned to the field
in 1887, when he became an editor of the *American
Musician*, which position he has held up to the present
time with significant results.

Apart from the foregoing, Mr. Freund has enjoyed a

distinguished connection with music trade history, and has a large circle of friends.

Mr. John Travis Quigg, Mr. Freund's co-editor on the *American Musician*, is a native of Philadelphia. He is an accomplished musician, an acute and scholarly critic of literature, drama, and the arts, and a journalist of varied and eminent experience. Personally he is a gentleman possessed of many charming traits, and is manly and outspoken to a fault. He became the editor of the *American Musician* in 1885. This paper was founded by the Musical Union in 1884, and was published in an insignificant form under another title. Mr. Quigg assuming charge gave it a new status and character, owing to the influence of his pen and general editorial capacity. In 1887 the *American Musician* became an independent journal under Mr. Quigg's management. The acquisition of Mr. Freund in this year and the collaboration of two such clever people resulted in building up the present successful weekly, which has a large circulation and prestige. The piano trade has helped this success and given the paper permanency and character.

Freund's *Music and Drama* is another weekly devoted to the interests of the music trades and the piano business. Mr. Harry E. Freund is the proprietor and editor of this journal. He is a native of London, where he was born May 19th, 1863, and is a brother of Mr. John C. Freund. He received a first-class education, and adopted journalism after completing his scholastic studies. Mr. Freund came to this country in 1880 and succeeded to the interests of *Music and Drama* upon the temporary retirement of Mr. J. C. Freund. He is a popular young editor, and highly esteemed throughout piano circles, professional and commercial.

The *Music Trades Review*, founded in 1879 by Mr. Charles Avery Welles, is another organ of the art industry treated in this work. This journal came into the possession of Mr. Jeff Davis Bill and E. Lyman Bill in 1887, and has since then been edited and perpetuated under that management. It commands a good circulation, influenced considerably by the personal popularity of Messrs. Bill & Bill.

The *Musical Courier*, another leading weekly, is a well-known journal of the music trades. It began in 1880 as the *Dramatic and Musical Courier*, and was edited by Mr. Nickerson up to 1885, when the present editors, Mr. Otto Floersheim and Mr. Marc A. Blumenberg, assumed control. Mr. Floersheim is a native of Germany, an excellent pianist, and a composer of considerable note in the higher forms of musical art. He has lived many years in this country, and has high literary qualifications and artistic discernment. Mr. Blumenberg is a native of Baltimore, Md. He is practically experienced in the piano business, is a good musician, and a clever writer, and his family have been largely associated with musical art in Baltimore and elsewhere.

Chicago, the metropolis of the West, bids fair to become a future rival of New York as an art, musical, and literary centre. Many of the New York manufacturers maintain large branch stores, and several piano factories have appeared there within recent years. As the chief city of a vast territory, peopled by a progressive and intellectual community, it is no surprise that two musical journals are known even now in Chicago. The *Indica-*

Very sincerely

John C. French

tor, a standard weekly well known to most readers as an organ of the music trades, is the pioneer publication of that city. It is published and edited by Mr. Orrin L. Fox.

The *Indicator* first appeared in 1880 in a modest form, but was so successful that it was enlarged to its present size shortly after publication. It has an able trade department, and although published some distance apart from the present home of piano manufacturing, all items of general import appear in its columns, while it reflects Western musical life and movement in a peculiarly able manner.

Mr. O. L. Fox is an experienced and clever writer. His connection with musical journalism and the trade is emphasized by the fact that his esteemed wife, Mrs. O. L. Fox, is an eminent figure in the Chicago musical world, and is a member of the faculty of the Chicago College of Music.

The Philadelphia *Musical Journal* and several other journals also chronicle musical events and piano manufacturing matters incidentally.

All of these journals mentioned are maintained through the support of the music trades principally, and are large factors in promoting the growth of musical and art culture in the United States. The music trades, in return for their support, receive substantial and incontrovertible benefits, too well known to need recital. The musical editor is a necessity of our civilization, and occupies a dignified position in relation to progress in the sphere of human development indicated, and is as much entitled to distinction as his brother of the daily newspaper press. This is given in a broad and general sense.

Thus we have seen in the phases of modern piano trade history dealing with the "materials," special business enterprises, and press, that it maintains, as shown, the growth and immense proportions of an art industry that contributes more to human happiness, to the elevation of mankind and the promotion of good-will on earth, than any other factor in our modern civilization.

To conclude this work without acknowledgment of the services rendered musical culture and the American pianoforte by the pianists, teachers, and other exponents of the pianoforte as a musical instrument that have appeared in the United States during the past century of national independence, would be but to show ignorance of all that pertains to the higher and truer meaning of the instrument as an expression of the divine art which it represents.   Going back to the early chapters of this work, the names of Hulett, Von Hagen, and Gilfert stand out in this relationship as teachers and pianists. Since these remote days, those who figured most prominently as pianists and teachers of the instrument are given in an addendum list, which includes teachers as well as virtuosi dead and living, native born and foreign. To attempt a classification or a critical biographical estimate of this vast array of talent would be utterly impossible.   More I cannot do than pay this humble tribute to their significant connection with the promotion of musical art in this country.

APPENDIX A.

PROMINENT PIANISTS AND TEACHERS
WHO ARE OR HAVE BEEN IDENTIFIED WITH THE AMERICAN PIANOFORTE.

Henri Herz.
Sigismund Thalberg.
Leopold de Meyer.
Louis Moreau Gottschalk.
Henry C. Timm.
Richard Hoffman.
Otto Singer.
Harry Sanderson
B. J. Lang.
James M. Wehli.
Henry G. Tucker.
Alfred H. Pease.
Joseph Poznanski.
J. N. Pattison.
William K. Bassford.
Charles Wels.
S. B. Mills.
Charles Fradel.
William Mason.
Robert Goldbeck.
William H. Sherwood.
Alexander Lambert.
Carlyle Petersilea.
David M. Levett.
Arthur Foote.
Mr. & Mrs. Edward Hoffman.
Louis Maas.
Otis B. Boise.
B. Bockelmann.
Anton Rubinstein.
Hans Von Bulow.
Rafael Joseffy.
Carl Faelten.
Constantin Sternberg.
Emanuel Moor.
Edmund Neupert.
Moritz Rosenthal.
George Magrath.
Ferdinand Von Inten.
Emil Liebling.
Louis Staab.
Arnim Doerner.
Henry G. Andreas.
Frederick Grant Gleason.
Charles H. Jarvis.
Frank L. Curtis.
George F. Bristow.
George W. Morgan.
Pierre Douillet.
Ferdinand Q. Dulcken.
George W. Sumner,
Herman Carri.
George Doelker.
George W. Chadwick.
H. C. MacDougal.
Joseph Comellas.
S. N. Penfield.
William R. Case.
George W. Colby.
Joseph H. Gittings.
Edgar S. Kelley.

Cecelia S. P. Cary.
Alida Topp.
Marie Krebs.
Anna Mehlig.
Teresa Carenno.
Clara E. Thoms.
Annette Essipoff.
Amy Fay.
Madeleine Schiller.
Julie Rive King.
Cecelia Gaul.
Mrs. Steininger Clark.
Josephine Ware.
Fanny Bloomfield.
Helen Hopekirk.
Neally Stevens.
Mrs. Sherwood.
Eugenie de Roode-Rice.
Mary O'Brion.
Douste Sisters.
Ida Mollenhauer.
Adele Margulies.
Alma Faunce Smith.
Adele Aus der Ohe.
Elizabeth Marsh.
Lydia Kunz Venth.
Emma Hahr.
Mr. & Mrs. William H. Neave.
Frederick Boscowitz.
Kunkel Brothers.
Epstein Brothers.
William G. Vogt.
Henry G. Thunder.
Robert Thallon.
Frederick H. Hahr.
E. S. Matoon.
S. N. Penfield.
Johannes Ziegler.
Alfredo Barilli.
F. Zech.
Asger Hamerik.
James M. Tracy.
John Orth.
Otto Bendix.
W. S. B. Matthews.
H. O. C. Kortheuer.
Mauritz Leefson.
Carl H. Lachmund
Walter Petzet.
Walter J. Hall.
A. R. Parsons.
George Schneider.
W. M. Semnacher.
Bernard Courlaender.
Christiania.
John S. Van Cleve.
Wilson G. Smith.
Johannes Wolfram.
George W. Hunt.
J. C. D. Parker.
Dr. F. Ziegfeld.

APPENDIX B.

LIST OF IMPORTANT PATENTS TAKEN OUT FROM 1796 TO 1890,
Including those Destroyed in the Fire of 1836.

1796, May 27.—J. S. McLean, New Jersey, Pianoforte.
1800, Feb. 12.—J. J. Hawkins, Philadelphia, Pianoforte.
" Oct. 24.—J. J. Hawkins, Philadelphia, Musical Instruments.
1807, July 2.—R. Shaw, Boston, Pianoforte.
1816, Oct. 8.—G. Chartres, New York, Pianoforte.
1817, Oct. 3.—J. Geib, New York, Pianoforte.
1818, Aug. 27.—J. A. Guttwaldt, New York, Pianoforte.
1819, Aug. 21.—R. Bury, Albany, Glass Strings for Piano.
1820, March 3.—P. Peltinos, Philadelphia, Chronometric Tuning Pen.
1822, Nov. 14.—J. Stewart, Boston, Pianoforte.
1824, July 29.—J. Dwight, Boston, Longitudinal Bar in Pianoforte.
1825, Dec. 17.—A. Babcock, Boston, Skeleton Metal Plate.
1827, May 15.—T. Loud, Philadelphia, Horizontal Pianoforte.
1828, March 18.—C. F. L. Albrecht, Philadelphia, Pianoforte.
" Aug. 14.—J. Mackey, Boston, Fitting Hammer Head for Pianoforte.
1830, May 17.—C. S. Sackmeister, New York, Pianoforte.
" May 20.—C. P. Seabury, New York, Pianoforte.
" May 24.—A. Babcock, Philadelphia, Cross-Stringing Pianofortes.
1831, April 22.—E. R. Currier, Boston, Horizontal Pianoforte.
" May 5.—J. F. Nunns, New York, Pianoforte Action.
" June 3.—T., H. O., G. T. & H. F. Kearsing, New York, Pianofortes.
" Aug. 6.—Jesse Thompson, New York, Pianoforte Action.
1833, July 22.—Louis Fissore, Baltimore, Pianoforte Plate.
" Dec. 31.—A. Babcock, Boston, Construction and Action of Pianoforte.
1835, July 7.—T. Loud, Philadelphia, Compensating Tubes for Pianoforte.
1836, Feb. 12.—J. Pethick, Mount Morris, N. Y., Pianoforte.

1836, March 2.—I. Clark, Cincinnati, Pianoforte.
" March 12.—H. Hartye, Baltimore, Pianoforte.
1837, Dec. 7.—T. Loud, Philadelphia, No. 504, Pianoforte Action.
1838, Nov. 20.—E. Brown, Boston, No. 1014, Pianoforte.
1839, June 27.—J. J. Wise, Baltimore, No. 1205, Pianoforte Action.
" Aug. 3.—W. Cumston, Boston, No. 1275, Pianoforte.
" Oct. 26.—H. Herrick, New York, No. 1379, Pianoforte.
" Oct. 31.—A. Babcock, Boston, No. 1389, Pianoforte.
1840, Oct 8.—J. Chickering, Boston, No. 1802, Pianoforte.
1841, Feb. 10.—T. Gilbert, Boston, No. 1970, Pianoforte Action.
" May 6.—J. Dwight & D. B. Newhall, Boston, No. 2081, Arranging Keys in Pianoforte.
" May 19.—F. C. Reichenbach, Philadelphia, No. 2099, Horizontal Pianoforte.
" July 10.—L. Gilbert, Boston, No. 2167, Pianoforte.
" Nov. 3.—D. B. Newhall, Boston, No. 2330, Pianoforte.
1842, April 1.—T. Loud, Philadelphia, No. 2523, Shifting Movement for Square and Upright Pianos.
" April 29.—C. Bosert & J. Schomacker, Philadelphia, No. 2595, Pianoforte.
1843, Jan. 27.—E. Brown, Boston, No. 2934, Pianoforte.
" Sept. 1.—J. Chickering, Boston, No. 3238, Pianoforte.
1844, March 26.—O. Gori and P. Ernst, New York, No. 3504, Pianoforte.
" April 17.—O. M. Coleman, Philadelphia, No. 3548, Pianoforte.
" June 24.—L. Reuckert, Baltimore, No. 3643, Pianoforte.
1845, March 12.—L. Reuckert, Baltimore, No. 3940, Pianoforte.
" June 25.—S. W. Draper, Boston, No. 4082, Pianoforte.
" Oct. 25.—E. Badlam, Potsdam, N. Y., No. 4241, Pianoforte.

1846, July 2.—L. Philleo, Utica, N. Y., No. 4612, Pianoforte.

" Oct. 29 —J. Schriber, New York, No. 4832, Pianoforte.

1847, April 24.—T. Loud, Philadelphia, No. 5086, Pianoforte Action.

" July 24.--T Gilbert, Boston, No. 5202, Metallic Frame for Piano.

" Aug. 7.—T. Gilbert, Boston, No 5216, Pianoforte.

1848, June 13.—J. H. Schomacker, Philadelphia, No. 5631, Pianoforte.

" Dec. 26.—J. J. Wise, Baltimore, No. 5990, Pianoforte Action.

1849, March 27.—J. A. Gray, Albany, No. 6223, Pianoforte.

" April 10.—C. Meyer, Philadelphia, No. 6282, Elevating the Tops of Pianos.

1850, June 18.—L. Gilbert, Boston, No. 7441, Upright Pianoforte.

" July 9.—C. Meyer, Philadelphia, No. 7494, Sounding Board.

" Aug. 13.—J. Pirsson, New York, No. 7568, Pianoforte.

1851, July 1.—M. Miller, Rochester, N. Y., No. 8104, Pianoforte.

" Aug. 26.—G. Bacon & R. Raven, No. 8320, Square Piano.

" Sept. 9.—R. Kreter, New York, No. 8350 Pianoforte Action.

" Sept. 9.—J. A. Gray, Albany, N. Y., No. 8352, Pianoforte Action.

" S pt. 23.—L. H. Browne, Boston, No. 8383, Pianoforte.

" Sept. 30.—T. Gilbert, Boston, No. 8389, Pianoforte.

" Oct. 24 —H. J. Newton, New York, No. 8452, Pianoforte String.

" Oct. 28.—F. Mathushek, New York, No. 8470, Pianoforte.

1852, April 20 —W. F. Furgang, Albany, No. 8887, Piano and Organ Key.

" June 27.—G. Brown, Boston, No. 8680, Pianoforte Action.

" Oct. 5.—J. J. McDonald, New York, No. 9304, Pianoforte.

1853, June 4.—R. Kreter, New York, No. 9326, Covering Piano Hammers.

1854, Jan. 21.—S. B. Driggs, Detroit, Mich., No. 10,416, Pianoforte Attachment.

1855, Feb. 6.—J. A. Gray, Albany, No. 12,362, Pianoforte Sounding Board.

" Dec. 18.—S. B. Driggs, Detroit, Mich, No. 13,942, Metallic Framing a d Sounding Board.

1857, March 17.—J. A. Gray, Albany, No. 16,832, Piano Action.

" May 5.—H. Steinway, New York, No. 17,238, Piano Action.

" May 19 —S. B. Driggs, New York, No. 17,320, Pianoforte Action.

" July 21.—G H. Hulskimp, Troy, N. Y., No. 17,838, Metallic Bridge.

1858, June 8.—J. V. Marshall, Albany, No. 20,500, Pianoforte Action.

" June 15.—H. Steinway, New York, No. 20,595, Pianoforte Action.

1859, May 24.—N. J. Haines, New York, No. 24 119, Pianoforte Action.

" July 26.—J. W. Fischer, New York, No. 24 905, Pianoforte.

" Aug. 30.—F. Marshall, New York, No. 25,305, Pianoforte Action.

" Sept. 13.—D. Decker, New York, No. 25,393, Pianoforte Action.

" Sept. 13.—F C. Lighte, New York, No. 25 426, Pianoforte.

" Nov. 29.—H. Steinway, Jr., New York, No. 26,300, Pianoforte.

" Dec. 20.—F. Mathushek. New York, No. 26,550, Pianoforte Action.

" Dec. 20.—H. Steinway, New York, No. 26,532, Grand Piano.

1860, Feb. 21.—F. C. Lighte, New York, No. 27,226, Grand Pianoforte.

" May 1.—J. A. Gray, Albany, No. 28,137, Pianoforte.

" May 22.—G. H. Hulskamp, Troy, N. Y., No. 28,374, Pianoforte Action.

" July 10.—J. W. Fischer, New York, No. 29,068, Pianoforte.

" Aug. 7.—H. Lindeman, New York, No. 29,502, Pianoforte.

" Oct. 2.—F. Mathushek, New York, No. 30,279, Pianoforte.

1861, April 23.—C. F. Chickering, New York, No. 32,119, Square Pianoforte.

" May 21.—H. Steinway. Jr., New York, No. 32,386, Pianoforte Action.

" May 21.—H. Steinway, Jr., New York, No. 32,387, Pianoforte Action.

" Oct. 8.—H. S. Calenberg, New York, No. 32,427, Pianoforte Action.

1862, Jan. 7.—T. Marschall, New York, No. 34,114, Pianoforte.

" Feb. 25.—A. II. Hastings, New York, No. 34 491, Pianoforte.

" April 8.—H. Steinway, Jr., New York, No. 34,910, Pianoforte.

" June 24.—S. T. Parmelee, New Haven, No. 35,704, Pianoforte.

" July 1.—F. C. Lighte, New York, No. 35,766, Pianoforte.

" Oct. 21.—G. H. Hulskamp, Troy, N. Y., No. 36,712, Piano Action.

1863, Feb. 17.—W. Bourne, Boston, No. 37,717, Pianoforte.

" June 2.—D. Decker, New York, No. 38,731, Pianoforte.

1865, Jan. 10.—D. Decker, New York, No. 45,818, Pianoforte

" March 7.—S. T. Parmelee, New Haven, No. 46,759, Pianoforte.

" Aug. 1.—T. Loud, Philadelphia, No. 49,127, Swell for Musical Instruments.

1866, Feb. 20.—A. Ludolff, New York, No. 52,725, Iron Frame for Pianoforte.

" June 5.—W. Steinway, New York, No. 55,385, Pianoforte.

" Aug. 14.—R. Raven, New York, No. 57,186, Pianoforte.

" Oct. 16.—W. H. Mason, Boston, No. 58,950, Pianoforte.

1866, Oct. 16.—P. Schuler, Philadelphia, No. 58,896, Pianoforte.
" Oct. 30.—W. V. Wallace, New York, No. 59,295, Pianoforte Action.
1867, Jan. 29.—J. J. & D. Decker, New York, No. 61,612, Pianoforte.
" Feb. 19.—H. Herrick, New York, No. 62,134, Pianoforte Action.
" April 2.—W. H. McDonald, Brooklyn, No. 63,547, Pianoforte.
" April 13 —T. Marschall, New York, No. 88,970, Pianoforte.
1868, May 26.—G. M. Guild, Boston, No. 78,276, Sounding Board.
" July 21.- H. Herrick, Boston, No. 80,073, Pianoforte.
" Aug. 18.—T. Steinway, New York, No. 81,306, Pianoforte.
1869, March 2.—D. T. Peck, New York, No. 87,509, Pianoforte.
" April 6.—C. F. T. Steinway, New York, No. 88,749, Piano Sounding Board.
" Aug. 10.—T. Steinway, New York, No. 93,647, Piano Action.
" Dec. 14.—C. F. T. Steinway, New York, No. 97,982, Pianoforte.
1870, March 1.—G. H. Davis, Boston, No. 100,266, Grand Pianoforte.
" March 15.—G. Steck. New York, No. 100,948, Iron Frame for Pianofortes.
" March 15.—A. H. Hastings, New York, No. 100,888.
" June 14.—W. Bourne, Boston, No. 104,256, Pianoforte.
" July 5.—D. Decker, New York, No. 105,049, Former for Bending and Gluing Cases of Grand Pianos.
1871, March 28.—F. Mathushek, New York, No. 113,073, Pianoforte.
" June 6.—C. F. T. Steinway, New York, No. 115,782, Pianoforte Action.
" June 20.—G. Steck, New York, No. 116,109, Grand Pianoforte.
" July 25.—J. B. Dunham, East Chester, N. Y., No. 117,393, Sound Board for Pianos.
" Oct. 10.—A. H. Hastings, New York, No. 119,760, Pianoforte.
" Nov. 28.—C. F. Chickering, New York, No. 121,334, Upright Pianos.
1872, May 14.—C. F. T. Steinway, New York, No. 126,848, Duplex Agraffe Scale for Pianos.
" May 28.—C. F. T. Steinway, New York, No. 127,383.
" May 28.—C. F. T. Steinway, New York, No. 127,384.
" Dec. 24.—C. F. Chickering, New York, No. 134,194, Piano Agraffe.
1873, Feb. 11.—C. F. T. Steinway, New York, No. 135,857, Piano Sounding Board.
" March 18.—R. Kreter, New York, No. 137,005, Upright Piano Action.
" Oct. 21.—G. Steck, New York, No. 143,789, Grand Pianoforte.
" Oct. 28.—G. H. Davis, Boston, No. 143,957, Upright Pianoforte.

1874, March 17.—A. Dolge & A. Gleitz, New York, No. 148,678, Piano Action.
" Aug. 11.—F. Mathushek & D. H. Dunham, New York, No. 154,062, Pianoforte.
" Aug. 18.—H. Behning & J. Diehl, New York, No. 154,116, Piano Agraffe.
" Oct. 27.—A. Steinway, New York, No. 156,388, Piano Attachment.
1875, Feb. 16.—F. Polster, Baltimore, No. 159,838, Piano Repetition Action.
" March 2.—H. Behning & J. Diehl, New York, No. 160,299, Piano Nameboard, etc.
" March 9.—W. F. Kearsing, New York, No. 160,600, Piano Stringing and Tuning Device.
" May 4.—Kranich & Bach, New York, No. 162,829, Piano Agraffe.
" June 1.—A. Steinway, New York, Nos. 164,052, 164,053, 164,054, Piano Attachment.
" Nov. 16.—E. Gabler, New York, No. 169,984, Upright Piano.
" Nov. 16.—E. Gabler, New York, No. 169,985, Piano Agraffe.
" Nov. 30.—S. Brambach, New York, No. 170,619, Upright Music Rack.
" Nov. 30.—C. F. T. Steinway, New York, No. 170,645, Grand Piano Action.
" Nov. 30.—C. F. T. Steinway. New York, No. 170,646, Pianoforte Agraffe.
" Nov. 30.—C. F. T. Steinway, New York, No. 170,647, Pianoforte Metal Frame.
1876, Feb. 15.—W. M. Cammon, Albany, No. 173,565, Pianoforte.
" March 28.—C. F. Chickering, New York, No. 175,336, Grand Piano Frame.
" June 13 —C. F. T. Steinway, New York, No. 178,565, Pianoforte.
" Aug. 1.—C. F. T. Steinway, New York, No. 180,671, Piano Sounding Board.
" Oct. 17.—M. C. Knabe, Philadelphia, No. 183,308, Piano Action.
1877, March 20 —Wessell, Nickel & Gross, New York, No. 188,706, Piano Action.
" May 8.—A. Steinway, New York, No. 190,639, Piano Attachment.
" May 29.—Kranich & Bach, New York, No. 191,444, Pianoforte.
" Nov. 6.—Kranich & Bach, New York, No. 196,912, Piano Action Frame.
" Nov. 20.—C. F. Chickering, New York, No. 197,332, Pianoforte.
1878, Jan. 15.—A. H. Hastings, New York, No. 199,154, Piano Action.
" Jan. 29.—E. Gabler, New York, No. 199,635, Pianoforte.
" Jan. 29.—J. Brinsmead, London, Eng., No. 199,687, Pianoforte Action.
" Feb. 26.—G. W. Lyon, Chicago, No. 200,741, Piano Sounding Board.
" April 2.—H. W. Gray, Philadelphia, No. 202,020, Piano String.
" May 7.—G. Bothner, New York, No. 203,407, Piano Action.
" May 21.—C. F. T. Steinway, New York, No. 204,106, Grand Piano.

1878, May 21.—C. F. T. Steinway, New York, No. 204,107, Piano Action.
" May 21.—C. F. T. Steinway, New York, No. 204,108, Pianoforte.
" May 21.—C. F. T. Steinway, New York, No. 204,109, Piano Agraffe.
" May 21.—C. F. T. Steinway, New York, No. 204,110, Piano Sounding Board.
" July 2.—C. F. T. Steinway, New York, No. 205,696, Piano Repeating Action.
" Nov. 26.—Wessell, Nickel & Gross, New York, No. 210,381, Piano Damper Action.
1879, Jan. 7.—G. Steck, New York, No. 211,115, Piano Damper Attachment.
" Feb. 4.—F. & H. Mathushek, Jr., New York, No. 212,029, Pianoforte.
" July 22.—C. F. T. Steinway, New Yo k, No. 217,828, Device for Levelling Keyframes of Pianofortes.
" Sept. 2.—C. F. T. Steinway, New York, No. 219,323, Device for Adjusting Piano Action Frames.
1880, Feb. 3.—C. S. Fischer, New York, No. 2 4,008, Piano Action Frame.
" April 13.—C. F. T. Steinway, New York, No. 226,462, Piano Action and Actionframe.
" April 20.—H. Praeger, Baltimore, No. 226,676, Music Desk for Piano.
" May 18.—G. M. Gould, Boston, No. 227,624, Upright Piano Action.
" June 15.—Carl Mahling, New York, No. 228,912, Piano Damper Attachment.
" July 13.—J. Hardman, New York, No. 229,820, Pianoforte.
" July 20.—C. F. T. Steinway, New York, No. 230,354, Upright Piano Action.
" Aug. 24.—C. F. T. Steinway, New York, Nos. 231,629, 231,630, Piano Hammer.
" Oct. 5.—C. F. T. Steinway, New York, No. 232,857, Key Frame Bed for Pia o.
" Oct. 19.—Kranich & Bach, New York, No. 233,103, Piano Action.
" Oct. 26.—C. F. T. Steinway, New York, No. 233,710, Piano Square Board Bridge.
" Dec. 14.—J. Hardman, New York, No. 235,357, Piano Action.
1881, March 1.—M. J. Chase, Richmond, Ind., No. 238,214, Piano Action.
" March 15.—A. F. Hellig, Little Ferry, N. J., No. 238,898, Stringing Pianoforte.
" April 19.—J. F. Conover & W. Brown, New York, No. 240,134, Pianoforte.
" June 7.—G. M. Woodward, Brookline, Mass., No. 242,732, Piano Damper Action.
" July 5.—M. J. Chase, Richmond, Ind., No. 243,689, Sounding Board.
" July 5.—G. M. Guild, Boston, No. 243,700, Upright Piano Case.
" July 19.—W. A. Lorenz, Brooklyn, No. 244,635, Upright Piano Case.
" Aug. 16.—Louis Stremmell, Lynchburg, Va., No. 245,672, Pianoforte.
" Sept. 13.—C. G. Buttkereit, Des Moines, Ia., No. 247,009, Bell Piano.

1881, Sept. 27.—C. E. & W. Bourne, Boston, No. 247,474, Upright Piano Case.
" Oct. 4.—C. F. Chickering, New York, No. 247,887, Pianoforte.
" Dec 14.—J. Hardman, New York, No. 235,357, Piano Action Frame.
1882, Jan. 17.—P. G. Mehlin, New York, No. 252,37 , Piano Action Frame.
" Feb. 28.—P. G. Mehlin, New York, No. 254,209, Wrest Block Bridge.
" May 23.—E. M. Cammon, Albany, No. 258,455, Pianoforte.
" May 30.—J. Hardman, New York, No. 258,751, Repetition Action for Pianos.
" July 25.—H. Behning, New York, No. 261,523, Sounding Board for Upright Piano.
" Aug. 1.—J. Jacobsen, New York, No. 262,047, Upright Piano.
' Dec. 5.—H. Sohmer, New York, No. 268,562, Piano Agraffe Bar.
" Dec. 19.—A. Gemundes, Columbus, O., No. 269,405, Piano Action.
1883, Jan. 23.—C. F. T. Steinway, New York, No. 270,914, Piano Action.
" July 3.—J. Diehl, New York, No. 280,362, Piano Sounding Board.
" Oct. 2.—F. L. Becker, New York, No. 285,785, Pivot Joint for Piano Action.
" Oct. 9.—P. G. Mehlin, New York, No. 286,425, Upright Piano Case.
1884, March 18.—Wessell, Nickel & Gross, New York, No. 295,317, Piano Damper.
" March 18.—P. G. Mehlin, New York, No. 295 383, Piano or Organ Key Rail.
" March 25.—J. R. Lomas, New Haven, No. 295,778, Stringing Device for Pianos.
' April 8.—G. W. Peck, New York, No. 296,612, Lid Raising Attachment for Pianos.
" April 29.—F. L. Becker, New York, No. 297,908, Repetition Action for Piano.
" May 6.—J. Swenson, New York, No. 298,040, Device for Cutting Damper Felt for Pianos.
" May 27.—H. Kroeger, New York, No. 299,479, Pianoforte Fr me.
" June 24.—H. S. Parmelee, New Haven, Conn., No. 301,068, Piano Sounding Bo rd.
1885, Jan. 27.—P. G. Mehlin, New York, No. 311,243, Pianoforte.
" Feb. 3.—E B. Haynes, Baltimore, No. 311,754, Piano Pedal Attachment.
" Feb. 24.—Wessell, Nickel & Gross, New York, No 312,776, Piano Damper.
" March 17.—F. Polster, Baltimore, No. 314,195, Upright Action.
" March 24.—A. Baus, New York, No. 314,310, Piano Agraffe.
" March 31.—C. F. T. Steinway, New York, No. 314,740, Piano Frame.
" March 31.—C. F. T. Steinway, New York, No. 314,741, Piano Pedal.
" March 31.—C. F. T. Steinway, New York, No. 314,742, Piano Frame.

1885. April 21.—W. C. Ellis, Worcester, Mass., No. 316,023, Piano Action.
" April 28.—G. Cook, Boston, No. 316,445, Pianoforte.
" May 12 —P. Menges, New York, No. 317,-660, Pianoforte Action.
" June 2.—J. Brinsmead, London, Eng., No. 319,189, Piano Sounding Board.
" July 14.—S. Brambach, New York, No. 322,009, Upright Piano Action.
" Aug. 4.—C. W. Brewer, Racine, Wis., No. 323 632. Piano Action.
" Aug 4 —F. G. Smith, Brooklyn, No. 323.-747, Upright Piano.
" Aug. 18.—E. Gabler, New York, No. 324,-467, Pianoforte.
" Sept. 1.—F. Engelhardt, New York, No. 325 401, Piano Action.
" Sept. 8.—l Fuso, Boston, No. 325,669, Upright Action.
" Sept. 8.—G. J. Couchois, Chicago, No. 326,020, Piano Agraffe.
" Sept 15.—C. E. Rogers, Boston, No. 326,-335, Pianoforte Action.
" Sept. 22.—F. Polster, Baltimore. No. 326,-586, Repeating Action for Square and Grand Pianos.
" Oct. 27.—J. F. Conover, New York, No. 329,277, Piano Stringing.
" Nov. 10.—F. Zech, San Francisco, No. 330,080, Piano Action.
" Dec. 22.—F. Imhorst, San Francisco, No. 332,716, Piano Action.
1886, Jan. 26.—S. Brambach, New York, No. 334,933, Upright Piano Case.
" March 9.—V. Bessier, New York, No. 337,-552, Pianissimo Stops for Piano.
" March 30.—J. W. Reed, Chicago, No. 338,779, Piano String Bridge.
" March 30.—W. & C. E. Bourne, Boston, No. 338,918, Upright Piano Action Frame.
" April 6.—J. Hardman & W. H. Dutton, No. 339,170, Harp Stop for Upright Piano.
" April 20.—S. La Grassa, New York, No. 34 ,219, Key Bottom for Pianos.
" May 4.—S. Hansing, Boston, No. 341,003, Stringing Pianos.
" June 15.—A Felldin, Ithaca, N. Y., No. 343,805, Piano Tuning Pin.
" June 29.—C. D. Pease, New York, No. 344,677, Action Rail for Piano.
" July 20 —R. E. Letton, Quincy, Ill., No. 345,706, Upright Piano Action.
" Aug. 4.—J. W. Hooper, Boston, No. 348,111, Pianoforte Action.
" Oct. 5.—C. F. Chickering, New York, No. 350,292, Pianoforte.
" Oct. 12.—F. L. Wing, Brooklyn, No. 350,-517, Piano Key-Bed Support.
" Oct. 19.—H. Kroeger, New York, No. 351,326, Capo d'astro Bar for Pianos.
" Oct. 26.—J. Gramer, Boston, No. 351,696, Metallic Frame for Pianos.
" Nov. 9.—J. F. Conover, New York, No. 352,300, Music Rack for Pianos.

1886, Nov. 9.—J. W. Carnes, Orion Ill., No. 352 395, Tuning Pin.
" Nov. 30.—P. G. Mehlin, New York, No. 353,301, Mute Bar Damper for Pianos.
" Dec. 14.—S. La Grassa, New York, No. 354,323, Upright Piano.
1887, Jan. 18.—W. C. Ellis, Worcester, Mass., No. 356,109, Pianoforte Action.
" Feb. 1.—P. G. Mehlin, New York, No. 356,759, Key Frame for Piano.
" Feb. 8.—J. E. Richardson & J. A. Warren, Detroit, Mich., No. 357,291, Upright Piano.
" Feb. 8.—P. Weber, New York, No. 357,-436, Pianissimo Pedal for Piano.
" March 8.—H. Sohmer, New York, No. 358,946, Pianoforte.
" March 28.—H. B. Nickerson, New Bedford, Mass., No. 359,808, Stringing Pianos.
" April 12.—A. Dolge, New York, No. 361,-144, Press for Forming Piano Hammers.
" April 19.—C. S. Weber, Cleveland, O., No. 361,384, Stringing Pianos.
" April 26.—S. Newhouse, Chicago, No. 361,967, Piano Sound Board.
" May 24.—E. Stroud, New York, No. 363,-488, Piano Action Frame.
" May 31.—S. Brambach, New York, No. 363,947, Upright Piano Action.
" June 7.—D. E. Dopp, Santa Rosa, Cal., No. 364,399, Piano Action.
" June 7.—A. Dolge, New York, No. 364,-496, Piano Hammers.
" June 7.—J. R. Perry, Wilkesbarre, Pa., No. 364,601, Piano Damper.
" June 28.—George Steck, New York, No. 365 412, Pianoforte.
" June 28.—A. J. Gillespie, Atlantic, Ia., No. 365,593, Stringing Pianos.
" July 12.—Wessell, Nickel & Gross, New York, No. 366 360, Piano Action.
" July 12.—W. Becker, Chicago, No. 366,-615, Guide Pin for Piano Keys.
" July 19.—C. Lutz, New York, No. 366,782, Piano Tuning Pin.
" July 26 —J. W. Cooper, Boston, No. 367,-272, Pianissimo Device for Piano.
" Aug. 16.—G. F. Dieckman, New York, No. 368,195, Electrical Piano.
" Aug. 23.—P. J. Keller, Bridgeport, Conn., No. 368,673, Bridge for Piano.
" Oct. 4.—W. H. Ivers, Dedham, Mass., No. 371,069, Pianoforte.
" Oct. 18.—V. H. Brown, Portland, Ore., No. 371 666, Piano Action.
" Oct. 25.—C. H. Mahling, New York, No. 372,035, Piano Frame.
" Nov. 15.—F. M. Antisell, San Francisco, No. 373,262, Piano Wrest Plank.
" Dec. 20.—F. E. H. Gardiner, Springfield, Mo., No. 375 150, Piano Tuning Pin.
" Dec. 20.—E. Q. Norton, Mobile, Ala., No. 375,327, Upright Piano Action.
1888, April 17.—S. R. Harcourt, Chicago, No. 381,1:9, Piano Action.

1888, May 8.—W. H. Ivers, Boston, No. 382,471, Piano Key Bottom.
" June 12.—W. H. Dutton, Philadelphia, Nos. 384,241, 384,242, 384,243, 384,244, Upright Piano.
" June 19.—P. Krumscheid, Boston, No. 384,917, Upright Piano Action.
" July 3.—F. G. Smith, Brooklyn, No. 385,380, Pianoforte.
" July 10.—J. McDonald, Brooklyn, No. 386,079, Piano Action.
" Aug. 7.—F. Feiling, Milwaukee, Wis., No. 387,503, Pianissimo Pedal for Pianofortes.
" Sept. 25.—W. H. Ivers, Boston, No. 389,966, Pianoforte Bridge.
" Sept. 25.—C. C. Hudson, Elmira, N. Y., No. 390,169, Upright Piano Case.
" Oct. 16.—H. R. Moore, Norwalk, O., No. 391,181, Piano Pedal Attachment.
" Oct. 23.—W. Umland, New York, No. 391,495, Damper for Upright Pianos.
" Nov. 6.—W. H. Ivers, Boston, No. 392,270, Damper for Piano.
" Nov. 13.—O. Lestina, Derby, Conn., No. 392,737, Piano Pedal.
" Nov. 20.—E. Q. Norton, Mobile, Ala., No. 393,024, Device for Beating Out Pianos.
1889, Jan. 15.—F. W. Hale, Boston, No. 396,155, Pianoforte.
" Jan. 29.—G. M. Guild, Boston, No. 396,740, Stringing and Tuning for Pianos.
" Feb. 5.—P. G. Mehlin, New York, No. 397,121, Piano Case.
" Feb. 5.—Kranich & Bach, New York, No. 397,239, Piano Action.

1889, Feb. 19.—S. Hansing, New York, No. 398,130, Muffler for Upright Piano; No. 398,151, Upright Piano Action.
" Feb. 26.—H. Mallebre, New York, No. 398,635, Upright Piano Action Frame.
" March 19 G. Steck, New York, No. 399,710, Pianoforte.
" May 21.—P. G. Mehlin, New York, No. 403 583, Piano Plate.
" June 4.—S. Hansing, New York, No. 404,704, Piano Action.
" June 11.—A. T. Strauch, New York, No. 404,876, Repeating Action for Grands.
" June 18.—C. R. Elias, Chicago, No. 405,465, Touch Regulator for Pianos.
" July 2.—S. R. Perry, Wilkesbarre, Pa., No. 406,405, Piano Action.
" July 16.—C. M. Richards, Fort Scott, Kan., No. 407,035, Shifting Piano Action.
" Aug. 13.—A. Richter, New York, No. 408,852, Piano Action.
" Aug. 20.—H. L. Howe, Lexington, Ky., No. 409,325.
" Aug. 27.—J. Swenson, New York, No. 409,810, Device for Cutting Damper Felts for Pianos.
" Sept. 3.—W. Umland, New York, No. 410,223, Divisible Upright Piano.
" Sept. 17.—Kranich & Bach, New York, No. 411,248, Piano Action.
" Oct. 1.—E. G. Schleicher, Mount Vernon, N. Y., No. 411,934.
" Nov. 5.—C. Brambach, New York, No. 414,923, Key Bottom for Pianofortes.

INDEX